Hampton Sides is a contribu[...] award-winning monthly maga[...] Mexico. His articles have app[...] *Magazine*, *New Republic* and the *Washington Post* among others. He lives in Santa Fe with his wife Anne, a journalist.

Praise for *Ghost Soldiers*

'Utterly compelling and impressively detailed, *Ghost Soldiers* dramatically recounts the story behind the Bataan Death March and the realities of survival in a Japanese prison camp. Hampton Sides has fashioned a true-to-life narrative as intelligently orchestrated and satisfying as the raid that ultimately liberated these men'
Stewart O'Nan, author of *The Circus Fire* and *A Prayer for the Dying*

'*Ghost Soldiers* took me on a queasy journey deep into the realm of pure evil – then rescued me in a blaze of heroics and righteous vengeance. There's grief, despair and terror here, but there's also adventure, courage and joy. It's a *Great Escape* for the Pacific Theater, but with a much more satisfying ending'
Erik Larson, author of *Isaac's Storm*

'With deft use of memories and words of actual survivors, Hampton Sides has forged a white-knuckled thriller that conjures this forgotten saga in all its horrifying and moving detail. *Ghost Soldiers* is a story of suffering, heroism and survival remarkable even in the dark annals of war'
Caroline Alexander, author of *The Endurance*

Also by Hampton Sides

Stomping Grounds

Ghost Soldiers

The Astonishing Story of One of Wartime's
Greatest Escapes

HAMPTON SIDES

timewarner
paperbacks

A *Time Warner* Paperback

First published in the United States of America by Doubleday in 2001
First published in Great Britain by Little, Brown and Company in 2001
This edition published by Time Warner Paperbacks in 2002

A CIP catalogue record for this book is available from the British Library.

ISBN 0 0 7515 3229 0

Maps designed by Jeffrey L. Ward

Printed and bound in Great Britain by Clays Ltd, St Ives plc

Time Warner Paperbacks
An imprint of
Time Warner Books (UK)
Brettenham House
Lancaster Place
London WC2E 7EN

www.TimeWarnerBooks.co.uk

To my Mother,
for her grace and equanimity,
and for teaching me to keep my eyes open

. . .

And to the mothers and wives of the men of
Bataan

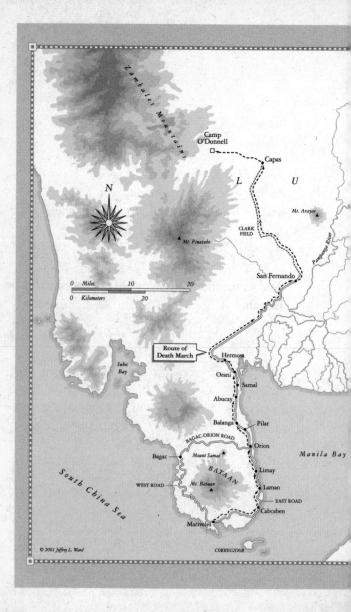

Zambales Mountains

Camp O'Donnell

Capas

L U

Mt. Arayat

CLARK FIELD

Mt. Pinatubo

N

0 Miles   10   20
0 Kilometers   20

Pampanga River

San Fernando

Route of Death March

Hermosa

Orani

Samal

Abucay

Balanga

Pilar

Subic Bay

BAGAC-ORION ROAD

Bagac

Mount Samat

BATAAN

Orion

Manila Bay

Limay

WEST ROAD

Mt. Bataan

Lamao

EAST ROAD

South China Sea

Cabcaben

Mariveles

© 2001 Jeffrey L. Ward

CORREGIDOR

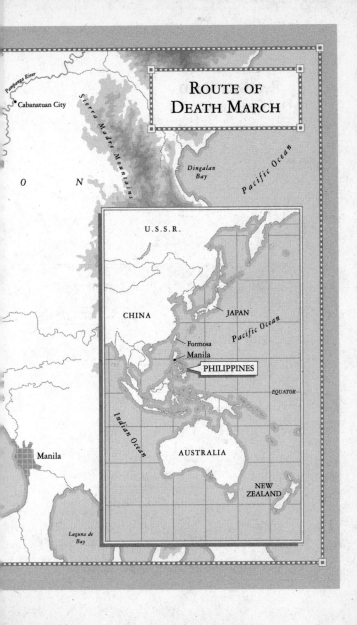

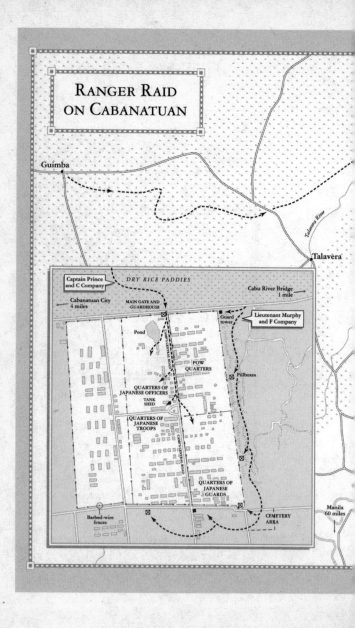

RANGER RAID ON CABANATUAN

Guimba

Talavera

Talavera River

DRY RICE PADDIES

Captain Prince and C Company

Cabu River Bridge 1 mile

Cabanatuan City 4 miles

MAIN GATE AND GUARDHOUSE

Guard tower

Lieutenant Murphy and F Company

Pond

POW QUARTERS

Pillboxes

QUARTERS OF JAPANESE OFFICERS

TANK SHED

QUARTERS OF JAPANESE TROOPS

QUARTERS OF JAPANESE GUARDS

Barbed-wire fences

Manila 60 miles

CEMETERY AREA

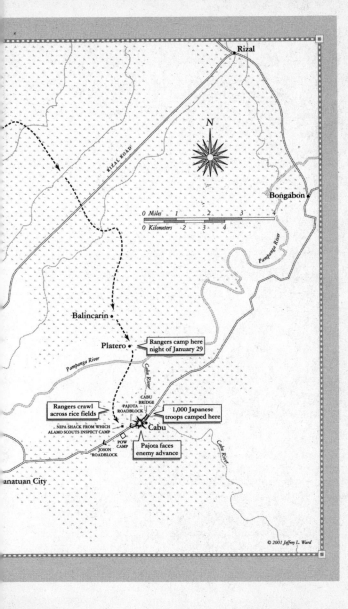

Rizal

N

Bongabon

0 Miles 1 2 3 4
0 Kilometers 2 3 4

Pampanga River

Balincarin

Platero

Rangers camp here
night of January 29

Pampanga River

Cabu River

CABU
BRIDGE

PAJOTA
ROADBLOCK

Rangers crawl
across rice fields

1,000 Japanese
troops camped here

NIPA SHACK FROM WHICH
ALAMO SCOUTS INSPECT CAMP

POW
CAMP

Cabu

JOSON
ROADBLOCK

Pajota faces
enemy advance

Cabu River

anatuan City

© 2001 Jeffrey L. Ward

Let us not speak of them; but look, and pass on.

Dante's *Inferno*

Alfred Oliver/James Duckworth/Lea Sartin/Jerry Steward/Robert Strong, Jr./Hjalmar Erickson/Albert Fields/William Galos/Robert Johnston/Edward Kallus/Donald Sawtelle/Thomas Wilson/James Green/William Knoblock/Stephen Sitter/Robert Hill/Paul Wing/Ralph Hubbard/John Borneman/Emil Reed/Robert Roseveare/Wilson McNeil/Bertram Bank/Matt Dobrinic/Robert Lewis/Robert Whiteley/Jules Yates/Frederick Amos/Curtis Burson/John Dugan/Robert Duncan/Lloyd Floyd/Ralph Hibbs/Charles Katz/Ben King/Raymond Knapp/Charles Leasum/Robert Sly/James Trippe/Dallas Vinnette/John Lucas/Caryl Piccotte/Denton Rees/Donald Robins/Homer Colman/Seaton Foley/Francis Lunnie/Walter Stone/George Kane/Hugh Kennedy/Merle Musselman/Herbert Ott/Earl Baumgardner/Knut Engerset/George Green/Isaac LaVictone/Alma Salm/Emmet Manson/Eugene O'Keefe/Frank Burgess/Donald Miller/Daniel Limpert/Charles Fox, Sr./Ambrose Wangler/Jerome Triolo/Edward Thomas/John Temple/Willard Smith/Melvin Johnston/Richard Hedrick/William Haines/Buerly Gibbon/William Gentry/William Duncan/Claude Daniel/Clifton Chamberlain/Robert Burke/Jerry Brown/Raymond Bliss/William Romme/John Zimmerman/Jack Jennings/Tony Wheeler/Grover Gilbert/James Pfeiffer/Ralph Ellis/Eric Lundblad/James Shimel/Stanley Bronk/Dale Lawton/Marvin Laycock/Orville Drummond/George Clow/Damon Howard/John Batcheler/Harold Beasley/Donald Bridges/David Chavez/Nathan Cleaves/Earnest Clements/Richard Claycroft/Frederick Crocker/George Darling/Wilber Disosway/John Kelly/Archibeque Esperidion/Julius Farrell/Jack Fogerson/Virgil Ford/Walter French/Fred Gaston/Samuel Goldy/Cecil Heflin/Elmer Howell/Everett Keyes/Joseph Knapp/William Lambert/Sylvester Lane/Burney Machovic/Lewis Taylor/Roy Smith/Austin Rogers/Hassel Short/Alma Owen/Charles Novak/Richard Neault/Charles Mortimer/Leon Tice/Harry Pinto/Clifton

Copeland/Kenneth Mize/Milo Folson/Edward Witmer/Gerald
Wagner/Charles Walker/Leon Swindell/William Thamos/Robert
Doyle/George Dunn/Abie Abraham/Ermon Addington/Louis
Albin/Robert Baker/Floyd Barnhardt/Chester Brown/Julian
Brown/Edward Burns/Roger Campbell/William Claxton/Floyd
Cooney/John Culp/Jacob Dusich/Roy Gatewood/Leonard
Gibbs/Harold Glass/Clinton Goodbla/Robert Guice/Frederick
Guth/George Gwin/Almer Hannah/Arthur Harrison/Roy
Hoblet/Oliver Hoover/Robert Howe/Melvin Johnson/Gus
Katrones/Marcos Keithley/Walter Ruig/John Ryan/Lavergne
Ritchie/Calvin Rhoades/Everett Reyes/D. C. Raines/Frederick
Rabin/Arnold King/Togan Kinnison/William Kippen/Charles
Kyllo/Stanislaus Malor/Charles Mokewen/Paul McKinley/Eldred
McPherson/Edward Miller/Walter Miller/Darvin Patrick/Alfred
Pharr/Charles Quinn/Donald Smith/Henry Staples/Blake Van
Landingham/Ari Vico/Stanley Wallace/Frederick Walther/Finas
Williams/William Smith/Milton Englin/Eugene Commander/Harry
Arnold/Millard Basinger/Lloyd Blanchard/William Davis/Hugh
Branch/Cecil Hay/Alfred Taube/Patrick Byrne/Paul
Nateswa/William Peterson/Richard Scott/Gareth Reed/Ray
Wilson/Deno Zucca/Neil Piovino/Edward Berry/Dennis
Rainwater/Max Greenburg/Neil Jovina/Glen Hagstrom/Richard
Chapman/Quentine Devore/Ted Easton/Paul Gernandt/John
Reiff/Frank Potyraj/Fred Schumm/Edward Seaman/Carl Stuard/Roy
Terry/Karl Tobey/Rufus Turnbow/Albert Parker/Lloyd
Anderson/Richard Barnes/Louis Barry/Eugene Clark/David
Coull/James Cowan/Howard Hall/Allen Gutridge/Spiriano
Griego/John Gordon/Frank Franchini/John Dugan/Lawrence
Hall/Joseph Henry/Raymond Holland/Louis Macholl/Robert
Paco/George Parrott/Don Robertson/Roy Jones/Samuel
Korrocks/J. B. Miller/Pat Parker/Carroll Sherman/Field Reed/Ralph
Rodriguez/William Shults/Ted Thomas/Robert Unger/John

West/Louis Zeliz/Dale Forrest/Jack Ostrom/Samuel
Horrocks/Sjpriano Srugo/Robert Strasters/Lester Vitek/Peter
Soppoknersky/Lorne Cox/Harold Amos/Richard Beck/Clarence
Bower/Paul Browning/Preston Bryant/Benjamin Cabreiro/Carl
Carlson/Julius Cobb/Sidney Coy/Robert Decker/Cecil
Easiley/Claude Gibbons/Herbert Herzog/Charles Jensen/Vernice
Kauffman/Norman Lev/Sanford Locke/George McHale/John
Moores/Winthrop Pinkham/William Rieck/William
Seckinger/Ernesto Serrani/Jeff Smith/Donald Snyder/Marshall
Stoutenburgh/Ira Taylor/Joseph Thibeault/Foch Tixtier/Charles
Tupy/Dale Vonlinger/Grandison Vroman/Eugene Watson/Ben
Williams/Chester Easton/Fred Vinton/Herman Silk/Lawdell
Yates/Thomas Wood/Frank Wilson/Herman Ancelet/John
Bailey/Lellon Barnes/Archie Bellair/Merwyn Chenoweth/Lawrence
Courtney/Carno Elkins/Eugene Evers/Travis Flowers/Thomas
Gorman/William Harrison/Dean Henderson/Charles Hickey/James
Hildebrand/Arthur Hilshorst/John McCarty/Vernon Jones/Willie
Jornogin/William Kirkpatrick/Walter Lawrence/Clarence
Mitchell/Lee Moore/James Ogg/Jack Peak/Felix Peterek/Edgar
Peters/Robert Ross/Jesus Santos/Edward Searkey/George
Sharpshire/Carl Smith/Ralph Spinelli/Joseph Stanford/George
Steiner/Melvin Baxter/Joe Chavez/Bruce Choate/William
Duncan/Elbert Easterwood/John Elms/Alfred Farrell/Burnise
Fay/Nelson Fonseca/Gordon Fultz/Dale Gilbert/Virgil
Greenaway/Lloyd Jackson/Troy Holt/Farley Hall/Edward
Johnson/Herman Kelier/Richard Kellogg/William Lash/Gerome
Leek/Vincent Lemely/J. M. Lillard/Joseph Limbaugh/Chester
McGlosson/Peter Connacher/Sam Sina/James Turner/Macario
Villaloboz/William Warren/Buster Wilkerson/Lawrence
Williams/James York/Edward Gordon/James Newman/Don
Adams/William Alschwede/John Alford/Uriah Ash/William
Baker/Lee Bennett/Russell Boatwright/Robert Body/James

Boyle/John Braunberger/Charles Buchanan/Joe Burks/Ben
Chavez/Harold Memmler/Norman Moen/Roy Morris/Henry
Peontek/B. S. Phillips/Loren Pierce/Peter Prinat/Ira Pitts/Earl
Quay/Frank Rawlinson/Lawrence Robinson/Marvel Ross/Alfredo
Sanchez/Joe Schneider/Lamar Wilkinson/Clarence Warton/Oliver
Wetzel/Joseph Wengronowitz/James Teel/William King/Willis
Vincent/Philip Rhode/John Walker/William Thompson/Walter
Kain/Ralph Ham/Everett Dillard/Ralph Taylor/George
Tarkanish/Delbert Sparks/Martin Seliga/Melvin Moritz/Robert
Monrow/Max McCoy/Orvin Kringler/Bernard Holen/Fern
Boaz/Lynn Brotherson/Joseph Burke/Clovis McAlpin/Charles
Kelly/Joseph Herron/Robert Pitchford/John Burtz/William
Girard/Clarence Hall/Paul Jackson/Paul Kelsey/Thomas
Krieger/James McCarthy/J. E. A. Morin/Ernest Rickett/Harry
Stefl/Virgil Wemmer/Harry Willis/Carl Silverman/Thomas
Slater/Thomas Mason/Otis Bills/John Cook/George
Distel/Kenneth Gorden/Albert Hayes/Olin Johnson/Alfred
Jolley/Ira Jeffries/Jearuld Drown/Edward Normandy/Osborne
Jones/Hugh Keays/George Weedon/Max Wait/Theodore
Rosenburg/Raymond Osborne/Leonard Menges/Frank
Ellsworth/William Fassoth/Ray Fouts/Hale Hutchins/Clyde
Jenkins/Jesse Light/Worden Clark/Vernon Booth/Mason
Blair/Robert Bary/Dean Albee/Joseph
Embree/J. W. Georgenton/John Huntley/Elmer McNeilly/John
Spradlin/Christopher Sullivan/John Thompson/Dick Verkey/Carl
Stoops/Robert Bell/Stanley Dellar/George Helley/Sidney
Stevens/Reginald Wyatt/George Laytol/Thomas Potter/Walter
Riley/Dennis Keating/John Allan/Lesley Palmer/Herbert
Markham/George Barber/John Cuncliffe/David Hallan/Gilbert
Maker/J. C. Slaughter/George Martin/George Shardlow/Leslie
McWilliams/Dutch Klein/Caspar Muelman/Gerard Van
Diggelen/Bjorn Leira/Aksel Svendsen

Prologue

December 14, 1944
Puerto Princesa Prison Camp, Palawan, Philippines

All about them, their work lay in ruins. Their raison d'être, the task their commandant had said would take them three months but had taken nearly three years. A thousand naked days of clearing, lifting, leveling, wheel-barrowing, hacking. Thirty-odd months in close heavy heat smashing rocks into smaller rocks, and smaller rocks into pebbles, hammering sad hunks of brain coral into bone-white flour with which to make concrete. Ripping out the black humus floor of the jungle, felling the gnarled beasts of mahogany or narra or kamagong that happened to be in the way. Above the bay, in a malarial forest skittering with monkeys and monitor lizards, they had built an airstrip where none should be, and now they were happy to see it in ruins, cratered by bombs.

One hundred and fifty slaves stood on a tarmac 2,200

meters long and 210 meters wide, straining with shovels and pickaxes and rakes. Ever since the air raids started two months earlier, Lieutenant Sato, the one they called "the Buzzard," had ordered them out each morning to fill the bomb pits, to make the runway usable again. This morning had been no different. The men had risen at dawn and eaten a breakfast of weevily rice, then climbed aboard the trucks for the short ride to the airstrip. As usual, they worked all morning and took a break for lunch around noon. But now the Buzzard said no lunch would be served on the strip, that instead the food would be prepared back at the barracks. The men were puzzled, because they'd never eaten lunch at their barracks before, not on a work-day. It didn't make sense to drive back now, for they still had considerable repair work to do. Sato offered no explanation.

The prisoners crawled into their trucks again and took the bumpy serpentine road back to the prison. In the meager shade of spindly coconut palms, they ate their lunches squatting beside their quarters in an open-air stockade that was secured with two barbed-wire fences. The entire compound was built at the edge of a cliff that dropped fifty ragged feet to a coral beach splashed by the warm blue waters of Puerto Princesa Bay.

Around 1 P.M. the air-raid alarm sounded. It was nothing more than a soldier pounding on an old Catholic church bell splotched with verdigris. The men looked up and saw two American fighters, P-38s, streaking across the sky, but the planes were moving away from the island and were too high to pose a danger. Having become discriminating appraisers of aerial threat, the prisoners ignored the signal and resumed their lunches.

A few minutes later a second air-raid alarm sounded. The men consulted the skies and this time saw an American bomber flying far in the distance. They didn't take the alarm seriously and kept on eating. Presently a third air-raid alarm sounded, and this time Sato and a few of his men marched into the compound with sabers drawn and rifles fixed with bayonets. Sato insisted that everyone heed the signal and descend into the air-raid hovels. "They're coming!" he shrieked. "Planes—hundreds of planes!"

Again the men were puzzled, and this time suspicious. When planes had come before, Sato had never registered any particular concern for their safety. Many times they'd been working on the landing strip when American planes had menaced the site. The Japanese would leap into their slit trenches, but often made the prisoners work until the last possible minute. The Americans had to fend for themselves, out in the open, as aircraft piloted by their own countrymen dropped out of the sky to bomb and strafe the airstrip. Several weeks earlier an American from Kentucky named James Stidham had taken a piece of shrapnel from one of the American bombers, a B-24 Liberator, and was now paralyzed. During the lunch hour he lay on a stretcher in the compound, silent and listless, with a fellow prisoner spoon-feeding him his ration.

"Hundreds of planes!" Sato shouted again, with even more urgency. *"Hurry."*

The slaves moved toward the air-raid shelters. They were primitive, nothing more than narrow slits dug four feet deep and roofed with logs covered over with a few feet of dirt. There were three main trenches, each about a hundred feet long. On both ends, the structures had tiny crawl-space entrances that admitted one man at a time.

Approximately fifty men could fit inside each one, but they had to pack themselves in with their knees tucked under their chins. The prisoners had constructed these crude shelters for their own safety after the American air raids started in October, to avoid more casualties like Stidham. With Sato's reluctant approval, they'd also painted "POW" on the galvanized-metal roof of their barracks.

Sato was behaving strangely today, the prisoners thought, but perhaps he knew something, perhaps a massive air attack was indeed close at hand. All the signs pointed to the imminent arrival of the American forces. The tide of the war was turning fast—everyone knew it. That very morning a Japanese seaplane had spotted a convoy of American destroyers and battleships churning through the Sulu Sea en route to Mindoro, the next large island north of Palawan. If not today, then someday soon Sato and his company of airfield engineers would have to reckon with the arrival of U.S. ground troops, and their work on Palawan would be finished.

Reluctantly, the American prisoners did as they were told, all 150 of them, crawling single file into the dark, poorly ventilated pits. Everyone but Stidham, whose stretcher was conveniently placed beside one of the trench entrances. If the planes came, his buddies would gather his limp form and tuck him into the shelter with everyone else.

They waited and waited but heard not a single American plane, let alone a hundred. They huddled in the stifling dankness of their collective body heat, sweat coursing down their bare chests. The air-raid bell continued to peal. A Navy signalman named C. C. Smith refused to go into his pit. Suddenly the Buzzard set upon him. He raised his saber high so that it gleamed in the midday sun, and with all his strength he brought it blade side down. Smith's head was cleaved in two, the sword finally stopping midway down the neck.

Then, peeking out the ends of the trenches, the men saw several soldiers bursting into the compound. They were carrying five-gallon buckets filled with a liquid. The buckets sloshed messily as the soldiers walked. With a quick jerk of the hands, they flung the contents into the openings of the trenches. By the smell of it on their skin, the Americans instantly recognized what it was—high-octane aviation fuel from the airstrip. Before they could apprehend the full significance of it, other soldiers tossed in lighted bamboo torches. Within seconds, the trenches exploded in flames. The men squirmed over each other and clawed at the dirt as they tried desperately to shrink from the intense heat. They choked back the smoke and the fumes, their nostrils assailed by the smell of singed hair and roasting flesh. They were trapped like termites in their own sealed nest.

Only a few managed to free themselves. Dr. Carl Mango, from Pennsylvania, sprang from his hole, his clothes smoldering. His arms were outstretched as he pleaded—"Show some reason, please God show reason"—but a machine gunner mowed him down.

Another prisoner crawled from his trench, wrested a rifle from the hands of a soldier, and shot him before receiving a mortal stab in the back. A number of men dashed toward the fence and tried to press through it but were quickly riddled with lead, leaving a row of corpses hung from the barbed strands like drying cuttlefish. A few men managed to slip through the razor ribbon and leap from the high cliff, but more soldiers were waiting on the beach to finish them off. Recognizing the futility of escape but wanting to wreak a parting vengeance, one burning prisoner emerged from his trench, wrapped his arms tightly around the first soldier he saw, and didn't let go—a death embrace that succeeded in setting the surprised executioner on fire.

All the while, Lieutenant Sato scurried from trench to trench with saber drawn, loudly exhorting his men and occasionally punctuating his commands with a high, nervous laugh. At his order, another wave of troops approached the air-raid shelters, throwing grenades into the flaming entrances and raking them with gunfire. Some of the troops poked their rifle barrels through the entrances of the trenches and fired point-blank at the huddled forms within. James Stidham, the paralytic who had been watching all of this from his stretcher, quietly moaned in terror. A soldier stepped over to him and with a perfunctory glance fired two slugs into his face.

When Lieutenant Sato was satisfied that all 150 prisoners were dead, he ordered his men to heave the stray bodies back into the smoky pits. The soldiers splattered additional gasoline inside and reignited the trenches. They tossed in more grenades as well as sticks of dynamite to make it appear as though the victims had perished in an air raid after all, with the shelters receiving several "direct hits" from American bombs. The immense pall of smoke curling from the three subterranean pyres was noted by observers five miles distant, across Puerto Princesa Bay.

Entries from Japanese diaries later found at the camp spoke hauntingly of December 14. "Although they were prisoners of war," one entry stated, "they truly died a pitiful death. From today on I will not hear the familiar greeting 'Good morning, Sergeant Major.'" Another mentioned that on the beach below the camp, the "executed prisoners [are] floating and rolling among the breakwaters." Said another: "Today the shop is a lonely place. There are numerous corpses . . . and the smell is unbearable."

———————

On January 7, 1945, an officer from the Army's intelligence branch, known as G-2, sat down with a man named Eugene Nielsen, who had a remarkable story to tell. Their conversation was not casual; it was an official interrogation, and the intelligence officer, a Captain Ickes, was taking notes. At the time of the debriefing, Nielsen and Ickes happened to be on the tropical island of Morotai, a tiny speck in the Spice Islands of the Dutch East Indies that had become a crucial stepping-stone in General MacArthur's drive toward Japan. Eugene Nielsen was an Army Private First Class who had been with the 59th Coast Artillery on the besieged island of Corregidor—directly across from Bataan—when he was captured by the Japanese in May 1942. Born and raised in a small town in the mountains of Utah, Nielsen was twenty-eight years old, and three of those years he had spent languishing in a prison camp near the Palawan capital of Puerto Princesa. There he had done backbreaking work on an airfield detail, crushing rock and coral and mixing concrete by hand.

Nielsen had been evacuated to Morotai along with five other ex-POWs. He was convalescing while awaiting shipment home to the United States. Although he was racked with the residual effects of the various diseases he'd contracted while starving in the tropics, he had recovered much of his strength since his escape from prison. He had two bullet wounds which were still on the mend.

The officer from G-2 sat horrified in his chair as Nielsen told his story, which concerned an incident on Palawan several weeks earlier, the full details of which no official from U.S. Army intelligence had apparently heard before.

The trench smelled very strongly of gas. There was an explosion and flames shot through the place. Some of the guys were moaning. I realized this was it—either I had to break for it or die. Luckily I was in the trench that was closest to the fence. So I jumped up and dove through the barbed wire. I fell over the cliff and somehow grabbed on to a small tree, which broke my fall and kept me from getting injured. There were Japanese soldiers posted down on the beach. I buried myself in a pile of garbage and coconut husks. I kept working my way under until I got fairly well covered up. Lying there, I could feel the little worms and bugs eating holes in the rubbish, and then I felt them eating holes into the skin of my back.

When he looked around, Nielsen realized that a surprising number of Americans had made it down to the beach—perhaps twenty or thirty. Some, like Nielsen, had torn bare-handed through the barbed wire, but the largest group had made it down by virtue of a subterranean accident: a natural escape hatch that led from one of the trenches out to a shallow ledge in the eroded cliff wall. Several weeks earlier, while digging the air-raid pits, some of the Americans had serendipitously discovered this small fissure, and they'd had the forethought to conceal it by plugging the opening with sandbags and a veneer of dirt so the Japanese would never see it. They had thought, in a not very specific way, that this tunnel might come in handy someday, and they were right. One by one, they escaped the incinerating heat of their shelter by crawling through the hole and burrowing out to the rock landing. From there they jumped down to the beach, where they hid among the various crevices and rock outcroppings.

By doing so they gained only a temporary reprieve, however, trading one form of butchery for another. Eugene Nielsen, still lying in the refuse heap, heard gunfire sputtering up and down the beach. Systematically, the soldiers were searching the rocks and hunting down fugitives. It was obvious that they intended to exterminate every last one. The prisoners camouflaged themselves with slathered mud and cringed in the rocky clefts and folds, lacerating their legs and feet on the coarse coral as they tried to squeeze into ever tighter recesses. Other prisoners took refuge in a sewage pipe that was half filled with stagnant water, while still others concealed themselves in thick mattresses of jungle weeds higher along the banks.

The seaside massacre went on for three or four hours. The Japanese would pluck the prisoners from their hiding places and slay them on the spot, either by gunshot or by bayonet. Squads of soldiers combed the weeds in tight formation, plunging their bayonets every foot or so until they harpooned their quarry. One American who'd been caught was tortured at some length by six soldiers, one of whom carried a container of gasoline. Seeing the jerry can, the American understood his fate and begged to be shot. The

17

soldiers doused one of his feet with gasoline and set it alight, then did the same with the other. When he collapsed, they poured the rest of the gasoline over his body and ignited it, leaving him writhing in flames on the beach.

Not far away, a prisoner from South Dakota named Erving Evans, realizing he'd been seen and hoping to avoid the same fate, leaped up from a trash pile where he'd been hiding and blurted, "All right, you bastards—here I am, and don't miss."

They didn't.

They were bayoneting guys down low and making them suffer. They shot or stabbed twelve Americans and then dug a shallow grave in the sand and threw them in. Some of these men were still groaning while they were covered with sand. Then the Japs started to cover the grave with rubbish from the pile where I was hiding. They scraped some of the coconut husks off, and found me lying there. Then they uncovered me from the shoulders on down. They thought I was dead, and seemed to think I had been buried by my friends. I lay there for about fifteen minutes while they stood around talking Japanese. It was getting to be late in the afternoon. One of the guys hollered it was time to eat dinner, and every one of the Japs there went off somewhere to eat. I got up and ran down along the beach and hid in a little pocket in a coral reef there.

Down among the coral, Nielsen encountered seven other survivors. One of them was very badly burned. His hair was singed and "his hide was rubbing off when he brushed against anything." They were all crouched among the rocks, hiding from a barge that was methodically trolling the coves and foreshores. Having exhausted their hunt by land, the Japanese were now searching by water. Aboard the barge were three or four soldiers armed with rifles as well as a tripod machine gun.

Nielsen peeked around the corner and saw the barge coming. He decided he was insufficiently hidden, so he broke off from the group and crouched behind a bush close by. From where he was secreted, he could watch the barge approaching. The Japanese were whispering among themselves and excitedly pointing out crannies that looked promising. One of the seven Americans, a marine from Mississippi named J. O. Warren, wasn't leaning back quite far enough. The Japanese saw his foot protruding from a rock and immediately shot it. Warren dropped in agony from his wound. In what seemed to be a sacrificial act intended to help his comrades, Warren hurled himself out in the open so as not to tip off the whereabouts of the other six. He was immediately shot and killed. The barge passed on.

I left that area and started down the beach. About fifty yards ahead I ran into more Japanese. Suddenly I realized I was surrounded. They were up above me and also coming in from both sides. I was trapped. So I jumped in the sea. I swam underwater as far as I could. When I came up there were twenty Japanese firing at me, both from the cliff and from the beach. Shots were hitting all around me. One shot hit me in the armpit and grazed my ribs. Another hit me in the left thigh, then another one hit me right along the right side of my head, grazing my temple. I think it knocked me out temporarily. For a short period I was numb in the water, and I nearly drowned. Then I found a large coconut husk bobbing around in the bay and used it to shield my head as I swam.

They kept shooting at Nielsen from the beach. He decided to swim back toward the shore so they'd think he'd given up and was coming in. He hoped they'd momentarily let up on their fire, and they did. Nielsen then angled slightly and swam parallel to the coastline for about a hundred yards. The Japanese followed him down the beach, patiently tracking alongside him, step for stroke. Occasionally they pinged a shot or two in his direction, but mostly they just kept a close eye on him.

I came down to a place along the shore where there were a lot of trees and bushes in the water. I knew they were following me, so I went toward shore and splashed to make a little noise. I wanted them to think I was finally coming in. Then I abruptly turned around and went out just as quiet as possible and started swimming across the bay. They never shot at me again. Probably it was too dark for them to see me. I swam most of the night. I couldn't see the other side of the bay but I knew it was about five miles. About halfway out I ran into a strong current. It seemed like I was there for a couple hours making no headway. Finally I reached the opposite shore and crawled on my hands and knees up on the rocks. I was in a mangrove swamp. I was too weak to stand up. It was about 4 A.M. I'd been swimming for nearly nine hours.

Washed up on the far shores of Puerto Princesa Bay, Nielsen was a pitiful sight—naked, nursing two bullet wounds, his skin crosshatched with lacerations. He rested for a few hours and then stumbled half delirious through the swamp until he encountered a Filipino who was walking along a path, wielding a bolo knife. In his current state, Nielsen was suspicious of anyone carrying a knife.

The Filipino seemed wary of Nielsen's hideous castaway appearance but was not especially frightened. "I couldn't imagine how he could be so cool," Nielsen said. At first Nielsen worried that the man was a Japanese sympathizer, but then the Filipino offered him water. Nielsen asked the man to take down a letter. "I think I am the only one alive from the Palawan prison camp," he said. "I want you to write to the War Department to tell them about the Japanese massacre of the Americans at Puerto Princesa." Without uttering a word in reaction, the Filipino began to walk away from Nielsen. Then he abruptly turned around and said cryptically, "You have friends here."

Perplexed, Nielsen followed his new acquaintance down a path through dense jungle to a hideout where Filipino guerrillas were stationed. There, to his amazement, Nielsen encountered two more American survivors from the camp, Albert Pacheco and Edwin Petry. "I didn't believe it at first," said Nielsen. "I thought I was seeing things." Each of the two men had his own grisly story to tell, the details varying only slightly from Nielsen's account. Pacheco and Petry had hidden together in a coral cave that was half flooded with seawater. "The crabs ate on us pretty good down there," Petry said. The two men were forced to vacate the cave when it became completely flooded at high tide. Like Nielsen, they started swimming across the bay around dusk, but they'd enjoyed more favorable currents.

Later Nielsen, Pacheco, and Petry hooked up with three additional escapees. Still others would wash up over the succeeding days, bringing the total of known Palawan survivors to eleven. One had endured an encounter with a sand shark. The last arrival, Glenn McDole, from Des

Moines, Iowa, was found clinging to a Filipino fish trap out in the bay. Local fishermen hauled him in, half alive, with the morning catch.

By guerrilla escort, Nielsen and the original five survivors made their way out of the Japanese-held province of Palawan, first by foot and then by an outrigger canoe, or banca, powered by blankets that were thrown up as makeshift sails. On January 6, the half dozen men were finally evacuated by a Catalina flying boat to the island of Morotai, where they came under the care of the U.S. Army.

———————

Two days after Eugene Nielsen told his harrowing story to Army G-2, General Douglas MacArthur waded onto the shores of Luzon in one of the largest land invasions in the Pacific War. There are more than 7,000 nicked and wrinkled islands in the vast archipelago of the Philippines, but Luzon is the principal isle—the most populated, most developed, and historically most important rock in the green volcanic chain, home of the port city and capital, Manila. In March 1942 when the defeated General MacArthur had vowed, "I shall return," no one needed to ask where he would return *to*. For practical reasons, MacArthur's forces had established an initial Philippine beachhead in October 1944 on the island of Leyte, four hundred miles to the southeast of Manila. But Luzon remained the prize, the sine qua non. Consequently, the Japanese dug in for what the War Ministry in Tokyo called "the decisive battle," although the War Ministry seemed to call every battle "decisive" now that the stakes grew higher and American forces steadily closed in on the home islands of Japan. Radio Tokyo had announced with characteristic hyperbole that American troops attempting to invade Luzon would be treated to "the hottest reception in the history of warfare." Propaganda aside, it was true that General Tomoyuki Yamashita, who commanded the Fourteenth Imperial Army, waited for MacArthur with more than a quarter of a million men.

The invasion took place on the balmy morning of January 9, 1945, at Lingayen Gulf, a broad crescent of beaches, swamps, and aquaculture ponds some 100 miles north of Manila. In terms of firepower and manpower, in terms of planes and warships and amphibious craft, the invasion at Lingayen Gulf was one of the most monumental operations of World War II, involving 164 ships, 3,000 landing craft, and some 280,000 American troops.

Such titanic force turned out to be unnecessary. Postponing his "hot reception" for later, Yamashita declined to contest the landing. American ships had encountered a number of devastating kamikaze attacks and bombings from enemy torpedo planes en route to Lingayen Gulf, but the Japanese ground forces on Luzon conserved their firepower for the protracted defensive war Yamashita planned to wage in the highland jungles in the north of Luzon.

Thus the great invasion, while epic in scale, bordered on the anticlimactic. The Japanese responded with an eerie calm that seemed out of character. Only a matter of hours after the big naval guns thundered in the predawn darkness, the first American troops waded ashore. Not only were the Lingayen beaches unfortified—they were empty.

Five hours later, Douglas MacArthur marched onto the strand with his usual pomp and circumstance. Then, with little of either, came General Walter Krueger, the decidedly businesslike and undramatic commander of the U.S. Sixth Army. Krueger was a career military man beloved by ordinary troops for his gruff and uncomplicated humility, which made him seem the antithesis of his Supreme Commander. He was sixty-four years old, the son of Prussian immigrants. As a young man, Krueger had fought with distinction across the plains of Luzon in the so-called Philippine Insurrection after the Spanish-American War. Now, thirty-six years later, he stood on the palm-fringed shores at the head of a mighty army.

MacArthur and Krueger established a beachhead and quickly regained their bearings in a land they both knew with intimacy and fondness. With the Japanese refusing to join the battle at the coast, the Americans were left with two separate goals: pursue Yamashita north into the mountains and drive south for Manila. But winning the capital came first, and MacArthur urged Krueger to move his Sixth Army down the Central Plain with all possible haste. "Go to Manila," MacArthur demanded. "Go around them, go through them, but go to Manila."

—————

It was in pursuit of this goal that two weeks later, on January 26, General Krueger was presented with a dilemma of enormous emotional import. The Sixth Army had driven halfway to Manila when he learned that a certain fragile obstacle stood in the way of his forces. His highest G-2 officer, a big, burly man from Nebraska named

Horton White, laid out the problem with all of its nuances. They sat in Krueger's field tent at Sixth Army headquarters in Calasio, a little town a few miles from Lingayen Gulf that was now completely overtaken by the U.S. Army, surrounded by Quonset huts and supply depots. The green canvas tent billowed in the sea breeze, and a large topographical map of Luzon was perched on an easel.

Earlier that day, White explained to General Krueger, he'd had a series of intense discussions with an American guerrilla leader named Robert Lapham. Lapham was a thin, shrewd, flinty man from Davenport, Iowa, who'd spent the past three years living in the shadows, directing a band of Filipino insurgents in a protracted fight against the Japanese occupation. Lapham had ridden his horse some forty miles from his hideout in Nueva Ecija province to alert G-2 about a situation that he believed could develop into a terrible disaster. He told Horton White that near the city of Cabanatuan (KA-ba-na-TWAHN), which lay some sixty miles to the east of Calasio, there were approximately 500 American soldiers living in a squalid prison camp. These prisoners, he said, had been captured by the Japanese after the fall of Bataan and Corregidor, the largest surrender in American military history. Many of them were survivors of the Bataan Death March. For three years they had starved and slaved. Their fellow prisoners had died by the thousands because the camp commandant refused to give them even the most rudimentary of medicines. At one time Cabanatuan camp had been the largest POW compound in all of the Philippines and one of the largest in all of Asia, housing as many as 8,000 Americans. It was the mother camp around which all the others had served as satellites. Nearly every American

25

who'd been captured by the Japanese had passed through its sordid gates at some point. The population had fluctuated over the years, with prisoners constantly coming and going and coming back again depending on the whims and changing needs of the Japanese Army. But in recent months, Lapham said, the camp census had dwindled dramatically. The Imperial Army had been sending all the able-bodied prisoners on ships to work as stevedores and coal miners in Japan.

Now all that was left at Cabanatuan were the dregs, the sickest and the weakest. The ghosts of Bataan, they called themselves, with a mixture of black humor and the peculiar proud toughness of the orphaned. When General MacArthur had abandoned the Philippines in March 1942, these were the men he abandoned—or, rather, what was left of them. They were a special lot, a subset of a subset of bad fortune, an elite of the damned.

Major Lapham knew all of this about Cabanatuan because the camp was in his backyard. For the past three years his area of operation had been Nueva Ecija, and Cabanatuan City was the provincial capital. His guerrillas had been keeping a close eye on the place. They knew everything about the camp—the black markets, the personnel changes, the executions, the work details. Since the invasion of Lingayen Gulf, they'd become increasingly worried about the fate of the prisoners. There was, Lapham said, a very good chance that the Japanese would massacre these prisoners. Paradoxically, the closer the Sixth Army drew to Cabanatuan, the greater the risks became. For years, Lapham and his guerrillas had dreamed of storming this thatch bastille and spiriting the prisoners to safety. Now, more than ever, the urgency of such an action impressed itself upon Lapham. He was a practical and steel-nerved man, but lately he'd felt what he called "forebodings." As Lapham would later write in his memoirs: "The plight of the prisoners at Cabanatuan had been on my mind for many months. I found it hard to think clearly when I was so emotionally committed to their rescue. We feared that once the Japanese thought the invasion was imminent, they would kill all the prisoners."

Such a mission would be tricky, Lapham suggested, because large numbers of Japanese troops, as many as 8,000 or 9,000, were building up around Cabanatuan City. On the other hand, Lapham said his guerrillas could provide invaluable assistance should the Army decide to proceed with such an operation.

Horton White was taken by everything Lapham had said. The intelligence reports that he had been seeing over the past month seemed to validate the guerrilla leader's fears. The Japanese were increasingly turning to frenzied acts of rage and bloodshed. As the possibility of defeat loomed nearer, they were sinking into a kind of madness. The horror of the Palawan massacre was only the most recent example of this fearful spiral. At the battle of Saipan in the early summer of 1944, the U.S. marines were shocked and amazed to find that hundreds of Japanese soldiers had committed suicide—in many cases by ritualistic disembowelment, or seppuku—rather than face capture. At the battle of Leyte Gulf three months earlier, the Navy had seen the arrival of a deadly new weapon, the kamikaze plane, which conveyed with ghastly eloquence the depth of the Japanese desperation.

Army intelligence already understood the contempt with which the Japanese Army viewed the prisoner-of-war status. The Military Field Code, which was promulgated by Hideki Tojo in January 1941, had made it expressly clear to all Japanese soldiers that falling into enemy hands brought irrevocable shame not only to the captured soldier but to his entire family. "Have regard for your family first," the Field Code stated. "Rather than live and bear the shame of imprisonment by the enemy, the soldier must die and avoid leaving a dishonorable name." The Field Code directed the Japanese soldier to save the last round of ammunition for himself, or to charge the enemy in a suicidal assault. Consequently, Japanese prisoners were a rarity indeed. Armies of Western nations fighting in World War II typically saw a ratio of four soldiers captured to every soldier killed on the battlefield. In the Japanese Army, the ratio was one soldier captured for every 120 deaths.

For the few Japanese soldiers who *were* taken prisoner, captivity was viewed in radically different terms than in Western armies. In August 1944, Army G-2 was apprised of an incident in Australia that dramatically pointed out this vast perceptual gulf. The incident occurred in the early hours of August 5, at a large POW camp that had been constructed for Japanese prisoners in the parched countryside of New South Wales, near the town of Cowra. That morning more than 900 Japanese prisoners charged the barbed-wire perimeter clutching baseball bats, crude clubs, and cutlery knives. Issuing banzai battle cries, they attacked the camp gun emplacements in what was later determined to be a mass suicide attempt. In this incident 234 Japanese died and 108 were wounded. At least 31 prisoners killed themselves outright—either by hanging or by other means—and twelve were burned to death in huts set afire by their own comrades. "I could not kill myself and had been waiting for some force to kill me," said one participant who survived the ordeal. Said another: "The shame of being a Japanese prisoner of war was beyond endurance. . . . The time to die, which had been our desire since the day of our capture, had arrived."

If this was the way in which the Japanese viewed their own prisoners of war, Horton White could well wonder, then how could they be expected to view American POWs with a sense of mercy? The Japanese had signed but had never ratified the Geneva Convention of 1929, which concerned the humane treatment of prisoners. When the war began, Prime Minister Tojo had issued instructions to the commandants of all the Japanese-run POW camps. "In Japan," he told them, "we have our own ideology concerning prisoners of war which should naturally make their treatment more or less different from that in Europe and America." Tojo proved tragically correct in his assessment of these differences. After the war, it would be calculated that the death rate of all Allied POWs held in German and Italian camps was approximately 4 percent. In Japanese-run camps, the death rate was 27 percent. One out of every four captives of the Japanese perished.

Given everything G-2 understood about the Japanese regard for prisonerhood, Horton White appreciated how a dire situation such as the approach of a massive army could upset the tenuous balance at Cabanatuan and provoke the enemy to annihilate the internees. Now that the caprices of war were turning against them, G-2 expected the Japanese to grow even more ruthless and unpredictable. The training and culture of the Imperial Army encouraged them to regard the POWs, in the narrowest possible terms, as contemptible men who could nonetheless be useful in the war effort; once their usefulness stopped, however, so did their existential lease. A massacre could come about as the spontaneous and passionate outburst of vengeance-seeking combatants who finally saw the writing on the wall. Or it could unfold as a matter of higher policy, one predicated on the cold math of a losing war and filtered through the austerities of the Bushido warrior code from the Samurai days.

In August 1944, the War Ministry in Tokyo had issued a directive to the commandants of various POW camps, outlining a policy for what it called the "final disposition" of prisoners. A copy of this document, which came to be known as the "August 1 Kill-All Order," would surface in the war crimes investigations in Tokyo. Bearing a chilling resemblance to actual events that occurred at Palawan, the directive stated:

> *When the battle situation becomes urgent the POWs will be concentrated and confined in their location and kept under heavy guard until preparations for the final disposition will be made. Although the basic aim is to act under superior orders, individual disposition may be made in [certain] circumstances. Whether they are destroyed individually or in groups, and whether it is accomplished by means of mass bombing, poisonous smoke, poisons, drowning, or decapitation, dispose of them as the situation dictates. It is the aim not to allow the escape of a single one, to annihilate them all, and not to leave any traces.*

— — — — — —

General Walter Krueger needed no further convincing from Horton White. By all means, by any means, a force must be immediately dispatched ahead of the lines to attempt a rescue of Cabanatuan. It was an eleventh-hour mission of mercy that Krueger knew would be near to General MacArthur's heart. "Sounds risky," Krueger said, "but it's a wonderful enterprise."

Krueger consulted the map and considered the date. It was January 26. In five days he expected that his forces would reach Cabanatuan City. With that in mind, Krueger asked White when he thought the rescue should be attempted.

White's reply was grave. "I would say that after the twenty-ninth, our odds of finding prisoners alive are quite remote." They had but a few days of latitude.

The mission, they decided, would unfold as a unilateral operation, discrete from all the other movements and actions being undertaken by the Sixth Army. No one else within the army would be told about it. "It was obvious that any rescue attempt would have to be kept absolutely secret," Krueger would write in his memoirs. "Success depended upon surprise. If the Japanese received any inkling of it they would probably massacre all the prisoners."

Then came the question of who would carry out such a mission. Krueger would need a group of men trained in stealth techniques and the tactics of lightning assault. The expeditioners must be in exceptional physical condition, as they would have to cover some thirty miles on foot in each direction, marching around the clock. They would have to be versatile, self-reliant, and extremely proficient with light arms, as the odds were better than good that they would encounter major enemy resistance somewhere along the trek.

As Krueger and White mulled it over, the answer suggested itself.

31

"There's Mucci," White said.

Lieutenant Colonel Henry Mucci was the commanding officer of a remarkable outfit known as the 6th Ranger Battalion. The Rangers were a new, relatively untested unit of elite infantry that had been loosely patterned after the British Commandos. Colonel Mucci, a West Pointer and second-generation Italian-American, was the son of a Bridgeport, Connecticut, horse salesman. Mucci had personally overseen every minute of the Rangers' training during the past year in the jungles of New Guinea. They hadn't started out as Rangers, however. Originally they had been Army mule skinners. They were large men, recruited mostly from farms and ranches, who had been assigned to a pack artillery unit trained to work in the remote mountains carrying howitzers that broke down into parts for transport on the backs of mules. Their outfit was known as the 98th Field Artillery Battalion, Pack. After an arduous stateside training that had included climbing with their mules up Pike's Peak in Colorado, the 98th had been shipped to New Guinea with the assignment of transporting their equipment up and over the 10,000-foot Owen Stanley Mountains. But by the time they got to Port Moresby in early 1943, the battle was winding down, and besides, the higher planners had decided that mules were an obsolete way of doing business for a modern, mechanized army. As was sometimes said of the sterile beasts of burden they led, the 98th had "no pride of ancestry, no hope of posterity." The mules were sent off to Burma, and the men, who in truth had grown tired of getting kicked and bitten and stepped on by their stubborn animals, happily awaited a new assignment. With a few clicks of a field typewriter inside a tent somewhere in New

Guinea, the 98th was disbanded and the mule skinners became the 6th Ranger Battalion under the command of a perfect stranger named Henry Mucci, who aspired to mold them in less than a year into a sterling fighting force of jungle commandos.

The new Rangers could see right from the start that Mucci (MEW-see) was a colorful and forceful personality. A Pearl Harbor survivor, he had been the Provost Marshall in Honolulu. Some of the Rangers came to call him "Little MacArthur," not only because he smoked a pipe incessantly but also because he had, like the Supreme Commander, a firm grasp of the theatrics of warfare—the salesmanship, the cajolery, the motivational tricks and public-relations gimmicks that, when applied in a certain magical combination, can give a unit both high morale and a high profile. Henry Andrew Mucci was such a lavish and convincing persuader that the Rangers supplied him with another nickname—Ham, an acronym formed naturally enough from his initials, but also a sobriquet that captured his incorrigible knack for laying on the bullshit with a very large shovel. His men didn't care—they adored him, in large part because anything he asked them to do and anywhere he asked them to go he was right there alongside them. Mucci was a fitness enthusiast who could outrun and outmarch most subordinates ten years his junior. Thirty-three years old, he was a short, sinewy man with a pencil mustache, thick black eyebrows, and enormous forearms bristling with dark hair.

He was also extremely ambitious. His expectations for the Rangers could not have been higher. During the invasion of Leyte in October, Mucci's Rangers had been given the special honor of securing three small islands that clogged the bay and had to be quelled before the true landing could begin. The Leyte assignment had the markings of a bold and potentially suicidal mission, but in the end most of his Rangers had seen little action, as the Japanese had largely vacated the islands just prior to their landing. Frustrated, Mucci had sent back a message to his headquarters: "Here we are, with all these goddamned bullets and no Japs." Ever since they had landed on Luzon, Mucci had been waiting for a big mission and none had been forthcoming. It was now more than two weeks after the Lingayen Gulf invasion and still they sat idle. An impatient, restlessly energetic man, the colonel was desperate to show what his troops could do.

Since they had little else with which to occupy themselves, some of the Rangers had been assigned to serve as Krueger's personal bodyguards at his Calasio headquarters. They were parked right outside the tent while Krueger and White conversed, standing sentinel like a line of stiff Beefeaters. It was plain to see they were bored out of their minds. Guarding Krueger was an honor, of course, but the drear inactivity of the post rather cramped the colonel's sense of Ranger style.

"Send for him," Krueger told White. "Mucci's the one."

———————

Colonel Mucci spent the following day at Sixth Army headquarters meeting with Horton White and Robert Lapham, reviewing all the details and requirements for his mission. Since he couldn't bring all 800 of his Rangers, Mucci decided to assign the mission to C Company, which was under the command of a sharp young Stanford graduate from Seattle with the auspicious-sounding name, for a rescuer, of Robert Prince. Mucci had such confidence in Captain Prince that he designated him "assault commander" and asked him to design the master plan for the raid on the prison stockade. The son of a successful Washington State apple distributor, Prince possessed the quiet optimism of a forward thinker, someone with a prudent, understated judgment about people and situations. Prince was blessed with the rarest of gifts: steady nerves. He had the take-it-or-leave-it equanimity of a citizen soldier, a non–West Pointer without long-range military ambition, someone who wanted to do his job as best he could and then get back home to Seattle as soon as possible, back to his new bride, Barbara, and the important stuff of living. His grandfather had been a Union soldier in the Civil War and was wounded at Petersburg, but the military had never particularly been a family profession. Prince had nothing grandiose to prove, no saber-rattling father to measure up to, no weird baggage passed down from an old Army clan.

Cool. That was the word everybody used to describe Prince. And in so many senses: circumspect, soft-spoken, methodical, bookish, hard to impress, slow to react, maybe a little standoffish. In a surprise commando raid, perhaps the hottest of all military engagements, coolness was the essential quality, the antidote. Prince had it.

When Colonel Mucci returned from Sixth Army headquarters on the afternoon of Saturday, January 27, he conferred with Captain Prince, and then the two officers called a meeting of C Company. The Ranger camp was keen with anticipation. Mucci's men had seen him leave for Army headquarters in a staff car that morning, and they were dying to know what he was coming back with. Now Mucci stood before them with an assignment finally in hand.

"It's going to be extremely dangerous," he said. "Some of you might not make it back."

He explained only the essence of it—the details would come later. The following morning at dawn, the men of C Company, along with one platoon from F Company, were to head east in a convoy of trucks to a little place on the brink of the American lines called Guimba. From there, they would walk thirty miles through enemy territory in a stealth operation considered so important and yet held in such tight secrecy that no one else besides General Krueger himself would know about it. There was a prison camp, he said, full of the last ill and stick-figured American survivors from Bataan and Corregidor. The task before the Rangers was to liberate these prisoners before the Japanese slaughtered them all. "You're going to bring out every last man," he said, "even if you have to carry them on your backs."

It was a plum assignment, but the risks were immense. As Mucci put it, they'd be "behind the eight ball" for the duration of the raid. The area around the camp was infested with enemy troops, he said. He urged anyone who had doubts to drop out then and there. He especially recommended that married men withdraw from the mission. Such was the difficulty of the operation that he wanted every last member of the expedition to be a volunteer. Mucci said, "I only want men who feel lucky."

The assembled Rangers studied each other in mute amazement. They all felt lucky. No one dropped out.

"One other thing," Mucci said. "There'll be no atheists

on this trip." Upon adjourning the meeting, he said he wanted every last one of them to meet with the chaplains and pray on their knees. Services would be held in a half hour. "I want you to swear an oath before God," he told them. "Swear that you'll die fighting rather than let any harm come to those prisoners."

Pivoting with a flourish, Little MacArthur bid his men adieu and left them to their swirling thoughts. Then all 120 of them, even the cynics and doubting Thomases in the ranks, went to church.

Book One

Blood
Brothers

Though all men
Across the seas of this world
Are brothers,
Why do the wind and waves
Yet so resound?

Emperor Meiji

Chapter 1

Dr. Ralph Emerson Hibbs lay delirious in a ditch at the tattered edge of the jungle, his teeth clicking with chills. The malarial attack came over him suddenly, as they always did, the strength dropping from his legs like an untethered weight. In their thousands the parasites were reproducing inside him, *Plasmodium vivax* bursting from his liver and into his bloodstream. The doctor had nothing with which to treat himself. He couldn't work, he couldn't think. He had to ride out the fever as everyone else did, helplessly, shivering in a ditch by the side of a battle-pocked road. An Army captain and a graduate of the University of Iowa Medical School, Dr. Hibbs was the surgeon of the 2nd Battalion of the 31st Infantry Regiment, a man responsible for the health of some 700 soldiers in the field, but he had no quinine. On the anopheles-infested peninsula of Bataan at the end of the first week of April 1942, there was virtually no quinine to be had.

Along with thousands of other malarial men, Dr. Hibbs had been walking out of the mountains down the zigzag road toward Mariveles. In great haste and confusion, the men were stumbling south to escape the turmoil and the butchery of the front lines, where for the past week the Japanese onslaught had been merciless. One participant later described the exodus: "Thousands poured out of the jungle like small spring freshets pouring into creeks which in turn poured into a river." As they walked, the soldiers picked their way around bomb craters and bits of embedded shrapnel. The jungle smoked all about them. Overturned wrecks of jeeps and half-tracks lay smoldering in the creeper ferns. The rattan vines were singed, the tree leaves wormed with bullet holes, the canopy torn open by artillery shells, letting the late-afternoon sun seep through.

The word had come from somewhere or other that General King would offer his surrender in the morning. Hibbs reacted to this news with as much relief as sadness. Everyone knew the situation was hopeless. "We were participants in a lousy game," Hibbs later wrote. "We couldn't live much longer, let alone fight." The men were gaunt, shell-shocked, addled with nerve fatigue. They were so exhausted, as one soldier put it, "that even our hair was tired." They were fighting with improvised weapons, living on improvised food. Day by day the regular had devolved into the irregular. Sailors were serving as infantryman, firing machine guns fashioned from parts cannibalized from crashed airplanes. Corned beef had segued to hardtack, and hardtack to iguana, and iguana to grubs and silkworms. Army veterinarians who under ordinary circumstances were supposed to care for the health of the pack mules and horses had instead been overseeing their slaughter for "cavalry steak." The lines had broken so many times it was absurd to persist in calling them lines anymore. The men of Bataan had fallen back to the place where there was no more back to fall back to. Densely packed with hospital patients, ammunition dumps, military hardware, and the scattered remnants of the troops, the southern tip of Bataan had become so crowded, recalled one American officer, that "bombers could drop their payloads at almost any point or place and hit something of military value." Whether one wanted to call it a retrograde maneuver, or a strategic withdrawal, or some other euphemism for retreat, they simply had nowhere to go. At their front was the Fourteenth Imperial Army, at their rear was the South China Sea.

And above them, Zeros. For weeks and months, the skies had droned with Mitsubishi engines. The bombing and strafing runs had been relentless, chewing up the little nipa huts in the Filipino barrios, leaving the brown grass fields and canebrakes, especially combustible in the dry season, consumed by enormous fires. Photo Joe, as the Americans called the enemy surveillance planes, had circled overhead with impunity, radioing the exact disposition of the Fil-American forces so the Japanese artillerymen on the ground could rain shells upon them with deadlier precision. There was even a doddering surveillance blimp which for some reason the Americans couldn't seem to bring out of the sky.

The planes not only dropped bombs, they dropped words. As the battle dragged on, propaganda sheets had fluttered down from the skies. One leaflet depicted a voluptuous woman beckoning soldiers to bed down with her. "Before the terror comes, let me walk beside you . . . deep in petaled sleep. Let me, while there is still a time and place. Feel soft against me and . . . rest your warm hand on my

43

breast." More recently the propaganda had turned from a tone of clumsy prurience to one of dark ultimatum.

> *Bataan is about to be swept away. Hopes for the arrival of reinforcements are quite in vain. If you continue to resist, the Japanese forces will by every possible means destroy and annihilate your forces relentlessly to the last man. Further resistance is completely useless. You, dear soldiers, give up your arms and stop resistance at once.*
>
> Commander-in-Chief of the Imperial Japanese Forces

Yet for the men of Bataan, disease was the real enemy, killing them and sapping their morale with even greater efficacy than the Fourteenth Army. Old diseases that modern medicine had long since learned how to treat. Diseases of vitamin dearth, diseases of bad hygiene, diseases of jungle rot, diseases of sexual promiscuity, and, of course, the vector-borne diseases of the Asian tropics. Their bodies coursed with every worm and pathogen a hot jungle can visit upon a starved and weakened constitution— dengue fever, amebic dysentery, bacillary dysentery, tertian malaria, cerebral malaria, typhus, typhoid. The field hospitals were rife with gas gangrene, spreading from wound to wound to wound. The men's joints ached with the various odd swellings of incipient beriberi, an illness of vitamin B deficiency which, as one soldier described the condition, left the legs feeling "watery and pump[ing] with pains" and made the racing heart "thump like a tractor engine bogged in a swamp."

Working at the front lines with the 31st Infantry, Dr. Hibbs had seen all of these conditions, and many others of even greater exoticism, but increasingly he'd found it impossible to treat the sufferers. It was a medical defeat. The hospitals overflowed to the point that the nurses were setting up outdoor wards among the gnarled folds and aerial roots of ancient banyan trees.

Of all the various units and outfits spread over Bataan, the 31st had seen a disproportionate share of sickness and death, especially in the last few weeks of the siege. Not only were its men in the thick of battle, but they generally ate less well than supply units situated closer to the quartermaster. It is an old hard fact of war that rations mysteriously shrink as they make their way to the front. And so the proud 31st, which before the war had been known as the Thirsty-first for its reputed drinking prowess, then came to be known as the Hungry-first, the most starved of all the American units on Bataan.

During the last few weeks of the fighting, the bloodshed had been horrific. Dr. Hibbs's memory of the last battles was a blur of despair and carnage. One morning Hibbs had found himself holding a leg whose owner could not be located. On another day, he had treated a kid with a ghastly shrapnel wound to the head, a wound large enough so that gray matter was protruding from his skull. Hibbs had declared the young soldier a goner, but then he had miraculously rallied, only to lapse into a coma. The battle raged so intensely that the whole unit was forced to pull back, but the medics had no litters or ambulances with which to transport casualties. Hibbs never forgot the sight of the blood-smeared boy dangling over the shoulders of the medics like a sodden rag doll as they retreated into the jungle. They would set the kid down on the ground and resume the fight, then pick him up and withdraw again, then set him down and fight some more. This went on all day,

45

with the boy becoming like a terrible mascot of the retreat. It hardly seemed worth the effort; the boy's brains were pushing out of his head, the color had washed from his face, his pulse was barely there—yet he kept on breathing. For Hibbs, the scene was a metaphor for what the fighting on Bataan had become, a heroic struggle to prolong a hopeless cause.

At night, when the fighting subsided, a lieutenant named Henry Lee would dash off lines of poetry from his foxhole. Universally beloved by members of the Philippine Division Headquarters Company, Lee was from Pasadena, California, and had been educated at Pomona College, where he first cultivated his literary aspirations. On Bataan he fought with the elite Filipino soldiers known as the Philippine Scouts. Whenever he wasn't holding a gun, he could usually be found with a pen in his hand. There was one snippet of Lee's verse that especially caught the spirit of the last weeks. Entitled "Prayer Before Battle," it was written as an homage to Mars.

> *Drained of faith*
> *I kneel and hail thee as my Lord*
> *I ask not life*
> *Thou need not swerve the bullet*
> *I ask but strength to ride the wave*
> *and one thing more—*
> *teach me to hate.*

Defeat had come slowly, steadily, over a period of four months. As in all great sieges, the fall of Bataan was not so much an emphatic decision of arms as it was an epic draw-down marked by increments of physical, spiritual, and material depletion. As John Hersey wrote at the time, the truth had come to the men of Bataan "in mean little doses." Hibbs had begun his tour of Philippine duty with a sunny nonchalance, even as the threat of war loomed. Manila was considered the easiest post in the Army, the "Pearl of the Orient," where officers lazed away the heat of the day and danced away the nights dressed in natty sharkskin suits, drinking gin and tonics and San Miguel beer at the Jai Alai Club. Hibbs had had a love affair with a Manila society girl named Pilar Campos, a beautiful young mestiza who was the daughter of the president of the Bank of the Philippine Islands. "Neither of us," Hibbs wrote, "sought help in finding the moral path." In late November, less than two weeks before the first Zeros came to attack Luzon, Hibbs had written a chipper note to his parents back in Oskaloosa, Iowa. "Things are peaceful here," he wrote.

> Life in the Orient is easygoing with emphasis on the mañana and siesta ethic. With the tremendous military buildup here, a Jap attack seems unlikely. If I had it to do over again, I would have gone to England. There's nothing going to happen here.
>
> Love, Ralph

By January, Hibbs recognized how misplaced his insouciance was, but he tried to put the best face on the situation. An optimist by nature, he endeavored to look for hope in the shadows, to ascribe the non-arrival of promised arms and medicines to honest mistakes that could be easily redeemed. A slender, bespectacled man with some of the bearing and affable features of the young Jimmy Stewart, Hibbs kept his sense of humor no matter how grim things got, his eyes always lit with a suggestion of mischief. In February, Hibbs sent another letter to his folks, which proved to be his last communication from Bataan—a letter notable for its facade of good cheer where plainly none existed.

> Life is not too bad. I have a bamboo bed, a blanket, plenty of water, a few too many mosquitoes. The food is fair—carabao, monkey, and occasionally mule. Everyone is content and in fairly good health. No need to worry.
> We have plenty of room in which to maneuver and fight and we have plenty of it left in us. Turn the calf out to pasture. I'll be delayed a while.
>
> Ralph

The letter ran prominently, and without a hint of irony, in the *Des Moines Register* under the headline "Things Are Not Too Bad."

In truth, Hibbs had found monkey to be considerably less than fair. The meat was unappetizing in hue and appearance, and if one had to clean and prepare the animal, consuming it made one feel rather like a cannibal. Hibbs later wrote, "After chewing on a piece it seemed to increase in size, requiring resting of the masseter muscle. Most monkey meat got placed back in our mess kits pretty much undisturbed." As trying as monkey was, the menu on Bataan grew progressively stranger. Meals consisted of cats, slugs, rats, various dried insects, and the meat and eggs of python. Some Filipinos were known to eat dogs;

the bow-hunting Igorot tribesmen who'd been brought in to teach the soldiers jungle survival skills were especially fond of a dish that might be described as hound haggis. "It was a custom to eat the stomach of a dog that had been gorged with rice before sacrificing it," Hibbs remembered. "The warm rice mixed with the mucus of the stomach was supposedly a delicacy."

On the evening of April 8, 1942, "things" were most assuredly bad for Dr. Hibbs. As he sat shivering in the ditch, half lost in the throes of his fever, the vast volcanic jungle clinked and snapped and exploded with the sounds of an army deliberately destroying itself. With surrender imminent, the men had been given the order to ruin their weapons and sabotage any hardware that might prove valuable to the enemy. Men were firing their last rounds of ammunition into the air, detonating their grenades, covering their gun emplacements with brush, dismantling their rifles and mortars and artillery pieces part by part and scattering the miscellaneous components into the jungle. Troops were pouring sand into the gas tanks of jeeps and armored vehicles, or pulling the drain plugs from the oil pans while the engines were left running. On the labyrinthine network of tiny trails that spread like capillaries over the southern tip of Bataan, the soldiers were not so much casting down their weapons as they were obliterating them, in preparation for General King's expected announcement of capitulation.

Suddenly the night erupted in a series of explosions that Hibbs described as "apocalyptic." He was hearing, and feeling, the dying gasp of the U.S. Army Forces of the Far East: The demolition squads were blowing up the last of the big American ammunition dumps to keep them from falling into Japanese hands. For a time that evening, the southern tip of Bataan took on the sheen of day, and one could limn the complex outline of the peninsula, with its deep ravines and extinct volcanoes, its innumerable points and promontories fingering out into the sea. The mighty island fortress of Corregidor could be seen shimmering in Manila Bay. Cringing in his ditch, Dr. Hibbs tried to shield himself from the rain of dirt and rocks and shell fragments that fell out from the explosions. The dumps contained several million dollars' worth of explosives—hundreds of thousands of rounds of small-arms ammunition and artillery shells. The detonations of TNT were unimaginably powerful, and they more than aroused Hibbs from his febrile stupor. "It was the biggest fireworks display I'd ever seen, even bigger than the Iowa State Fair," Hibbs said. "With each blast, my body would bounce clear into the air."

The fires from the ammunition dumps gradually dwindled, leaving a thick gunpowder haze over the jungle. Hibbs returned to a fitful sleep, only to be awakened sometime later in the night by another disturbance. The ground was rumbling, and although the night was otherwise still, the ipil-ipil thickets seemed to be twisting and swishing as though brushed by a strong wind. Nearly every soldier on Bataan felt it, a distant violent grumble in a low bass tone lasting perhaps twenty seconds.

"You'd think it was an earthquake," Hibbs muttered drowsily as he rose up on one elbow.

A Filipino runner who knew the situation happened to be stationed nearby. "Sir," he said. "It *is* an earthquake."

A few minutes after nine o'clock on the following morning, April 9, Major General Edward King crawled into a jeep and rode north from his command post toward Japanese lines to confer with representatives of General Masaharu Homma. As King and his small entourage of four men bounced along the rutted road with white flags fluttering in the wind, the general from Georgia brooded over a certain matter of historical irony. On the very same day in 1865, General Lee had met with Grant at Appomattox Court House to capitulate to the Union Army. Now, seventy-seven years later, King planned to lay down his arms in what would prove to be a surrender larger than any other in American history *except* for Appomattox. Approximately 78,000 American and Filipino soldiers were fighting on Bataan under his command; in addition, some 20,000 Filipino civilians had been drawn into the conflict.

That morning King had put on his last clean uniform so that he might look as dignified as possible under the circumstances. Gracious, mild-mannered, and taciturn, King was a career artilleryman with a law degree from the University of Georgia. A zealous student of Civil War history, King remarked that he felt as Lee must have felt before meeting with Grant, when the Confederate general had said, "I would rather die a thousand deaths."

Yet King understood that he had no choice. His troops were scattered and demoralized, many having resorted to looting food depots and hijacking supply trucks at gunpoint. King noted that in the five days since the start of the massive Japanese assault that came to be known as the Good Friday Offensive, the combat efficiency of the Luzon Force was "rapidly approaching the zero point." His quartermaster reported that he had only one more half-ration of food to dole out to the men, and even that last meal would be problematical because the distribution system had collapsed. As many as 24,000 men were crowded into the field hospitals and aid stations of southern Bataan. "If I do not surrender to the Japanese," King said at the time, "Bataan will be known as the greatest slaughter in history." He reasoned that "already our hospital, which is filled to capacity and directly in the line of hostile approach, is within range of enemy light artillery. We have no further means of organized resistance."

The Japanese aerial attack on Luzon had begun on the same day as the attack on Pearl Harbor—December 7 in Hawaii, December 8 across the International Date Line in the Philippines. By a series of incomprehensible blunders and incredibly bad luck, the Japanese bombers and Zeros caught a large portion of the American Air Force of the Far East on the ground at Clark Field north of Manila. In a matter of hours, the United States had lost control of the skies.

For the first few days of the attack, Douglas MacArthur, who was then in command of the defense of the Philippines, lapsed into something of a fugue state. He stayed secreted inside his penthouse in the Manila Hotel, virtually unreachable and apparently unable to react. When he finally emerged, he somewhat reluctantly invoked a defensive strategy, known as War Plan Orange, that had been on the drawing boards for many years. The plan was executed brilliantly and with alacrity. Declaring Manila an "open city," the outgunned Americans systematically withdrew from their positions around the capital and funneled down into the Bataan Peninsula to prepare for the onslaught of Homma's Fourteenth Imperial Army.

A few days before Christmas, Homma's troops landed at Lingayen Gulf and made their way south toward Manila, many thousands of them on bicycles. Encountering only weak and erratic resistance, Homma stormed into the undefended capital to find that the bulk of MacArthur's forces were already deeply entrenched on Bataan, which, with its roadless jungles and steep volcanic headlands jutting out into Manila Bay, was perfectly suited for a protracted defensive war.

Bataan was perfectly suited, that is, as long as the trapped defenders could receive reinforcements of food and munitions from the outside world. War Plan Orange had always been predicated on the assumption that the Army would have to hold out on Bataan only long enough for the Navy to steam across the Pacific Ocean and save the day. But, of course, there *was* no Navy: the Pacific fleet had been virtually destroyed at Pearl Harbor. Without warships to break the Japanese blockade, it was nearly impossible for sufficient shipments of supplies to reach the men of Bataan and Corregidor, the massively fortified island just off the tip of the peninsula that controlled access to Manila Bay. And so the defense soon devolved into a brutal war of attrition—a war, as one participant later put it, of "consumption without replenishment."

Nearly from the outset, Bataan bore the markings of an American Thermopylae, a desperate act of heroic defense that seemed destined, ultimately, to fail. One Japanese officer likened the American predicament on Bataan to that of "a cat entering a sack." Lieutenant Henry Lee, the poet in the Philippine Scouts, described Bataan as "our own little rat trap . . . a rear guard with no main body." The men were stranded on a finger of land, forced to fight on rations of less than fifteen ounces a day with rusty, antiquated equipment that dated back, in some cases, to World War I. The War Department in Washington briefly weighed more ambitious schemes to relieve the Americans on a large scale before it was too late. But by Christmas of 1941, Washington had already come to regard Bataan as a lost cause. President Roosevelt had decided to concentrate American resources primarily in the European theater rather than attempt to fight an all-out war on two distant fronts. At odds with the emerging master strategy for winning the war, the remote outpost of Bataan lay doomed. By late December, President Roosevelt and War Secretary Henry Stimson had confided to Winston Churchill that they had regrettably written off the Philippines. In a particularly chilly phrase that was later to become famous, Stimson had remarked, "There are times when men have to die."

Still, during the four months of the siege there were repeated intimations that food, ammunition, and medicines were on their way. President Roosevelt made a number of promises that he knew could never be kept, at one point pledging the Philippine people by radio that "every vessel available" was en route to Luzon. Roosevelt wired MacArthur with the stirring report that "every ship at our disposal is bringing to the southwest Pacific the forces which will ultimately smash the invader." MacArthur was both a victim of Roosevelt's deceit and a purveyor of false hope himself—for he was inclined to view even the most guardedly worded cable from the War Department in an unrealistically sanguine light. MacArthur rightly felt betrayed by Washington, yet at the same time he burned with an optimism that bordered on the pathological. The most resounding promise of relief had been issued by MacArthur himself in the form of a January 15 communiqué written directly to the troops in a prose style that was histrionic even by his standards. "Help is on the way," he pledged.

Thousands of troops and hundreds of planes are being dispatched. The exact time and arrival of reinforcements is unknown as they will have to fight their way through Japanese attempts against them. It is imperative that our troops hold until these reinforcements arrive. No further retreat is possible. Our supplies are ample; a determined defense will defeat the enemy's attack. It is a question now of courage and determination. Men who run will merely be destroyed, but men who fight will save themselves and their country. I call upon every soldier in Bataan to fight in his assigned position, resisting every attack.

General MacArthur had done his part to resist every attack by directing the action from the confines of his concrete bunker deep inside the Malinta Tunnel on "the Rock," as Corregidor was known. He made but one trip across the two miles of water from Corregidor to inspect his beleaguered troops on the peninsula. Fairly or not, his molish habits soon earned him the nickname "Dugout Doug" among the increasingly bitter foot soldiers. In truth, MacArthur had demonstrated his personal courage on countless occasions; apparently oblivious to danger, he had a habit of emerging from his tunnel at odd hours, without a helmet, and paying surprise visits to his Corregidor gunners during the full heat of an aerial attack. But the Bataan men never saw MacArthur in this light. Starving in their foxholes, they took to reciting a chant, originally penned by an American newsman, that captured their sense of abandonment mixed with a certain hard-bitten pride:

> *We're the battling bastards of Bataan,*
> *No mama, no papa, no Uncle Sam,*
> *No aunts, no uncles, no nephews, no nieces,*
> *No pills, no planes, no artillery pieces,*
> *. . . and nobody gives a damn.*

In March, when the situation grew truly desperate, President Roosevelt ordered MacArthur to leave his Corregidor bunker. With utmost stealth the general and his family were evacuated by PT boat and then by airplane to Australia. Upon MacArthur's departure, General Jonathan Wainwright, a beloved, hard-drinking stick of a fellow universally known as "Skinny," had crossed over from Bataan to assume command of the Philippines from Corregidor, and, in turn, General Edward King had taken Wainwright's place as commander on Bataan for the final doomed weeks. Even as he assumed his thankless post, King knew that he would be the one who would have to surrender. "He understood the inevitable tragedy of his position," one military historian would write, "and bore his cross unflinchingly."

— — — —

What made surrendering doubly painful for General King was that he had no official consent to do so. In making what he called his "ignominious decision," King had secured approval from no one in the high command, and in fact his superiors were adamantly opposed—or would have been opposed had he consulted them. MacArthur had expressly stated that Bataan was not to fold. From the safe remove of his offices in Melbourne, MacArthur had cabled Army Chief of Staff George C. Marshall that he was "utterly opposed, under any circumstances or conditions, to the ultimate capitulation of this command. . . . If it is to be destroyed it should be upon the actual field of battle taking full toll from the enemy." Skinny Wainwright was equally unyielding in his stated position on the matter. To President Roosevelt, Wainwright had pledged "to keep our flag flying in the Philippines as long as an American soldier or an ounce of food and a round of ammunition remains." The moment Wainwright heard about King's decision to surrender that morning, he tried to contact him and countermand the move. But King proved unreachable by telephone or radio. Wainwright wrote MacArthur that he "disapproved of [King's] action and directed that there would be no surrender. I was informed it was too late to make any change, that the action had already been taken."

General King's unilateral decision to surrender on his men's behalf was thus courageous in several ways at once. He could only assume that he would be court-martialed after the war for acting contrary to orders. Yet he insisted on acting alone so that no one above him, neither Wainwright nor MacArthur nor Marshall, would be "saddled with any part of the responsibility." It was a soberly thought-out move very much in keeping with the sacrificial nature of so much of the Bataan campaign.

Since King could speak only for the forces on Bataan, Corregidor would still hold, at least for the time being, and

Wainwright could decide for himself whether to surrender the citadel or languish until the last ounces of food and the last rounds of ammunition were expended. Various personnel, including the Bataan nurses, would be ferried across the water to Corregidor before it was too late. The 8,000 men on Corregidor had the supplies and morale to continue the fight. The Rock had been the target of a relentless aerial siege so massive that every tree and plant had been obliterated, leaving the surface of the island denuded and riddled with craters. But within the vast network of tunnels, fortifications, and catacombs, the Corregidor forces enjoyed access to considerably more food and ammunition than King's men did. Wainwright could hold out for perhaps a month.

General King had another difficult problem to ponder as he motored north to meet the Japanese. He knew that a large percentage of his men were in such sorry shape that they would be unable to walk to wherever the Japanese intended for them to go. As King put it in a memo: "The physical condition of the command due to long siege, during which they have been on short rations, will make it very difficult to move them a great distance on foot." Foreseeing this eventuality, King had reserved a significant number of American troop-carrying vehicles and ample stores of gasoline expressly for the purpose of trucking the prisoners north to wherever the Japanese might designate. He recognized that it was highly unusual for a defeated general to request that the victors allow him to transport his own army into captivity, but he dearly hoped that General Homma would accept his proposal, for he feared that the Japanese did not possess sufficient numbers of vehicles to accomplish such a large task—and if they did, that they would find more pressing military uses for them.

In spite of the white flags flying conspicuously from the two jeeps, King's forward progress was almost immediately halted by several attacking Japanese planes. The aircraft dove low and proceeded to bomb and strafe the road, aiming straight for King's jeeps. Earlier in the morning King had sent envoys ahead to alert the Japanese that he would be proceeding north to discuss terms for a surrender—and the Japanese had promised safe passage—but somehow the word had failed to spread to the pilots. Every few hundred yards King and his entourage would have to leap from the vehicles and crouch in the roadside ditch to avoid being hit. The planes kept circling back to drop more bombs and pepper the road with machine-gun fire.

King's group crept northward, dodging the planes for more than an hour, until they spotted a Japanese reconnaissance aircraft banking over the road and tipping its wings in greeting. From that point on they continued unmolested. Finally, they passed through the Japanese lines and were met by a soldier who politely escorted them to a farmhouse not far from the town of Lamao. They were shown to a table and chairs that had been arranged outside the house. Still rattled by the perilous jeep ride north, King sat down and tried to wipe some of the roadside dirt from his uniform. Presently a black Cadillac pulled up to the house and out climbed a short, grim-faced man, Colonel Motoo Nakayama, General Homma's senior operations officer. Homma, who was back at his headquarters in Balanga, had declined to appear in person because he had assumed King to be merely a representative of General

Wainwright and refused to conduct negotiations with a man of lower rank.

From the start Nakayama was greatly confused about the nature of General King's relationship to General Wainwright and just what it was that King was offering to surrender. Nakayama took a dim view of King's notion that Bataan should be considered separately from Corregidor—although geographically distinct, the two commands were militarily one and the same as far as the Japanese were concerned. "It is absolutely impossible for me to consider negotiations . . . in any limited area," Nakayama curtly stated. In any case, Nakayama insisted that Wainwright had to be present before General Homma would entertain any serious discussions of surrender. Eventually King prevailed upon Nakayama to hear him out and to agree, at least informally, to a cessation of hostilities. King raised his concerns about the condition of his men and expressed his firm hope that the American and Filipino troops would be treated in accordance with the terms of the Geneva Convention. He then requested that he be allowed to transport his men, under Japanese supervision, in U.S. Army trucks to wherever Homma desired. Nakayama categorically denied these requests. He made it clear that Homma would hear no terms or conditions from King— *certainly* not until Wainwright appeared at the table. When King reiterated his concern for the safety of his troops, Nakayama brusquely cut him off, saying, "The Imperial Japanese Army are not barbarians."

King understood that he was utterly without leverage. Even as they sat conversing, he could hear the rumbling of Japanese artillery. Every minute spent dallying in fruitless negotiation spelled further death for his men. He had no choice but to surrender unconditionally. In lieu of a sword, he removed his .45 pistol and set it upon the table at approximately half past twelve.

Bataan had fallen. General Edward King was a captive of the Imperial Army.

＊＊＊＊＊

When he received the news, Edward "Tommie" Thomas had absolutely no idea what to do, where to go, how to comport himself. Surrender was not on the technical or emotional map of the U.S. Army, nor was it a subject that had been discussed in his training. The word was never even mentioned.

Thomas was a lieutenant with the Signal Corps, and he had been spending the last week on Bataan with his field crew rigging up emergency phone lines across the jungle near the front. Thomas had gleaned strong hints that the end was near, for the designated routes of the phone lines kept changing, and changing again. Stringing wire across dense tropical woods was hard and slow-going work. He and his crews would climb up into the trees with safety belts and spiked shoes, cutting slashes into the bark with bolo knives to mark the route. Later they would come along with a mule rigged up with heavy spools of copper wire. They'd unspool the cable and string it up in the trees, using little more than a compass and an old topo map to guess their way across the gloom of the jungle toward a point that had been previously fixed. On one occasion they were menaced by a Japanese plane, and on another they were shot at by a Japanese sniper, but most of the time they worked alone without incident in the fastness of the rain forest, with bright-feathered birds screeching in the upper story and unseen artillery rumbling in the distance. There were Filipinos in his crew who knew the forest and helped fill out their rations by harvesting berries, bamboo shoots, jackfruit, camotes, cassava roots, and other wild offerings in the thickets. When they spotted tribes of monkeys scampering above them, one of the Filipinos in Thomas' crew would shoot them out of the canopy with his .45 automatic pistol. Unlike Dr. Hibbs of the 31st Infantry, Thomas thought monkey stew tasted "delicious" and in his extreme hunger found eating it conceptually uncomplicated until he came across an intact hand or leg, which to him "resembled that of a baby."

Thomas was a loud, friendly giant of a man, a beaming six-foot-four strawberry blond from Grand Rapids, Michigan, where he'd been a star end on the Godwin High School football team. He'd had a difficult upbringing, even in comparison to the hard-luck stories typically found in the Bataan army. His father left his mother when he was a baby, his young brother had lost an arm in a streetcar accident and then had died of scarlet fever, and during the depths of the Depression his family had sunk into a poverty so extreme that after a series of moves and a stream of bad men constantly coming through the house, Thomas struck out on his own. His mother loved him dearly, but couldn't provide for him. Thomas spent his last two years of high school camping out of a rattletrap car on Buck Creek, living off the meager proceeds of his paper route and his summer wages from tending lettuce in the region's famously rich muck gardens. He had wanted to go to college but he couldn't afford it, so he joined the Army, which in comparison to his life in Grand Rapids seemed a radiant existence, holding out the promise of good wages ($21 a month) and three hot meals a day.

After basic training he entered the Signal Corps School in Monmouth, New Jersey, where among other things he learned to be a radio technician. The Signal Corps had much to teach him as he wended through its ranks, took his shipment to Manila, and rose to second lieutenant. But the Army remained silent on the subject of how he might go about laying down his arms in a jungle 7,000 miles from home and offering himself over to an especially foreign enemy. In addition to all the old myths about American invincibility—America never lost a war, Americans don't quit, God is on our side—there was an unspoken superstition within the ranks that talking about surrender was itself a perilous thing, the germ of disaster. Thomas said, "Surrender was never spoken of. *Never.* Not even when we knew it was coming. We knew it was hopeless, that we'd been abandoned and were fighting a lost cause. But still we couldn't bring ourselves to plan for the inevitable day. To acknowledge the possibility of it was to admit weakness."

Consequently the defeated foot soldiers on Bataan had no protocol to follow. All across the peninsula men were in the same throes of confusion that Thomas found himself in. Many decided to run into the hills to become guerrillas. Taking longer odds, a few attempted to escape Luzon by native boat, sailing south in the direction of the Visayan Islands and, they hoped, Australia. But most soldiers on Bataan knew they would have to submit to the Japanese. For them, the question became: *In what manner?* Should they come out in ones and twos, straggling from the jungle with their hands up? Should they emerge onto the main roads a whole unit at a time, or should officers make the initial overtures as representatives of enlisted men? What sort of personal possessions should they bring with them into captivity? Would they be expected to feed themselves? And what about the 68,000 Filipinos who'd been fighting on Bataan—did they have to surrender in the same fashion as the Americans or should they try to melt into the thickets and return to their civilian lives?

Of greater uncertainty—and more pressing concern— was the question of what would happen to them once they gave themselves up. The men of Bataan had little inkling of what to expect. Some Americans clung to slender hopes that the Japanese would follow more enlightened ideals for the treatment of prisoners as had been laid out in the Geneva Convention, while others who had read or heard about large-scale atrocities in Japanese-occupied China feared the onset of another Nanking. Like most Americans, Thomas was extremely fearful of what his captors would do with him, but at other times he visualized a bright scenario, based upon no particular evidence, in which the Japanese would ultimately give the Americans over to the Red Cross in a mass prisoner exchange.

Never had the U.S. Army fought against an enemy about whom it knew so little. The initial encounter between victor and vanquished would involve an extreme clash of two proud cultures whose profound ignorance of one another predictably generated intense feelings of racial animus and mutual disdain. There was a sense in which the defeated Americans had become victims of their own blithely held notions of racial superiority. Before December 1941, many Americans stationed in and around Manila had scoffed at the Japanese threat, firmly believing that if war ever broke out, the conflict would be decided in a matter of days. To them, Japan was a queer nation of flower arrangers and Zen Buddhists. They were "slope-heads" and "slant-eyes," strange little people who wore bathrobes and sandals with split-toed socks. Americans stereotypically portrayed the Japanese soldiers as buck-toothed simianlike creatures who were neither clever enough nor well-enough equipped to withstand a modern Western army. It was widely believed that nearly all Japanese suffered from a kind of tribal nearsightedness that made them lousy pilots; despite their best efforts they hopelessly missed their targets and often crashed their little tin-can airplanes into the sea. Various Japan experts argued with a straight face that Dai Nippon would not pose a significant threat because the brain of the average Japanese soldier was overtaxed from having to learn the inordinately complex systems of alphabets and Chinese characters that formed the foundation of his written language.

For his part, Thomas had never given a moment's thought to the enemy—his background, his culture, his beliefs. Clearly the stereotypes concerning the Japanese soldier had been wrong, but the Americans had little notion what to replace them with. Said Thomas, "The Japanese were just the Enemy. I had no idea what would happen when I finally met them face to face."

———————

Thomas spent the evening of April 9 hidden with his telephone maintenance crew in the cavelike folds of an immense tree just a few hundred feet from the main road, which was thronged with tattered American soldiers moving south in great confusion toward Mariveles. The following morning, Thomas' Filipino crewmen decided to head north through the jungle and attempt to reunite with their families. Thomas wished them well and waved them off with tears in his eyes. Then he decided to go surrender himself. He slipped off his undershirt and tied it to a long branch that he'd stripped from the jungle underbrush. Slowly, he crept down to the road and started walking in the direction of Mariveles. Almost immediately he spied a group of Japanese soldiers marching crisply in his direction. They wore khaki uniforms with combat packs, and their field hats, fashioned with long sun flaps in the rear, sported a single gold star. Bayonet blades gleamed brightly from the barrels of their .25 caliber rifles.

Thomas hoped that the Japanese would be inclined to treat a Signal Corps engineer like himself less harshly than a fighting soldier from the front lines. With his heart pounding like a mallet in his chest, he stood in the road waving his dingy undershirt. A jeep pulled up to him and the Japanese driver motioned for him to hop in. In a few minutes they came to a Japanese camp and Thomas was met by a young lieutenant who spoke nearly perfect English. He had studied at UCLA, he said, and he was fond of the United States. "Someday, after all this, I will go back."

Then the lieutenant surprised Thomas. "Do you want to stay here with me and be my prisoner?" he asked. He pointed to a big white truck parked nearby and said he didn't know how to drive it. "Maybe you can?"

So Thomas agreed to serve as the lieutenant's chauffeur. In return, the officer was kind to him and offered him cigarettes and ample food. "You won't try to escape, will you?" he asked.

Thomas shook his head. "Where would I go?"

"Good—I trust you."

That night, after a dinner of dried fish, rice, and sake, the officer motioned for Thomas to follow him into the woods. They came to a place where the jungle had been cleared and flattened to make a crude wrestling ring. Several large wrestlers wearing only G-strings were stretching and warming up in the ring while a group of spectators stood around and watched. The style of wrestling was akin to sumo but more informal and free-form. After a few matches, the officer nudged Thomas and said, "Your turn."

"I don't know how," Thomas protested.

"You learn quick."

Thomas stripped down to his underwear and the bout commenced. At six feet four, Thomas was considerably taller, but his opponent was heavier and extremely well muscled. "I put my hands on my hips, snorted, and jumped as I had seen them do," Thomas later wrote in his memoirs. He looked over at the lieutenant, not sure what was supposed to happen next. He grabbed his opponent in an armhold, but the Japanese wrestler soon broke free. "Suddenly, he slammed me to the ground and jumped on top of me. I couldn't move." The referee indicated that the match was over. Then the Japanese wrestler graciously helped Thomas up from the ground.

When he rose to his feet, the soldier spectators gave Thomas a rousing applause. "They like you," the lieutenant said.

Thomas spent the next several days driving the white truck for the Japanese lieutenant, hauling goods this way and that along the road, looking for other vehicles abandoned by the Americans that might be nursed back to health. One night, gathered around the fire of the Japanese camp, Thomas asked the lieutenant what would become of the American prisoners. "Maybe the Red Cross will take us," Thomas said optimistically.

The lieutenant nodded his head in vague agreement and then said, "But you cannot fight anymore."

"I've had all the war I want," Thomas replied.

Thomas broached an idea that had been turning over in his head all day. The lieutenant had treated him generously and had shown a friendly spirit that seemed genuine, but Thomas yearned to be with his comrades. He was lonely and uncomfortable being the only American in a camp full of Japanese. It was an odd arrangement that couldn't last. Delicately, he asked his new friend if he would take him to wherever the surrendered Americans were being held. With a sympathetic expression, the lieutenant stepped away for a moment to consult with a superior and then returned. "Tomorrow," he said. "I take you."

The next morning Thomas gave the lieutenant driving lessons so he could fend for himself. Then they drove to a place not far from Mariveles where a group of nearly fifty American officers had been assembled behind a hastily strung fence of barbed wire. There was some confusion about where Thomas had come from, but eventually he crawled under the fence and joined the Americans. Thomas thanked the lieutenant for his many kindnesses and then said goodbye.

The guards had separated the officers from enlisted men and grouped them together in order to interrogate them about various war plans and installations. The Japanese were especially interested in confirming a rumor that had apparently taken on mythological proportions within the Imperial Army—that there was a secret tunnel connecting Corregidor to Bataan. Individual questioning went on much of the morning, and then later in the day a Japanese colonel who spoke fair English came to address the entire group. He said it had come to the attention of the Japanese Army that a number of atrocities had been committed by the Americans during the defense of Bataan and those atrocities would have to be avenged. There was a particular incident that had occurred at a place called Quinauan, where the Japanese had made a surprise landing by boat behind the lines and had proceeded to dig themselves into a series of hillsides that swept precipitously to the sea. The fighting, much of it hand-to-hand, had indeed been horrific, with a high death toll for both sides. When the Japanese refused to surrender, the Americans forced the Japanese out of their intricately connected burrows by driving tanks over the foxholes and dropping firebombs directly into the entrances.

In any case, the Japanese colonel now insisted that the Americans would have to pay a price for the Quinauan incident. He instructed the officers to select ten individuals from within their ranks. These ten men, he said, would face a firing squad in the morning.

After much discussion, ten Americans of different ranks were chosen. Some of them, including Thomas, volunteered. "I don't know why I did it," he said. "I didn't reason through it much. Part of it, I think, was that I was single and young and most of the others were married with families. But really, it was an impulse decision."

The next morning the ten men were brought over to a hill and made to watch a group of Japanese soldiers as they practiced marksmanship and bayonet skills on a series of targets set up in the trees. Thomas and the other nine men were handed shovels and pickaxes and forced to dig a hole large enough to accommodate all of them. As a courtesy to the damned, they were given cigarettes to smoke and sake to drink and then told to kneel at the threshold of the grave. The colonel asked them if they wanted blindfolds and they declined.

The ten men in the firing squad hoisted their rifles. Each American looked his executioner in the eye. The colonel gave the signal with his sword and the firing rang out with a ragged stitch.

Thomas lay awkwardly in the hole, entangled with other bodies. He was breathing but he wasn't sure of his condition. Then he looked from side to side and saw that other comrades were still alive. Confused, Thomas slowly extricated himself and peered "like Kilroy" from the lip of the grave.

The assembled Japanese erupted in laughter. "I was really going to shoot you," the colonel said, "but then I decided on this joke."

The men in the hole hugged each other with tears of disbelief welling in their eyes. The target practice, the gravedigging, the sake and cigarettes—it had all been an elaborately contrived prank. The colonel was toying with their fate as a cat toys with a shrew. A few of the men needed a splash of water to revive themselves, proving, as Thomas put it, that "the imagination can be very real."

—————

Although he was the victor, Lieutenant General Masaharu Homma did not feel victorious, nor did he take pleasure in any of the usual glories or spoils. He was enormously relieved that Bataan had finally succumbed, but for the Fourteenth Army the war was far from over. Homma still had not won the true prize his superiors in Tokyo demanded of him, the prize which they insisted was long overdue. There was little point in occupying the Philippines if the Japanese Navy or merchant marine could not freely use the docks and wharves of Manila Bay, the finest natural harbor in Asia. Yet one could not control Manila Bay without controlling Corregidor. Fixed with cannons that could fire twenty miles, honeycombed with deep tunnels and lateral shafts, Corregidor was stuck like a steel bit in the mouth of Manila Bay. The island was shaped like a tadpole, its squirmy tail pointing off toward Manila, its bulbous head aimed at Bataan. The Rock, it was called. The Impregnable Fortress. The Asian Gibraltar.

There was only one way for Homma to take Corregidor, and that was for him to move his forces into southern Bataan, array his artillery pieces high along the southern flanks of Mount Mariveles, and rain unmerciful fire down upon the island, softening it up until an amphibious assault could be reasonably undertaken. Confronting this complex interlock of land and water, Homma realized that Bataan was but the first key.

It is an axiom of Euclidean geometry that two points cannot occupy the same space, and therein lay Homma's problem. Before he could move his forces into southern Bataan, the surrendered Americans and Filipinos would have to be moved out. In their crippled thousands, they were underfoot, directly in the line of fire, like so much human debris. They were concentrated along the southeastern rim of the peninsula, precisely the area that afforded Homma the best vantage point for attacking Corregidor. Constantly chastised by Tokyo for moving too slowly, the ordinarily cautious Homma was under enormous pressure to expedite his artillery bombardment of the island. Thus Wainwright's refusal to surrender Corregidor meant that the Bataan prisoners would have to be hastily cleared away—swept off the stage, in effect, so the next act could begin.

General Homma had foreseen this enormous evacuation problem a month earlier and had commissioned some of his ablest officers to address it. The officers had presented their ideas to Homma on March 28. On paper, their plan appeared decent and humane. The prisoners were to be incarcerated at a place called Camp O'Donnell, a former training installation for the Philippine Army that lay approximately seventy-five miles north of Bataan's tip. The prisoners of war would be brought up the East Road of Bataan, passing through the towns of Cabcaben, Lamao, Limay, Orion, Pilar, Balanga, Orani, Lubao, and finally San Fernando, where they would then take a twenty-five-mile train ride to Capas, which was located very near the camp. Those soldiers who were physically able would be expected to march, but the distances would be reasonable—on average, no more than ten miles a day. Food and shelter would be provided. Hundreds of vehicles would be furnished to transport the sick. Two field hospitals would be set up, each one capable of treating as many as 1,000 patients.

The plan had two fatal flaws, however, flaws which would not become fully apparent until several days after the surrender. The first was that his officers grossly underestimated the number of prisoners who would offer themselves up. Based on wildly inaccurate intelligence reports of enemy troop strengths made earlier in the siege, Homma's planners projected that only about 25,000 Filipino and American troops would surrender. The actual number, counting civilians, was closer to 100,000. All the logistical elements of the evacuation plan—arrangements for food, water, shelter, and vehicles—were based upon this fabulously erroneous calculation. Homma had immediately sensed the figure was off. "You go back and estimate again," he curtly told one of his subordinates, and the new number came back in the neighborhood of 40,000, still off by 60,000 souls.

The second major mistake made by Homma's planners was that they grossly overrated the health and strength of the prisoners. By their reckoning, well over 70 percent of the Luzon Force could easily make the trip to Camp O'-Donnell on foot. They had no sense of the scale of the starvation and disease that racked the Fil-American troops. "We were vaguely aware that the food situation in the defense force was not good," Homma would later say. "But we judged that the Luzon Force could hold out several months longer, at least as far as food was concerned."

Overall, Homma seemed pleased with the plan. Although he was preoccupied with strategies for the coming offensive against Corregidor ("My first and last concern was how I could assault the impregnable fortress in the shortest time possible," he said), it was important to Homma that the prisoners be handled fairly. Homma instructed his officers to treat the American and Filipino captives "with a friendly spirit" in accordance with the Geneva Convention—and also within the spirit of the Imperial Army's noblest, if often overlooked, ideals. While the War Ministry in Tokyo took an extremely harsh view of its own troops falling into the hands of the enemy, Homma was aware that the Emperor himself had instructed Japanese soldiers to view foreign POWs as "unfortunate individuals" and to handle them with "the utmost benevolence and kindness." During the Russo-Japanese War of 1904–05, the Imperial Army had been widely praised for treating its prisoners decently. A standard Army instruction that had been written in 1904 had plainly outlined a policy of mercy. "Prisoners of war," it said, "shall be treated with a spirit of goodwill and shall never be subjected to cruelties or humiliation."

Homma took this sort of language to heart, at least in the abstract, for he was a compassionate general with views that might be described as liberal and internationalist. Considered by many the most brilliant military theoretician of his generation, Homma was a moody, sensitive, eccentric man of striking good looks. Standing nearly six feet two, he was regarded as a virtual giant for a Japanese man of his era. The son of middle-class landowners who had farmed rice for centuries, Homma was born and raised on the island of Sado, a remarkable place off the west coast of Honshu that had historically served as a land of banishment for exiled writers, priests, and politicians. As a young man, Homma became a devotee of Noh theater and pursued a scandalous love life that continually threatened to derail his career. Though hopelessly devoted to his first wife, he had divorced her after learning that she'd become a prostitute. His rise to prominence had been controversial and wildly erratic, his career marred with gossip concerning his drunken binges and reckless liaisons with beautiful but socially undesirable women.

Among his various posts, he had served as head of the Army Propaganda Department in the mid-1930s, during which time he befriended Japan's preeminent writers, painters, and dramatists. His colleagues viewed him as fiercely intelligent, highly principled, and vaguely effeminate. A prominent novelist named Hidemi Kon, who knew Homma well, wrote that the imposing and large-statured general seemed like "a man made for command." Yet he was a kind of living contradiction, with the personality of an idiosyncratic aesthete unhappily trapped inside the confines of Bushido discipline. Homma was known for painting and composing verse during the heat of battle, a habit that won him the nickname "the Poet General."

It was a matter of some irony that General Homma should have been assigned to attack the American Philippines, for in both his philosophy and his personal style, Homma was democratic-minded and openly pro-Western, a public stance that had set him at odds with Hideki Tojo. General Homma spoke fluent English. He had traveled in America and was a great lover of American movies. He was a self-described Anglophile, having lived and studied for years at Oxford and having traveled with British units throughout Europe and Asia. His second wife, Fujiko Takata, fifteen years his junior, had seen much of the United States. Among his numerous foreign assignments, Homma had attended the disarmament conference at the League of Nations following World War I. Openly critical of the fanatical ultranationalism that came to grip his country in the late 1930s, Homma had been a committed moderate in the years leading up to the war. In 1938, he had reportedly traveled to Nanking and authored a stinging document recounting the atrocities that had occurred under the Japanese occupation and berating the commanding officers there—a courageous stand that is said to have diminished his stature within the Japanese military.

If Homma had a tragic weakness it was that in his deeply introspective moments—of which there were many—he could be grossly inattentive to the details of his command, preferring to delegate all the messy responsibilities and minutiae to subordinates. A colleague once called him a "paper genius," the sort of brilliant theorist who could instinctively grasp subtleties of strategy in the abstract but who was slightly out of sync with the day-to-day realities of a fluid battle situation. The Poet General was a dreamer, an absentminded optimist. If his intentions toward his new prisoners seemed compassionate, the question remained whether he would be steadfast and forceful enough to convey his compassion to the many officers and enlisted men in his vast army's lower echelons who would be charged with transporting the prisoners into captivity.

On April 9, as untold thousands of Americans and Filipinos stumbled out of the jungle sucking stalks of sugarcane and waving towels and bedsheets, Homma had buoyant confidence in the Fourteenth Army's evacuation plan. Speaking in crystalline English that was accented with a certain Oxonian lilt, Homma told one captured American officer whom he met near his headquarters in Balanga, "Your worries are over. Japan treats her prisoners well. You may even see my country in cherry-blossom time, and that is a beautiful sight."

Chapter 2

Crickets fiddled in the grass as the first rays of dawn seeped through the night fog. A rooster was crowing in a nearby barrio, and a breeze stirred from Lingayen Gulf, rattling the palm trees. At four-thirty in the morning of Sunday, January 28, 1945, it was still too dark to see, but the Ranger encampment at Calasio bustled with life. Jeep engines revved, generators hummed, cauldrons clanged in the mess tents. The Rangers were wide awake, dressed in their combat boots and jungle greens, sipping cups of Nescafé. Some fussed with their weapons, while others loaded up the big six-by-six GI trucks parked in the dusty field. As the men worked in the feeble light, the sandy soil beneath their boots periodically shuddered from artillery shells exploding far in the distance.

Among the camp noises was the chatter of a monkey busily scrabbling over someone's leftover can of corned-beef hash. Eugene Dykes, an F Company Ranger from Wisconsin, had found the monkey back in Finschhafen, New Guinea. The monkey, which Dykes had named

Keezel, had become his inseparable pet. Keezel was a spider monkey, with furtive eyes and tiny nervous hands. Dykes planned to bring him along for the raid—probably not a good idea, but Mucci didn't seem to mind. Quiet and unobtrusive, the monkey had become a kind of Ranger mascot, a memento from the long training days in the steam and stinking mud of New Guinea. Dykes tied Keezel on a leash attached to his belt. Every time he grew frightened—as when the big shells thundered in the distance—the monkey would tug at Dykes's collar and drop down his shirt.

Keezel wasn't the only one—everybody had the jitters that morning. The collective adrenaline surge was palpable. Hardly anyone had slept. For many of the Rangers, this was their first true assignment, their first brush with combat. All their training back in Port Moresby couldn't quite prepare them for the knot of emotions they felt now. The men were scared and thrilled in equal measure, touched by a kind of awe. Missions like this one were exceedingly rare. People assumed Rangers were always off on one swashbuckling exploit or another, but it rarely worked out that way. Usually their duties came down to something far more prosaic. A platoon of Rangers might pull patrol through hostile territory and bring back a tiny nugget of information about the disposition of the enemy. Or perhaps one night a couple of guys would go prowling over to a Japanese ammunition dump and blow it to smithereens.

To go in and liberate a camp of doomed POWs was an entirely different matter. This was a genuine prison break. And not just any prison, but a prison full of *those* guys—the men they'd read about in the papers or knew firsthand, their friends and cousins and older brothers, seniors when they were sophomores. The guy from down the street whose mom was now in permanent mourning. All those fate-fucked men whose boats left just before theirs was supposed to, who sailed on to this American colony halfway around the world to be sacrificed like goats.

Captain Robert Prince had two such friends who'd been sent over to the Philippines ahead of him—close friends, men he'd trained with. They'd gotten trapped on Bataan and hadn't been heard from since. Prince wondered whether they were still languishing in Cabanatuan camp. "I didn't know if they were alive or dead, but I thought maybe there's a chance," Prince recalled. One of them was named Reed Shurtleff, "a big easygoing guy from the University of Utah, a good friend of mine." The other was an artilleryman from Santa Clara University, a young man named Van Geldern. "As a practical joke," Prince said, "a group of his friends had put his name on a bulletin board list of people who were volunteering to go to the Philippines. Van Geldern denied it. He said, 'I didn't volunteer, I didn't sign this.' But the orders were already cut. So off he went. Fate is fickle—it could have been me."

The men from Bataan and Corregidor had already suffered hardships that seemed beyond comprehension. A small number of them had escaped from Philippine prison camps and had managed to reach Australia. Eventually, American newspapers carried harrowing tales of their ordeal, including depictions of the Death March and the camps, so the Rangers, like most Americans, were generally aware of the prisoners' travails. When Colonel Mucci suggested that in all likelihood the Japanese planned to sweep these guys into a ditch and slaughter them, the Rangers were thus fired with a zealous outrage. "It made us so damn mad," Prince said, "we couldn't see straight."

With this mission the Army was operating on something like emotion, if the U.S. Army could be said to have emotion. The Rangers had to recognize that the sentimental allure of raiding Cabanatuan outweighed its strategic value. In the narrowest battle analysis, one could legitimately ask whether it was worth risking the lives of these elite young men in a romantic action that might be viewed as desperately ad hoc. What if the intelligence was wrong and the Japanese weren't planning to massacre the POWs after all? In a full-out war, many armies wouldn't think of gambling so much on an emotional rescue—certainly not the Japanese Army, with its famous contempt for its own countrymen who fell into enemy hands. Some commanders might resort to a stone-hearted calculus: The Cabanatuan POWs were all casualties, weren't they? What could these spent and stick-figured soldiers contribute toward the war effort against Yamashita?

Probably nothing, but that was a reckoning not one of the Rangers cared to make. The force of Mucci's argument was irresistible: These men had to be rescued. The colonel made the endeavor sound so grand that to be part of it felt like the honor of a lifetime, a glorious entrustment. As Captain Prince's first sergeant, Robert Anderson, put it: "This was the most thrilling thing I had ever been a part of, and I'da died before I would have missed it." Colonel Mucci had proposed the sweetest imaginable use of force, to defend and avenge in the same act.

At approximately five o'clock that morning, January 28, 121 Rangers—and one chattering monkey—climbed into the canvas-topped beds of their GI trucks and the convoy pulled out of Calasio, aiming east toward a ripening sun. At the head of the column, in a staff jeep, rode Colonel Mucci, tobacco smoke pouring from his pipe, his Colt .45 tucked in a sidearm holster. Something about Mucci looked different, and it took a while for the men to figure out what it was: He'd shaved off his pencil mustache, the one he took such meticulous care of. "Too damn much trouble for this assignment," he told one of his men. Getting rid of it left the colonel with one less thing to worry about.

In a few short minutes the convoy reached the Sixth Army headquarters near Dagupan. The headquarters was a vast hive of Quonset huts and green canvas sprawled along the shores of Lingayen Gulf, whose waters bulged with gray warships. Dagupan was just a pit stop for the Rangers. While some of the men loaded a cache of antitank grenades and bazookas, a crew of four official Army photographers sidled up to one of the trucks. These young men were from the 832nd Signal Service Battalion and they'd been ordered to join the Rangers for the duration of the raid. They were lugging an impressive arsenal of heavy photographic gear—4 x 5 Speed Graphic cameras, twin-lens Rolleis, a 35mm Bell & Howell movie camera, plus a mess of tripods, cables, lenses, and countless rolls of film. The Rangers had seen Signal Corps photographers before, but they were a little puzzled to learn that these four cameramen, burdened with all their heavy accoutrements, were coming along for this mission.

The photographers were Mucci's idea. The Colonel had

always gone in for PR flourishes, and he had a notion that this operation would prove to be historic. Documenting the raid, he felt, was well worth the risks. So the team of four young specialists from Combat Photo Unit F, led by First Lieutenant John Lueddeke, was going to be there.

As with the Rangers, the Signal Corps photographers instantly regarded this mission as a plum. Because they all wanted to go, Lueddeke had set up a kind of lottery to make the selection fair and square. He asked his men to jot their names on scraps of paper and drop them into his helmet, from which he then plucked the three lucky winners—Robert Lautman, Wilber Goen, and Frank Goetzheimer. Now here they were with 121 Rangers in a convoy bound for what they hoped would be *the* photographic assignment of the Philippine campaign.

Within fifteen minutes, the convoy pulled out of Dagupan, and headed southeast through the Central Plain. The men rode for miles on a slender highway pitted by bombs and artillery shells, one of the main arteries that ultimately fed into Manila. They sped through flat sugar country bordered on either side by jagged mountains—the Zambales off to the right, the Cordillera Central to the left. The Rangers tried to catnap in their trucks as the lazy vistas of Pangasinan province spooled past—nipa shacks, cane fields, green volcanoes puncturing the morning mist. At this early hour, the road was empty save for a few straggling refugees on calesa ponies, moving as fast as they could to get out of war's way. By the time the Rangers crossed the Agno River, it was already quite hot and humid, and the skies swarmed with American fighter planes. On the horizon, a half dozen plumes of smoke curled toward the pink sky—targets still smoldering from the night's bombing runs.

General Yamashita, it seemed, was giving up the Central Plain without much of a fight. The Japanese were running scared now, making a ragged retreat toward Baguio, in the north, where Yamashita was now establishing his headquarters. The might of America was bearing down on them, the might of Pittsburgh and Detroit, the hardware of a New World hegemon finally and fully aroused. Without the option of surrender, the Japanese Army had no choice but to head for the terraced mountains and jungles of northern Luzon, some of the most impenetrable terrain in the Philippines, where upland tribes were said to hunt the occasional human head and kill wild boars with darts. Here in these highland rain forests, Yamashita and his 250,000 depleted troops would hang on as long as their endurance and battle savvy would allow. For the Japanese, it would be Bataan in reverse, with the same sort of desperate battle logic the Americans had employed there: extort every advantage from the geography, hang on past the point of starvation, and then await inevitable doom.

Although Yamashita was conceding the Central Plain, he did not intend to let the retreat devolve into a rout. A large, well-coordinated withdrawal is perhaps the trickiest maneuver in battle; every war college professor knows that it's virtually impossible for an army to defend itself well while moving backwards. Yet if any Japanese general was capable of executing this ungainly backpedal it was Tomoyuki Yamashita, the unflinching commander dubbed "the Tiger of Malaya" for his dazzlingly swift triumph over British forces at Singapore. Rather than throw up a massive line of defense across the Central Plain, Yamashita planned only to delay the inevitable American advance toward Manila while protecting his own forces as they retreated along two north-south arteries, the Rizal and San Jose highways. To accomplish this task, Yamashita intended to concentrate troops in just a few places strategically situated along these major roads so as to remain in control of his evacuation routes until the retreat to the northern mountains was completed.

One of these strategic places was the provincial capital of Cabanatuan. With a population of 50,000, Cabanatuan (meaning "place of rocks") was the largest and most important town in Nueva Ecija province. The city was located just four miles west of the POW camp. Even now, as the convoy of Rangers hurtled toward their designated jump-off point, more than 7,000 Japanese troops were massing in the vicinity of Cabanatuan. Most of the Japanese were bivouacking in the city, but others were using the camp itself as a place to regroup for the night, sleeping in the empty barracks and dressing their wounds before returning to the front. The camp had become an enemy way station.

The Ranger convoy reached Guimba around seven-fifteen that morning. An agricultural outpost of a few thousand people in the somnolent rice country of northwestern Nueva Ecija province, Guimba sat on the edge of the American lines. For the Rangers it was the mission's true starting point. From here, they'd be on foot for thirty miles—and then for thirty more, if all went well at Cabanatuan. A field radio would be set up if Mucci needed to call the Sixth Army for emergency help, but otherwise the Rangers would observe strict radio silence, for it was feared and assumed that Japanese radio operators would be listening.

The convoy stopped and the men heard Colonel Mucci yelling, "Everybody *out!*"

Yawning, stretching, the Rangers emerged from their trucks into the glare of a tropical morning. They were nervous as they stared out over the flats to the east. The land appeared to go on forever. A steady heat shimmer rose off the rice fields, which were stippled with the remains of the harvest and framed in hard-packed dikes, perfectly square, block after block stretching out as far as the eye could see. To the distant south, Mount Arayat, a vast, solitary volcano, swelled almost four thousand feet over the plain.

The prison camp was out there in the no-man's-land, a barbed-wire vision thirty miles off. The Rangers faced a twelve-hour march across roads patrolled by Japanese tanks, across Japanese-held bridges, across open country infested with Japanese pillboxes. Getting there sounded chancy, and getting there was the easy part. The return was what had them worried. How were they supposed to beat a retreat through enemy territory with 500 cripples in tow? What if the Japanese followed with tanks? What if just one village harbored just one spy? The men preferred not to dwell on all the things that could go wrong. They had to keep their minds fixed on the prisoners. Let Mucci and Prince sweat the details—and then pray for bucketfuls of luck.

There was a naïve optimism, and a certain improvisational boldness, in the way Ranger battalions operated, and Mucci's outfit was no exception. Although they borrowed the name and drew on the heritage of other so-called "ranger" groups throughout American history—spirited outfits such as Robert Rogers' rangers from the days of the French and Indian War and, of course, the Texas Rangers—the Army Rangers were actually a brand-new concoction, having been created at the outset of the war as an American answer to the famed British Commandos. Billed as surgical-strike specialists who carried out their missions with a certain brash independence, the U.S. Rangers quickly garnered much favorable press for their reputedly superhuman talents behind enemy lines. But in truth the concept of elite infantry units, or "special forces," was still novel, and the Army high command remained uncertain just how to train and use them—or even whether they were a good idea. In Europe, Ranger units had often ended up functioning essentially as front-line infantry troops, sometimes with disastrous results. Almost exactly one year before Mucci's mission, on January 30, 1944, the 1st and 3rd Ranger battalions had made an overly bold and poorly scouted infiltration attempt at a place called Cisterna, near Anzio, Italy, only to be surrounded by German forces. Cisterna proved a terrible debacle, culminating in a mass surrender with hundreds of American casualties. Only eight men made it back to friendly lines. A year later, the Ranger ranks were still reeling from the catastrophe.

Mucci's 6th was the only Ranger battalion operating in the Pacific theater; it was, in effect, the untested Asian branch of a potentially impressive new franchise whose true business plan had yet to gel. With the raid on Cabanatuan, Mucci's outfit at least had an assignment that rang truer to the Rangers' original intended purpose. Yet, in a sense, his men were all neophytes. "Spec ops" was in its infancy, a romanticized kind of soldiering, the skills and techniques still crude. Their training, while extremely challenging, did not particularly qualify them to storm prison camps, let alone serve as personal saviors. They were simply winging it.

Surprise. That was the thing they had in their favor, the thing they must keep at all costs: the element of surprise, invisibility right up until the last moment. They had to cling to it, every second, every step. And yet, precious as it was, surprise was a funny sort of advantage—fragile, future-tense, perpetually subject to doubt. And so easy to lose. All it would take was a single Japanese scout with a good set of binocs looking in just the right place. Or one Filipino quisling. Then in a flash it would be over and the mission would go down as one of the war's great fiascoes, a first-rate slaughter in the order of Cisterna.

The men lay down and tried to rest for a few hours in a grove of mango trees. Then, after a hot lunch, they selected a two-day supply of K rations—small cardboard boxes filled with a few canned goods, two cookies, several cigarettes, and a tiny roll of toilet paper. They were also given foil-wrapped bars of milk chocolate to present to the prisoners as a gift on their way out of Cabanatuan if the raid was successful. It was a nice touch after three long years in a death camp: Hersheys, the first beneficence of Uncle Sam.

At two o'clock Colonel Mucci gave the signal and the Rangers headed out on foot, marching eastward in a long, single-file column with two young Filipino guerrillas as guides. Soon the train of Rangers spread out over a hundred yards, with Mucci marching in the vanguard and Captain Prince bringing up the rear. They followed a road for about ten minutes, and then at a place called Consuelo they turned south for several miles, cutting through an open field of dry grass.

Henry Mucci was ecstatic finally to be out on an assignment after nearly three weeks of sitting idle at Lingayen Gulf. As he marched ahead, the colonel burned with a certain bug-eyed intensity that made the men pay attention to his every move. Mucci had an incandescent temperament that he himself once described as "Mediterranean." He could be quick to anger, and once he was riled he could seem, as one Ranger put it, "mean as a junkyard dog." Sometimes, back at headquarters, he liked to play poker with some of the noncoms in his tent. One night when he drew a particularly lousy hand, he became so incensed that he hurled the whole deck outside. Mucci was a stern disciplinarian. "He could certainly let you know when you were wrong," Bob Prince said. Prince remembered a seemingly minor incident in New Guinea in which the colonel "got right up in my face and ate me out good for what seemed like a half hour, although it was probably only a minute. Boy, he could really dress you up, down, and sideways." But then, just as quickly, Mucci's pique would subside and he'd drop the matter as though it never happened.

Mucci's great charm was hard to parse. He was not a handsome man in the classic sense—he stood only five feet eight, his hair was fast receding, and his nose was so pronounced that in college some of his friends teased him with the nickname "Cyrano." He was a quick study, but certainly he was not a cerebral person. He was accepted into West Point on his second attempt, and graduated 264th in a class of 276 members. The 1936 *Howitzer,* the

West Point yearbook, noted that the cadet from Bridge-port "does not choose to be a classroom expert, but rather the field leader he is: the man who thinks on his feet, who inspires others beyond the powers of persuasion." He boxed, swam, and played basketball. He was an accomplished marksman and a "bruising" lacrosse player. His class squib went on to note that "he has a penchant for bringing beautiful girls to West Point . . . Color, action, and life will mark the path of 'Prince Henri.' "

In the first few days of their training near Port Moresby, New Guinea, in 1944, many of the Rangers hated Mucci. They thought he was a blowhard, and the physical demands he put on them seemed to border on cruelty, especially in the fierce tropical heat. Yet the colonel soon won them over. He was fair, he had a sense of humor, and everything he made them do—hand-to-hand combat drills, marches in the jungle, treacherous river crossings—he would undertake himself. The fire in his eyes was infectious.

The most grueling part of the Ranger training was conducted near their camp site on a steep hill that came to be called Misery Knoll. Mucci built a platform at the summit and would stand up there, blowing his whistle and barking orders. The men would have to double-time it up the hill or scramble their way to the top using only one leg and one arm. When they reached the top, Mucci would yell, "Now turn and knock down the man on either side of you!" At other times he would personally demonstrate a certain knifing technique or show the men with great relish how to disarm the enemy. He taught amphibious maneuvers, night warfare tactics, jungle survival skills. He oversaw marksmanship and bayonet practice, and accompanied his troops on innumerable runs and swims. "Physical endurance, that was his thing, taking it to the absolute limit of physical ability," said Alvie Robbins, a Ranger from a small mining town in northern Alabama. "He was not what you would call a wishy-washy individual. He said, 'If you're going to be Rangers, you either fish or cut bait.'"

Now, as the men advanced across the plains of Luzon, all those months of intensive training under Mucci began to make more sense. "We were glad for every minute of Misery Knoll," said Robbins. "We were in the best shape of our lives, and with this mission we understood why he had driven us so hard."

–––––––

As the Rangers marched, American artillery shells would occasionally lob high over their heads and explode deep into Japanese territory, sending up magnificent clouds of dust. The Yank firepower was impressive, Mucci thought, so impressive as to be worrisome. In fact, the colonel was almost as concerned about friendly fire as he was about any dangers posed by the Japanese. In the confusion of a porous and fast-moving front, there was the distinct possibility that forward units of the Sixth Army could momentarily mistake the Rangers for Japanese troops or, just as likely, that a single haphazardly aimed shell could fall in their midst.

Theirs was a secret assignment, but it was secret in *both* directions. Except for General Krueger himself and his G-2 people, hardly anyone in the Sixth Army knew the Rangers were out here. Perhaps most troubling, no one had breathed a word about the Cabanatuan raid to the air force.

Which meant that there were American fighter pilots flying around above them—restless and trigger-happy pilots—who hadn't the vaguest idea what the Rangers were up to. As Mucci and his men pressed farther into enemy territory, they began to realize, with an excitement cut with deepening dread, that they'd never been more vulnerable.

The grass field yielded to a vast expanse of rice, paddy after paddy, the checkerboard pattern broken only by the occasional slash of bamboo growing along the banks of a meandering creek. The Rangers found it hard to establish a rhythm as they crossed these endless quadrants. They tried to walk down in the dry paddies, but they were so hard and clumpy, and so thoroughly pocked with the deep footprints of draft animals, that the exercise was like walking over cobblestones. They tried to walk along the wet edges of the fields, but the mud sucked at their boots. They tried to walk on the tops of the dikes, but that didn't quite work either. The crude retaining walls were just piles of dirt that had been thrown along the verges and cooked by the sun. They might have served as a ready-made network of paths had they been a little wider and more stable, but too often they crumbled under a man's weight.

The result was an annoying obstacle course that went on for miles, with the Rangers tripping over the stumps of shriveled rice plants, veering to avoid mud bogs, scaling another dike, then hopping back into the next paddy. This kind of marching was brutal on the feet. After just a few miles, many of the men were starting to develop blisters. Captain Prince—whose feet were already raw from a bad case of "jungle rot" which he'd contracted on those long, wet hikes back in New Guinea—was noticeably limping, his soles burning with fresh blisters.

It wasn't much good for marching, but the Central Plain of Nueva Ecija was beautiful country. The rice had been harvested a month earlier, and now the paddies dozed in the languor of the dry season. The beige-brown fields swallowed the Rangers in their stillness. A carabao—the domesticated water buffalo of the Philippines—turned its massive head and stared dully in their direction. Doomed frogs and pond fish churned in shrinking puddles. The booms of the American cannonading had faded away, and now the men were aware of only the rustling rice stalks and the smell of rich black clay.

In such wide-open country it would have been impossible for the Rangers to camouflage themselves, yet they were unobtrusive enough, stitching like a dull green thread across the fields. They sported no rings or jewelry, or anything else that might glint in the sunlight. They all wore faded fatigues that bore no insignia of rank. Mucci wanted to keep the dress as drab and inconspicuous as possible, with nothing unusual that might catch the eyes of Japanese snipers—who generally preferred to shoot officers and noncoms first.

Likewise, the Rangers wore soft fatigue caps. Mucci had stipulated that there would be no "brain buckets" on this mission: metal helmets were too heavy, they made too much noise, and sometimes they gave off a faint sheen when the sun hit them just right. There was no point in jeopardizing the operation with one stupid clank of a chin strap or a gun stock thudding against the lip of someone's helmet as the men crawled like exposed garden snakes beneath the noses of the Japanese guards.

Then again, there was no way the Rangers could keep entirely silent as they marched toward Cabanatuan, not with all the guns and ammunition they were hauling. Nearly every Ranger had two bandoliers of ammo slung over his shoulders along with several fragmentation grenades and a jagged trench knife strapped to his leg. Each man carried the gun of his choice. Most Rangers, like Captain Prince, opted for the M-1 Garand, the standard-issue semiautomatic infantry rifle—a light and loyal weapon fed by an eight-round clip. Colonel Mucci and Dr. James Fisher, the battalion surgeon, brought only .45 caliber pistols, while the medics carried carbines, which were lighter versions of the M-1. Some of the noncoms preferred the Thompson submachine gun, the "tommy" of Prohibition fame, hopeless for long-range targets but murderous close in. Specialists assigned to the Weapons Section carried the Browning automatic rifle (BAR), heavy as a barbell, but with a range of more than 1,000 yards. Mash down the trigger and it could spit out 550 bullets in under a minute.

And then there were the bazooka men, with their big pipes folded in half as they marched. The bazooka was an unlovely, fire-breathing thing with an electric fuse, a newfangled rocket launcher not even dreamed of during the dark days of Bataan. Mucci hoped against hope that the bazooka guys wouldn't be needed, but in case the Japanese came at them with tanks, the Rangers at least would have something with which to retaliate.

Watching his men lug their miscellany of lead, Mucci began to see that, frustrating though it was, this slow-going terrain offered certain tactical advantages. Out here it would be virtually impossible for the Japanese to pursue them in vehicles. Even tanks would be slowed down on this hard-baked grid. And while the Rangers were utterly exposed, at least they could spot the Japanese coming; there was little danger of ambush. Since the Americans had all but destroyed the Japanese air force on Luzon, an attack from the skies seemed remote. As long as the Rangers stuck to the fields, Mucci felt, they'd be okay. The Japanese Army controlled the roads and the principal cities and towns, but the open country was theirs.

After a few miles they came to the Licab River, ordinarily a substantial tributary but only knee-deep now in the parched and cloudless days of the dry season. They quickly forded the stream, then passed through a tall stand of bamboo that clothed the far bank in a shimmery green. The bamboo gave way to another open field. The men squished across the dry grassland in their soaked fatigues and soggy boots, heading straight for a barrio called Lobong. The village dogs snarled on the outskirts, and the men could see clusters of pigs dozing in the cool shadows thrown by the high, stilted shacks.

Just outside the barrio, Mucci called his Rangers to a halt.

"Captain Joson?" he cried out.

Standing before them was Eduardo Joson, the leader of a group of Filipino guerrillas that would accompany Mucci's men on the raid. Lobong, Joson's headquarters, was the designated rendezvous point. From here, Joson and his men would guide the Rangers to the next barrio, where they would hook up with a second, and even larger, contingent of guerrillas.

"*Mabuhay!*" Joson called out. "You are Colonel Mucci?"

Mucci flashed a guarded smile.

"*Magandang hapon!* And welcome to Lobong," the captain said. Then he offered an expansive gesture. "My men—"

Behind him, the guerrillas casually tipped their straw buri hats and grinned. They were a ragged band—rice farmers clutching bolo knives, teenagers straddling ponies, a few old-timers stooped alongside their mud-streaked carabaos. Many of the men were unarmed and barefoot, wearing sturdy peasant clothes, their teeth stained with betel. Among their diverse ranks stood sixty or seventy well-trained soldiers, men hardened by three long years of hectoring the despised Japanese. Their khaki uniforms were threadbare and faded, and they carried old Springfield bolt-action rifles from the battlefields of Bataan.

Joson (ho-SOHN) was a short, generous-spirited man in his mid-thirties, bright but of limited education. He was a natural politician with a knack for gentle persuasion and a broad smile full of good teeth. Major Lapham, the American guerrilla leader, had always considered Joson one of his most capable officers. Joson couldn't count the run-ins he'd had with the Japanese over the past three years—skirmishes and ambushes and moonlight raids. Joson thrilled to the idea of attacking Cabanatuan. His runners had brought him the news last night. He and his lieutenants had gone out into the countryside, canvassing the surrounding barrios to round up as many able-bodied men as possible. Now here they were, mustered and ready to join the mission.

Without their help, the raid was scarcely even possible. The guerrillas were intimately familiar with the backcountry trails and knew the size and location of every Japanese garrison. They knew which snakes were poisonous and which pools were drinkable. They knew all the easiest places to cross the rivers and streams. Joson and his men would flank the Americans all the way to Cabanatuan and all the way back. They would assume the same risks as the Rangers, and in one regard, they assumed far more: If an enemy scout learned who the guerrillas were, the Japanese could take revenge by wiping out an entire village. It wasn't an idle threat. The Japanese had visited these sorts of reprisals upon barrios throughout the Central Plain for the past three years.

For the Rangers, the intensely pro-American loyalty of Filipinos like Joson and his guerrillas was both touching and a little hard to understand. Yes, they shared the same enemy—and if anything, the Filipinos hated the Japanese even more virulently than the Americans did. But why should the Filipinos worry over the fate of 500 American prisoners when they had their own immeasurable tragedies and sufferings to contend with? Their country was going up in flames all around them. Once again, two nations from across the seas were thrashing it out on Philippine soil, and once again, they were caught in the maelstrom. Like history's stepchildren, the Philippine people repeatedly seemed to bear the brunt of other people's arguments.

The Filipino friendship toward the United States was complicated by America's racial paternalism and the miscellaneous affronts of a half century's colonial rule. The United States had "won" the islands from Spain as a result of the Spanish-American War of 1898, and then went on to fight a vicious campaign against the Philippine people which came to be known, inappropriately, as the Philippine Insurrection, as though the local citizenry were displaying an outrageous insubordination for seeking a voice in the future of their own archipelago. In the end, more than 200,000 Filipinos died at the hands of United States soldiers, who called their Asian adversaries "gugus" and tended to see the conflict as an extension of the Indian extermination campaigns for which they had been trained. With the "insurrection" quelled and their new prize firmly in hand, the Americans set out in their peculiarly self-righteous way to prove to the European powers that there could be a different sort of colonialism—more compassionate, more progressive, less rapacious. With equal parts idealism and condescension, William Howard Taft, the stunningly corpulent first governor of the Philippines, argued that America must show "our little brown brothers" the way to democratic enlightenment. Relative to the other Western powers in other parts of Asia, the Americans had proven to be decent landlords, all in all. They built schools and bridges and roads, they introduced the rudiments of free enterprise and democracy, they sent over teachers by the boatload. America took on like a skin graft—American songs, American movies, American cars. English was spoken everywhere. Except for the patrician upper classes in Manila, the Spanish influence began to fade. Yet by the 1930s the United States was entertaining serious doubts about its experiment in "enlightened colonialism." Washington had promised independence by 1946 and the promise was well on its way to becoming a reality when Homma's troops landed and put everything on hold.

The Japanese mistreatment of the Filipinos had underscored for the average citizen the relative benevolence of American rule. Still, one might ask, to a peasant on the Central Plain who knew only rice and love and death, what did America really mean? In practical terms, what had allegiance to any foreign power ever brought? One would think that Joson and his men might resent America for all the trouble that seemed to come in its long wake, or at least that they'd think twice about endangering their own village to help solve an American problem.

But the guerrillas seemed as excited about the raid as the Rangers did. For whatever reason, or combination of reasons, they still regarded the Yanks with a curious and almost brotherly affection. They were even willing to die for them.

———————

The Rangers stayed in Lobong for a few hours, sitting out the worst of the late afternoon heat. Over a dinner of K rations, the men discussed some of the fine points of that evening's march, and then at six-thirty they gathered up their weapons and started hiking east, their backs to a sinking sun. It was only an hour before dark and the western skies over Lobong were clotted in reds and tangerines. Mucci's force now numbered some 200 soldiers—121 Rangers and 80 guerrillas. Joson's men fanned out to the sides and the rear of the Ranger column to guard against a surprise attack. For a half hour they all marched in silence through the twilight. Bats chased insects overhead, and farther up, two American fighter planes streaked across the darkening bowl of the sky, intent on deadly errands.

Soon the trail led into a dense forest. The Rangers stumbled blindly over limbs and roots until their eyes adjusted to the darkness. For several miles they followed the winding trail through the tenebrous woods. No one spoke; each man was absorbed in thought, trying to make out the warped shapes of the forest, listening to the clomp of boots on moss and the swish of the canteens.

The Rangers emerged onto a carabao trail that threaded through a field of tall grass, passing just south of a barrio called Baloc. Here they confronted their first real—and potentially perilous—obstacle. Mucci and Joson stopped their men in a bamboo brake to confer. Just ahead, across an open expanse of rice paddies, was the first national highway they would have to cross. The road was ensnarled with Japanese traffic heading north. The Rangers could see the long convoys of tanks and transport vehicles creeping up the road, a river of metal that flowed for miles. Now and again the trucks gave off resounding booms that sounded like gun reports—backfiring, the Rangers eventually realized, caused by all the alcohol and coconut oil the petrol-starved Japanese were forced to put in their gas tanks.

This highway was the main road leading from Cabanatuan City up to San Jose, an artery vital to the larger scheme of the Japanese withdrawal. The retreating army had taken to moving only at night to elude American attacks from the air. The trucks were motoring at a good clip, maybe thirty miles an hour, but the column seemed to continue endlessly in the distance.

The men whispered skeptically among themselves:

"How're we supposed to get through *that?*"

"Looks like the whole damn Jap Army coming through!"

In the shadows, Mucci milled among his men, outlining the plan. "Once there's a lull," he said, "I want you to crawl toward the road and leapfrog across the pavement, one at a time. Then run like hell across the field."

Mucci's plan was far from elegant, and it could take the better part of an hour to slip 200 men across the busy road one at a time. Still, what were the alternatives?

Thirty minutes later, the Japanese convoy trickled off to nil. At last the road was empty and quiet. Mucci gave the signal and the men began crawling across the field. It was a luminous night, with a full moon well launched in the eastern sky, affording plenty of light to see by—and plenty of light by which to be seen, should any Japanese stragglers appear on the road. In ones and twos, roughly half of the Rangers dashed across the road, their shadowy forms melting into the grass of the distant field. It was taking a while, but Mucci's plan seemed to be working fine.

Then, in a soar of nerves, Mucci did a double take. There was something on the road, maybe a hundred yards to the north.

"By God, it's a tank."

"Jesus, it's aimed right at us."

The Rangers crouched lower in the grass. Everyone tried to catch his breath. A tank? How had they missed it before? Had it been there all along, or did it just pull up? They watched the tank intently for a few long moments, but mercifully it didn't budge.

Maybe they hadn't been spotted, but clearly they would need a new plan. Captain Prince pulled out an Army topo map and began studying it in the moonlight. "Looks like there's some sort of ravine up there, with a bridge over it," Prince said. He ogled the stretch of highway where the tank was parked, trying to square the details of the map with the actual terrain.

One of the Rangers proposed using the ravine to their advantage. The Japanese tank crew would be looking up and down the road, but they wouldn't be watching the ditch directly below them. The Rangers could safely approach the tank by crawling along the ravine. Then they could slip beneath the bridge, single file, without making a sound, right under the noses of the Japanese.

The maneuver would be as delicate as threading a needle—and risky as hell—but Mucci gave the okay.

The Rangers crept toward the ravine and dropped into it, relieved to learn that it was only a dried-up streambed. Crouched low in the silty bottom, they followed the ravine east toward the highway. The Japanese tank was still up there, parked squarely on the bridge. In the vivid moonlight, the Rangers could plainly see the outline of the turret and the glint of the gun barrels. Soon they were skulking in the dark directly beneath the tank. The ignition must have been switched off recently, for some of the Rangers could hear the popping and ticking of various engine parts as they cooled. Others heard the voices of two Japanese men—muffled, metallic—conversing unawares inside the tank's cabin. The voices were so close it was as if the Rangers were inside the vehicle with them.

For a half hour, the long column wormed through the ditch, one man at a time. The Rangers tried to move in perfect silence, without so much as a whisper, their breathing measured and shallow. Still it seemed to them, in their apprehensive state, that they were making far too much noise. Every sound—the rustle of fatigue cloth, the tink of their guns, their own galloping hearts—seemed magnified a hundredfold.

Finally the rear guard slipped beneath the bridge, and they all dashed across the field to reunite with the others in a copse of trees at the far edge of a rice paddy. It was about nine o'clock, and the moon had climbed high overhead, throwing a milky emulsion over the land. Dogs barked somewhere in the middle distance.

The winded Rangers were sprawled in the grass beneath the tall trees, laughing giddily, comparing notes with the Filipino guerrillas. They'd come twelve miles since Guimba without incident. While Colonel Mucci assembled the ranks, the men gazed back toward the national highway, their faces lit with cheating grins.

Chapter 3

The water was pure and cool and raced from the hillside, as though from a natural spigot. Abie Abraham stared at it lustfully, as did the dozen or so other Americans in his group, who all stood at attention, impaled by the afternoon sun. The Japanese guard had halted the column along the East Road at a spot only a few yards from the spring, but he would not permit them to take a drink. Sergeant Abraham couldn't tell at first whether the guard's decision to rest at such a tantalizing place was deliberate or absentminded torture, but it was torture nonetheless. Clean artesian water, filtered by stone, splashing in brisk freshets from a hole in the jungle. The sight of it was unbearable—the *thought* of it, the thought of not having it. Abraham tried to avert his gaze, but he couldn't. His mouth was cottony, his lips were cracked, his tongue fell thickly over his teeth. For five cruel minutes on the afternoon of April 10, 1942, Abraham and his comrades stared.

Abie Abraham was a staff sergeant in the First Battalion

of the 31st Infantry, the same regiment in which Dr. Ralph Hibbs had served. A Syrian-American, Abraham had grown up in the wrinkled steel country of western Pennsylvania and had done a tour in Panama before shipping out to the Philippines in 1939. A gregarious, pug-nosed man with tattoos coursing down his arms, Abraham had been a champion Army boxer before the war. He was a fast-talking plug of a fellow—scrappy, stubborn, and hard—and yet now even he was beginning to flag.

Abraham had a small piece of shrapnel lodged in his back and a slow-healing bullet wound in his thigh, but his immediate problem was thirst. He hadn't had any water since morning, when his group first stumbled out of the jungle and assembled on the main road. In the stifling heat, the Japanese had rounded them up and inspected them. The guards walked down the line of prisoners, stealing whatever struck their interest. Watches and rings, pocketknives, cigarettes, canteens—the trifling spoils of war. One prisoner had his teeth bashed out by a Japanese soldier who fancied his gold fillings. Another guard greedily eyed an officer's West Point ring. The Japanese soldier motioned to the officer to remove the ring, but because his hands were swollen with beriberi, the American was unable to slide it off his finger. He tried to explain that it was impossible, that it simply wouldn't come off, but the Japanese guard suspected that he was lying. Becoming more and more frustrated, the guard tried to wrench it off himself. When that proved ineffectual, he finally took the American's hand and placed it against a tree. Then he brandished his sword and chopped off the whole finger to get at the coveted souvenir. The officer whimpered in shock and returned to the ranks, gingerly holding his maimed hand.

For the most part, however, the guards were not gratuitously cruel, at least not at first. In fact, most showed notable courtesy and restraint. The battle of Bataan had not been easy for them. Abraham could see that they too were exhausted, diseased, and half starved. Most of them were kids, seventeen- or eighteen-year-old peasants fresh from the misty rice paddies and terraced valleys of Nippon. Many of them seemed scared. Although they had the guns, they were outnumbered and surrounded by a spiteful foe. Accepting the surrender of a foreign enemy, on foreign soil, they found themselves in the midst of a vast and unpredictable drama for which there was no script.

For Abraham, the most obvious and impressive fact was that the Japanese were in a terrific rush to get them wherever they were headed. Bounding alongside the columns, or trundling slowly on black bicycles, the guards yelled, *"Speedo! Speedo!"* and seemed animated by an acute sense of deadline. Evidently, their superiors had ordered them to move X number of prisoners X number of miles by nightfall. They were preoccupied with their task and clearly overwhelmed by its enormity as the full scale of the surrender gradually became apparent to them. More and more prisoners trickled out of the ipil-ipil thickets to surrender, some of them waving bedsheets which they had radiantly stained with Mercurochrome to resemble the Rising Sun, in hopes of adding further inoculation value to their limp flags of truce.

The growing exodus of prisoners marched all day along the East Road, four abreast, in long columns of approximately one hundred men. But the Japanese were falling behind their deadline. Abraham could see the urgency lining their faces, could hear the mounting frustration in the way they sucked air through their clenched teeth. The Americans couldn't move fast enough. As morning burned into midday, the cumulative effects of their battle wounds and their myriad ailments and infirmities began to exhibit themselves, and the pace began to slip even further. "We staggered like drunken men," Abraham later wrote. "Our bodies had been whittled away, our eyes looked like burned-out sockets. We were scarecrows."

The Japanese became increasingly irritated at the prisoners' halting progress. Their exhortations grew louder and more shrill. With greater frequency, they punctuated their demands with the flash of steel blades. At one point Abraham misinterpreted a command of some kind, and in punishment for his peccadillo received a bayonet tip through his hand.

The April day was hot and bright and dry, and the smoky air stank with the fetor of rotting corpses that had never been claimed from the battlefields. The men in Abraham's group limped on makeshift crutches, the strong holding up the weak, the weak holding up the weaker. Abraham recalled, "We dragged along in slow, mechanical motions, looking straight ahead, hearing only the crunching of pebbles beneath our feet and the deep, hacking coughs of the sickest men." Begowned patients who'd come straight from the field hospitals winced in agony as the dressings of their often gangrenous wounds pulled apart from the steady strain of walking. Wave after wave of Japanese planes could be seen streaking over Manila Bay toward the hunched rock of Corregidor. A minute later, the plumes of the incendiary bombs would rise ominously over the island and scatter off to sea.

The narrow, winding road from Mariveles was choked

with traffic and veiled in thick clouds of dust and fumes. As the Americans and Filipinos marched north to prison camp, the Japanese troops marched south to take up positions for the coming amphibious assault on Corregidor. A steady stream of artillery pieces, ammunition, and supplies pressed south, reminding the prisoners that they were, in effect, refugees left in a most infelicitous position, caught in the teeth of an ongoing war. Convoys of tanks and troop-carrying vehicles pushed through the crowds. Many of the Japanese soldiers smiled and waved at the Americans as they passed by in their trucks, while a few, taking advantage of the anonymity of the situation, would reach down and bash unsuspecting prisoners over the head with bamboo sticks, or sneak in a quick blow with their rifle butts. "We couldn't predict what they'd do," Abraham said. "Some of them wished us well, and some of them just wanted revenge."

As they marched through the barrios of Cabcaben, Lamao, and Limay, the deepening chaos grew more combustible by the hour. Military order was deteriorating fast. The official commands and injunctions, whatever they may have been, were not effectively trickling down to the foot soldiers. Vengeance spread over the road like a fever. Coming face to face with the enemy they'd battled for nearly four months, the Japanese burned with the natural contempt of the victor. They had reason to hate the Americans for holding out so long (since Tokyo had expected Bataan to fall months earlier), and they had reason to hate the Americans for giving up so soon (since according to the Bushido Code surrender was beneath the dignity of a true soldier). With the clusters of prisoners now isolated from each other and spread out for miles, each guard realized that he could do whatever he wanted, that he was, in this temporary context, omnipotent.

Abraham thought this was the case with the Japanese soldier who was guarding his group as they stood at attention beside the artesian spring. The guard, he felt, was intoxicated by his new power. Abraham could not conceive of any other explanation for how a person could be so cruel. The men were dying of thirst, and water was *right there*. It was plentiful and free and it would not take much time for the men to get a drink. Yet the guard made the prisoners stand there and listen to the soft babble.

Finally, one of the men in Abraham's group could take it no longer. He bolted from the ranks and threw himself upon the spring. With relish, he splashed the water on his face, slurping and lapping it up. Then the guard materialized, "swaggering over like a goose," as Abraham put it. He shouted something in Japanese, and the American, coming to his senses, pulled away from the stream. Abraham watched in dull disbelief as the guard unsheathed his sword. With a "quick ugly swish," he brought the blade down and cleanly decapitated the American. The head plunked into the spring and sank in a thin roil of blood. The body lingered for a moment, suspended in an upright position, and then it, too, toppled over into the spring, with the arms dancing in the water current. Abraham noticed that the man's hands nervously opened and closed, like the pincers of a crab.

— — — — —

The helplessness was the most dreadful part of it, the feeling of absolute impotence in the face of evil. For them, the shock of the gore was not unmanageable. For four months they'd been close to death. They'd seen killing, and many themselves had killed. But the emotional texture of warfare was vastly different from that of prisonerhood. Fighting, even fighting a losing battle, was mercifully busy work. There was always something to do, and having something to do could be a godsend. It kept one's mind off the brutal panorama, it kept the focus on martial craft and the necessities of personal survival. Not being able to take action to save oneself or one's comrades, not being able to pick up a weapon and strike back, was a terrible, unnatural feeling. Prostration and inactivity violated everything they had learned as soldiers. "It did something to us," Abraham said. "It's hard to describe. We had been exposed to a whole new world. We saw these things, but we couldn't react. We could only watch and shuffle away, grumbling under our breath. Our minds were full of questions that didn't seem to have answers. The anger burned us up inside."

This was not the life Abraham had envisioned when he joined the Army in 1932. Unlike most of the enlisted men who had come lately to the colors, Abraham had devoted himself to the Army; it was his career, his whole life. He loved Manila and the Philippines, loved everything about this fair post in the tropics. His wife, Nancy, and their three young daughters had not made it out in time. They were caught by the Japanese invasion, and now they were doubtless interned at a civilian prison camp somewhere around Manila, although he didn't know where. He thought about them every minute and despaired for their safety.

Abraham was the son of Syrian immigrants. His

parents came from a little village called Mazra not far from Damascus and emigrated to the United States around the turn of the century, passing through Ellis Island. His father took a foundry job in Lyndora, Pennsylvania, a little smokestack town in the steel belt north of Pittsburgh. The family lived in an immigrant section called Red Row, which was a long strip of shotgun shacks snuggled beside a plant that manufactured wheels for trolley cars and trains. Abraham was one of eleven children. Running out of names, his parents decided on the redundant but sturdy Abraham.

Abraham Abraham proved his perseverance at an early age. When he was sixteen, he broke the world record for sitting in a tree. The dubious endeavor of tree sitting had become something of a national craze in the 1920s, much like goldfish eating or phone booth stuffing would become in later years. In the summer of 1929 Abraham took a fancy to an ancient apple tree in Alameda Park. He erected a five-by-five platform and hauled up the seat from an old Model T to serve as a bed. He climbed into the tree one day in late June, his eyes fired with ambition. From time to time one of his brothers or sisters would appear beside the trunk to send up food in a bucket attached to a rope. Some days they'd forget to come, or there would be a mix-up about who was supposed to deliver the food, and he would go hungry. "Come down from there, Abie," his brothers and sisters implored in July. Their pleas became more insistent as August slipped into September, and September into October. It was getting cold outside, and the apple tree was losing its leaves. Abraham stayed put for nearly four months. It was a confirmed world record, so down Abie came. Aside from some national press coverage, his only winnings consisted of hearty congratulations from his relieved parents and "a good bath." Someone asked him why he had sat up there all alone for 121 days. Abie answered, "It was something to do."

The Abraham family was so poor they couldn't afford a radio and their only source of heat was a decrepit coal stove in the kitchen. But Abraham's childhood memories were happy ones, marked by the haunting wail of the company steam whistle, the bells of the Ukrainian Orthodox Church, and the bleating of sheep on the green hills that rose over Conoquessing Creek. In the kitchen he would don an apron and help his mother make stuffed grape leaves and tabouli. Summertimes he would go with his father up into the hills and pick berries for elderberry wine. In the fall they'd hunt wild turkey and deer in the foothills. For spare change Abraham kept the local doctor's chickens, set pins at the town bowling alley, and worked in a shirt factory. But his real love was boxing, and when he joined the Army in 1932, the sport became his ticket to fame. In Panama he won fifty-four out of sixty bouts, fighting with guys with names like Kid Biasi, Frankie Konchina, and Joe Gorilla. He was the welterweight champion of the Canal Department, and later became the Army's head boxing coach in Panama. Then he was off to the Philippines for what looked like a carefree tour of duty.

Abraham was angry at the Japanese for all sorts of reasons, but chief among them was for coming to the Philippines in the first place and wrecking what was, for him, an island idyll. "Why did Japan have to destroy our paradise?" Abraham said. "Life in the islands was the greatest." He had never been more happy than in the months before the war. He raised ducks in his backyard. He hunted wild pigs on Bataan, and was an avid denizen of the nightclubs and cockfight arenas. He had become what more recent American arrivals in the Philippines called a "dhobie citizen," which simply meant that he had gone native, or at least that he was happily headed in that direction. He loved the Filipino people, their friendliness, their easy way of life. Having lived in Panama, he felt at home in the torpid heat of the tropics. Everything grew in the islands—hibiscus, bougainvillea, jasmine, the most delicate orchids. Geckos scrambled along the walls of his house, and exotic birds squawked in the mango trees around his neighborhood. "Nothing bothered me in the Philippines," Abraham recalled in his memoirs. "I loved the lazy, warm days, the palmy shores, the extravagant butterflies, the jungles dense and green."

One of the soldiers Abraham prowled around Manila with during those halcyon days was Arthur Houghtby, a first sergeant in the 31st. Close friends and fellow noncoms who trained in the same unit, they had done practically everything together before the war. Now they were marching out of Bataan together, side by side, keeping each other's spirits up.

Sergeant Houghtby started having trouble early on. The insidious combination of malaria and dysentery had sapped his strength to the point that he could no longer keep pace. He faltered and weaved conspicuously. The Japanese guards eyed him with increasing annoyance. They could see that a problem was developing.

Abraham was deeply worried for his friend. All along the march they had seen what happened to those who collapsed from heat exhaustion or straggled too far behind. Sometimes a prisoner would stumble and then get up, and then stumble again, only this time he wouldn't get up fast enough. The guards would grimace at their watches and the tension would throb in their necks. Exasperated, they realized that they held the solution to their problem in their hands. In some cases the guards took relative pity and gave the malingerer a beating about the head with a rifle butt—leaving him, alive but often unconscious, for his compatriots to carry in makeshift litters fashioned from blankets slung over bamboo poles.

In other cases, however, the guards exploded with rage and came in with bayonets flashing. Regarding bullets as precious commodities, the Japanese were adroit with their bayonets. They practiced their skills zealously. Usually they would go for the abdomen. The guard would drive his blade in deep and give it a jagged *twist twist twist* in the shape of a "Z" to scramble the bowels. The victim's legs would kick in nervous spasms. Stepping on the dying man's sternum, the guard would remove the blade with a flourish. He would spend a few minutes wiping his blade clean with a handkerchief—Japanese soldiers were expected to keep their bayonets immaculate. The guard would then give an impatient gesture and the column would move on, leaving the dead straggler behind. After the first instance of this, the unspoken rule became clear: Those who could not keep pace were dead men. As Abraham marched, he saw scores of American and Filipino bodies that had been dispatched in this fashion and left to rot on the side of the road.

Abraham took Houghtby's right arm and draped it over his shoulders, and the two walked together. This worked for an hour or so, but Houghtby was growing steadily weaker.

"Let me lie down," Houghtby said. "My legs are heavy."

"They'll kill you," Abraham said. "You want that?"

Another American stepped up and took Houghtby's left arm and they began to walk as a wobbling triumvirate, with Houghtby's legs miming the stride but not actually contributing to the forward progress. The guard did not seem to mind that Houghtby was being helped so long as the pace was not affected. For Abraham, it was a strange and dreadful feeling to know that he literally held Houghtby's life in his arms. "Death was with us every step," Abraham said, "watching us like a buzzard."

What Houghtby most desperately needed, of course, was a drink of water, but his canteen was empty, and the schedule-obsessed guard had no intention of stopping. Later in the afternoon, however, there was a changing of the guards. Almost immediately Abraham could sense that the new soldier responsible for his group was kinder and more sympathetic. He did not raise his voice. He slowed the pace a little. To Abraham's amazement, he gave one obviously struggling prisoner a bar of candy and a commiserating pat on the shoulder. After a while they came to a rivulet that was almost dried up. In the center of the stream was a deep pool brimming with dark, stagnant water—an old carabao wallow. A layer of green foam floated on the surface, and bluebottle flies swarmed in thick clouds. "Even so," said Abraham, "it was water." Abraham consulted the guard for approval. Although obviously skeptical about the hygiene, he understood the men's predicament and readily nodded his consent. Abraham helped Houghtby over to the wallow. They knelt down and raked the scum back with their hands. Then they immersed their faces in the tannin-dark liquid and drank like wild animals at a watering hole. "The water tasted as if it were sent from heaven," Abraham recalled. "When we started down the road again, somehow we felt better, even though we knew that those of us who didn't have dysentery already were sure to get it now."

———————

For the average soldier, the trek north to Camp O'Donnell took about a week. Yet because there were so many tens of thousands of prisoners in such varying states of health and mobility who began marching at different times from many starting places, the Japanese needed more than three weeks to accomplish the ungainly evacuation. The staggering logistics were surpassed only by the staggering carnage. Estimates vary wildly, but a median guess is that 750 Americans and as many as 5,000 Filipinos died from exhaustion, disease, gross neglect, or outright murder. Although most of the killings were committed in ones and twos, there was one notable mass execution in which 350 members of the Philippine 91st Army Division were herded up, tied with telephone wire, and systematically beheaded by sword. An unknown number of Americans were killed by shells fired from Corregidor, for the Japanese deliberately detained groups of prisoners to serve as "screens" for their artillery positions on Bataan in the cynical hope that the Corregidor gunners would not return fire for fear of hitting fellow Americans (Corregidor *did* hold its fire, but not indefinitely). Prisoners along the route were given little water, and fed only an occasional dollop of sticky rice the size of a baseball. For all too many men, the provisions were insufficient to keep them marching—

and a man who could not march was as good as gone. Had the deaths been apportioned evenly over the entire seventy-five-mile route, one would have encountered a corpse every twenty yards.

Yet for all its horrors, the march was not a premeditated atrocity. For the most part, the brutalities occurred in a piecemeal fashion against a backdrop of escalating confusion and seething racial hatred. Miscues, bad intelligence, cultural misunderstandings, sweltering heat, and a devolution of Imperial Army discipline all conspired to create an environment of tragic drift. The Bataan Death March, as the event later came to be called by the American media (most prisoners at the time simply called it, with characteristic understatement, "the Hike"), took place not according to plan, but rather as a result of the chaos that flourished under a plan that was fatally flawed. Once it became apparent that the original evacuation scheme was radically out of step with the circumstances on the ground, the Japanese failed to alter the plan to accommodate new facts. Their estimate of the number of prisoners was off, incredibly, by as many as 60,000 people, and their assessment of the health and stamina of the Fil-American forces was equally off base.

Realizing this, the Japanese should have instantly begun a wholesale rethinking of the logistics. Arrangements would have to be made for more vehicles, more food, more hospitals. Most obvious of all, more time would be needed to complete the move. But the Japanese Army, for all its many strengths, had rarely demonstrated a talent for reversing course in midstream once an error was recognized. Steeped in a rigid Confucian-influenced culture in which an order was considered final and any attempt to change it impugned the wisdom of the superior who conceived and issued it, the Japanese war planners were bold in action but often deficient in the improvisational skills needed for quick and supple reaction. Instead of alerting General Homma to the new exigencies on Bataan, the planners forcibly tried to make the old provisions—and timetables—work. The results were catastrophic.

For whatever reason, the Japanese elected not to honor General King's request that American vehicles be used to transport his men to prison camp. In truth, some of the trucks had been irreparably sabotaged by Americans who mistakenly thought they were supposed to destroy *everything* of potential value the day before the surrender. Many of the American vehicles were confiscated for military purposes, and were later seen towing Japanese artillery pieces toward southern Bataan. The Japanese Army was not heavily motorized; it remained, to a great extent, a foot army. This was partly a matter of choice and partly a matter of necessity, for Japan suffered from a desperate shortage of oil and enjoyed access to few outside sources of petroleum. Japan's extreme oil scarcity, exacerbated by the oil embargo that had been put in place by the United States and other Western powers before the war, had been one the major factors that precipitated the outbreak of hostilities. Capturing the oil wells of the Dutch East Indies became Japan's paramount goal upon initiating the war. Because every drop of gasoline was considered virtually sacred, the Japanese Army chose to invest little in troop-carrying trucks, jeeps, and other modes of ground transport. What little gasoline existed was reserved primarily for planes, ships, and tanks. Soldiers were expected to hike long distances—twenty-five or thirty miles a day—as a matter of course. Marching represented a much more significant part of the Japanese training regimen than it did for the American foot soldier. Japanese troops generally marched more often, for longer duration, and at a faster pace than did the Americans, who relied heavily on vehicles in large part due to the U.S. Army's ready access to cheap and plentiful gas. This major difference in the two armies contributed to a gulf in the perception of what constituted a reasonable distance for a day's march. The Japanese unrealistically expected the starved and diseased Filipino-American forces to meet the Imperial Army's norms for marching—again, with tragic consequences.

There was another major cultural difference that influenced many encounters between the Japanese and their new captives: The two armies entertained radically different views on the matter of corporal punishment. Beating had long been an acceptable and routine method of discipline within the Japanese Army. Soldiers could strike subordinates with no questions asked and no explanation warranted. The slightest distinction between ranks was of critical importance because it meant the difference between who could inflict blows, and who could expect to receive them. This sort of institutionalized brutality had a tendency to work its way down the ranks to the lowliest private. One can imagine what would happen when an enlisted man, hardened by this psychology of top-down violence, found himself suddenly thrown into a foreign and not altogether distasteful situation in which *he* was the superior, in charge of a group of helpless prisoners. For some, the temptation to beat proved irresistible. For others, beating was only the beginning.

It was also true that many of the Imperial Army

soldiers were themselves desperately hungry and ravaged by the same diseases that ravaged their captives. Although they hadn't deteriorated as far as the Americans had, many Japanese soldiers were showing signs of emaciation and battle fatigue. "We were all starving," recalled Shiro Asada, a Fourteenth Army soldier on Bataan. "We had dried fish paste and pickles to eat, that was all. Canned goods like the Americans had were a luxury to us. It seemed to us that some of the Americans were better fed than we were." As a matter of official policy, the Imperial Army showed a remarkable reluctance to provision its own troops. Army quartermasters provided only a bare minimum of such staples as miso and rice, but soldiers were expected to forage and steal to make up the caloric deficit. Thus, swiping rations or canteens from American prisoners wasn't merely a matter of the strong taking advantage of the weak—it was practically an Imperial Army imperative. The Americans, already living so close to the bone, would have to make do with even less, for how could an army that barely fed its own be expected to provide adequate meals for 78,000 enemy prisoners?

General Masaharu Homma, preoccupied with his plans for assaulting Corregidor, apparently remained oblivious to the enormity of the disaster that passed by his Balanga headquarters each day. Certainly General Homma was operating under enormous pressures from Tokyo; his career and professional honor were on the line. The Imperial Army chief of staff, General Hajime Sugiyama, had threatened on several occasions to remove Homma from his command. In Sugiyama's estimation, Homma was feckless, indecisive, and far too "soft" on the enemy. The master plan had called for Homma to take the Philippines by February, but the war had dragged on until April, and Corregidor still held. Refusing to consider the possibility that the master plan was unrealistic in the first place, Sugiyama thought the delays inexcusable and placed all blame at Homma's feet. In fact, the chief of staff's doubts about Homma went back a number of years. He had taken a dim view of Homma's pro-British leanings before the war, and had reluctantly offered the Poet General the assignment to invade the Philippines only out of deference to Homma's established brilliance as a strategist.

In the last weeks of the Bataan siege, Sugiyama, growing more and more frustrated with what he perceived as Homma's foot-dragging, had sent a trusted lieutenant to Luzon to infiltrate Homma's command. This odd sort of plenipotentiary spy was a remarkable, Rasputin-like character named Masanobu Tsuji. One of the dark legends of the Pacific War, Colonel Tsuji was an intense, bespectacled militant who held a mysterious power within the Imperial Army that was far out of proportion to his rank. Whenever trouble would flare up, Sugiyama would dispatch Tsuji to serve as his personal eyes and ears and, sometimes, hatchet man. Tsuji claimed to possess all manner of magical powers, including an immunity from death, and although he was despised by gentleman warriors like Homma, he had a small coterie of young officers who were fanatically loyal to him and would do anything he asked. "The God of Operations," they called him. He argued vehemently that it was Japan's destiny to control the entire Orient—*Asia for the Asiatics,* as the slogan went. Perhaps more than any other officer, Tsuji fanned the flames of race hatred and endlessly harped on the theme of the purity and superiority of the Yamato race. Wherever he went, atrocities seemed to follow. He was said to be personally responsible for the death of more than 5,000 Chinese. Tsuji advocated eating the flesh of the enemy to build fighting spirit—on one occasion, he is reported to have dined on the liver of a downed Allied pilot.

Many of the stories surrounding Tsuji had a mythological quality, but there was no question about his genius as a warrior. Because of his forceful charisma and the fact that he was almost always right, Tsuji enjoyed a rare measure of latitude to contradict and reprimand superior officers with seeming impunity. His appearance struck fear in the hearts of field commanders, for he was viewed as Sugiyama's surrogate; his presence could only mean that the chief of staff was displeased.

Predictably, soon after Tsuji touched down in Luzon, trouble ensued. He sent back numerous cables to Tokyo casting aspersions on Homma's command. "Homma lacks ability," he told Sugiyama. "His staff are dull and stupid." Tsuji managed to persuade a few of the field officers that the Philippine conflict was fundamentally a race war that required extreme measures and an absolute ruthlessness of the sort that the weak-willed General Homma could not muster. Tsuji was seen on Bataan when the atrocities began to occur, and one unconfirmed report had it that he personally killed dozens of prisoners. Almost certainly, he directly incited other officers to acts of cruelty against American and Filipino prisoners. Japanese historian Murakami Hyoe wrote that on one occasion Tsuji gave a live demonstration to subordinates on how to treat the captives. "Tsuji said, 'Here is the way to treat bastards like this,'" Hyoe wrote. "He then pulled out his pistol and shot one of the prisoners to death."

121

A few days after the surrender, Colonel Takeo Imai, a commander loyal to Homma, received a call over a field telephone from a "mysterious" figure. The person on the other line identified himself, opaquely, as a "division staff officer." He ordered Imai to immediately "kill all prisoners and those offering to surrender." Imai responded by saying that surely Homma had given no such command and demanded to know from whom the order originated. The voice then insisted that this order came straight from Imperial Headquarters and was to be strictly obeyed. Outraged, Imai hung up the telephone. Fearing that a mass execution might indeed occur, he took an extraordinary measure of precaution. He told his officers to liberate some one thousand American and Filipino prisoners who had recently surrendered themselves. The prisoners were released into the jungles and actually given tips on the best routes for escaping from Japanese forces on Bataan.

The same mysterious officer then conveyed the identical "kill all" order to Major General Ikuta via field telephone. Ikuta likewise ignored the command, certain that it could not possibly have emanated from Homma's headquarters. Throughout the day, this same false order was relayed to numerous other commanders in the field. Tsuji was universally assumed to be the culprit, although his guilt was never absolutely established. In any case, Ikuta's suspicions were correct: It was a rogue order. Homma had nothing to do with it. "Unfortunately," wrote British war historian Lord Arthur Swinson, "some other officers, not so closely acquainted with Tsuji's curious character, did as they were told."

Captain Bert Bank witnessed some of the worst of the horrors. One day he was nearly decapitated by a soldier who wildly swung his sword from a passing truck. He saw the corpse of a man whose penis had been cut off and stuffed in his mouth. He watched in terror as an American lieutenant colonel, whom Bank had been holding up for hours, suddenly slipped from his grasp and dropped from exhaustion, only to be run through with a bayonet. He was forced at gunpoint to bury several Filipinos who had been severely wounded but who were still alive—he saw their bodies twitch as he spread on the dirt. When a guard assaulted Bank with a metal club, fellow Americans carried him, semiconscious and with a deep gash in his head, for six hours.

It was a chaplain on the battlefields of Bataan, Father Cummings, who had coined the famous phrase *There are no atheists in foxholes*. Certainly the aphorism resonated with Bert Bank. He was not a particularly religious person, but he found himself praying a great deal during the five days and five nights it took him to reach Camp O'Donnell. Although he was the son of Russian Jews who had somehow landed in the hard red hills of Alabama, he prayed not as a practitioner of Judaism but as a supplicant to any deity or spirit who would listen. "You're not supposed to pray for results," Bank said, "but that's what I did. I didn't pray in any particular tradition. I just prayed for myself, for my friends. Prayed for the strength to make it through this. I was not angry at God. Who was I to second-guess God? But I was theologically confused. Why had I been spared? Why had my friends died? They were good people. They loved their families. They were honest and true. You ask these sorts of questions all the time, and you never get a satisfactory answer. God does strange things. But sometimes you can feel a presence. You can sense that this is all happening to teach us something about the nature of free will."

By disposition, Bert Bank was a joker, someone unaccustomed to making hard assessments of the world. He was a lively, garrulous man with a sharply pointed nose, keen eyes, and bushy black eyebrows that bounced with wild independence as he talked. He was the consummate Southern storyteller, an instigator, an imp—the kind of person who, as he put it, "always liked to carry on a lot of foolishness." He spoke with the deep drawl and custardy lilt of west-central Alabama. He could strike up a conversation with anybody and instantly make a lasting connection. "He never knew a stranger," one Bataan survivor said of him. There was nothing dark about Bert Bank; he was all brightness and joviality. Even now as despair closed in on him and his eyes drank in the unimaginable, he found a way to shut it off, isolating himself in an envelope of optimism, biding the hours in the warm trance of prayer.

Bertram Bank had been raised in Searles, Alabama, a little mining town just outside of Tuscaloosa. His parents had immigrated to the United States from a small Russian village close to the Polish border; his father ran a restaurant and then had a wholesale plumbing business, but he lost everything during the Depression. Somehow Bert was able to save enough to go to college at the University of Alabama. He was an extremely popular student, the business manager of the school paper, and a close friend of Paul Bryant, who would later become the legendary football coach of the Crimson Tide. Bank never gave much thought to the Army. He decided to enroll in ROTC because one of his buddies "thought I'd look good in a uniform." He received his commission in 1940 and underwent artillery training on the coast of South Carolina, where he dated Miss Georgia, Emma Minkowitz, the lovely Savannah belle who much later in his life would become his bride. Switching gears slightly, he joined the 27th Bomb Group of the Army Air Corps, and received his orders for the Philippines in the fall of 1941. He arrived in Manila in late November. After just two weeks largely spent barhopping and "catting around" in the old walled city of Manila, he found to his dismay that the war was on.

Since the air force was virtually destroyed in December, many members of Bank's 27th Bomb Group were given old Springfield rifles and placed near the front lines as infantry troops. Bank became a regiment S-2 officer. "I was supposed to be doing intelligence work, determining where the enemy was," Bank recalled. "But that wasn't hard to figure out—the enemy was *everywhere*." One day Bank was sitting in a jeep when a Japanese Zero shot over the treetops, came in low, and strafed him with machine-gun fire. He received a gruesome bullet wound in his left hand, and quite nearly lost it.

Later, when the food supplies dwindled to starvation levels on Bataan, some of Bank's foxhole buddies gave him a new nickname that would stick with him all through captivity—Garbage Mouth. "I acquired a deserved reputation for having a not very discriminating palate, even by Bataan's low standards of cuisine," Bank said. "I would eat anything that wouldn't eat me first. A group of us would be having our mess together, and then someone would find some little piece of something in their food that looked suspicious. They'd say give it to Garbage Mouth, he'll eat it. And I would."

Some time in March, Bank wrote his last letter home to his parents in Tuscaloosa.

In the field
Somewhere on Bataan Penin.

Dear Folks,

I am writing this letter with plenty of sadness in my heart, because I know that when you receive this you will cry with joy to hear that I am well. I know that I am going to return home some day, and I hope it will not be very long off. I have always said that with Mother praying for me, I don't see how anything but safety could accompany me through this war. I plead with you not to worry about me. I only hope that this letter will find all of you in good health. I know you will be happy to hear that I am a Captain now, as I received my promotion Feb. 16, 1942.

Everything is not convenient during these perilous times. It can get tough, but I hope that the situation in its entirety will be relieved in the very near future. I am giving you fair warning right now when we get together in Calif. I will probably spend my entire time drinking milk and eating. I haven't had a good fresh glass of milk since I left home. But I am not complaining at all, and I will go on eating rice and fish, just let me get back to Ala. and no one will ever get me away from Tuscaloosa again. When I return I promise that you will find a changed boy. I will never give you any arguments but will agree with you on every subject.

You know this is the most difficult letter I have ever attempted to write. This war is demoralizing. It is really bad that I am here, but if I wasn't here some other boy would be in my place. I guess I should go now. I can't give you a return address. It will do no good to write me as it will probably not be received by me. Kiss Lottie and Mother for me, Dad. When I return I want to see Mother as pretty as she was when I left.

LOVE TO ALL,
Capt. Bert

The surrender did not come as a great shock to Bank. Since he'd been closely following the disposition of the enemy troops, he had long understood that the defense was hopeless. Even though he agreed with General King's decision to surrender—"If he hadn't, the Japanese would have eliminated every one of us"—Bank was outraged by the calculated neglect from Washington that had made surrender inevitable. "I was extremely bitter when I began the march," he recalled. "Where was America? How did this happen? Why had we been left out here like this? Why had we not been more prepared? I felt like I was witnessing one of the greatest failures in our history."

All through the march, Bank attempted to figure out what the patterns and rules were—or even if there *were* any. The Japanese guards were often arbitrary. Bank couldn't predict how they would react. Each one had different peeves, applied different standards, demanded different levels of servility. What incensed one might go unnoticed by another. An infraction that in the morning could provoke a grisly beating might only draw inscrutable smiles in the afternoon. The violence came in random gusts.

Not entirely random, however. Gradually, a few

tendencies seemed to suggest themselves. One had to do with stature. Big guys, Bank noticed, generally came in for more punishment. Bank, who was fortunate enough to be a slight-statured, fine-boned man, heard this observation widely discussed among the prisoners. Many of the guards had evidently never encountered Westerners before, and some clearly derived a perverse pleasure from physically dominating the tallest among the prisoners. At the very least, large men visually stood out from the crowd and presented a more obvious target for a guard's wrath.

Another general rule that impressed itself upon Bank concerned the searches to which prisoners were repeatedly subjected. Prudence dictated that an American prisoner carefully study all belongings on his person and discard anything that displayed, even microscopically, the words "Made in Japan." The guards automatically assumed that these items were stolen off the corpses of Japanese soldiers. It was true that, during the siege of Bataan, Americans on the front lines had routinely taken "souvenirs" from dead Japanese troops—Rising Sun flags, photographs, the ornate "thousand-stitch belts" that had been sewn by female well-wishers back in Japan. But the Japanese guards on the march made no distinction between such war booty and, say, a small Japanese-made mirror that an American enlisted man might have purchased in a Manila department store before the war. Many Americans were thus beaten, and some were even executed for possessing innocuous objects which, upon closer scrutiny, bore the signature of having been manufactured in Dai Nippon.

Bank also became aware of the benefits of constantly shielding himself with other bodies. "You always wanted to keep away from the guards as much as possible and never give them an opportunity to hit you," he said. The Japanese usually marched the prisoners four abreast in segmented columns of as many as a hundred men. Trouble almost always seemed to come to those who walked along the edges. These perimeter marchers were more directly exposed to the ire of Japanese guards as well as to the gratuitous bashings and potshots sometimes taken by Imperial Army troops who happened to pass by. Since everyone quickly grasped this trend, jockeying for a choice vacancy became a competitive enterprise. "If at all possible," said Bank, "you wanted an inside slot. If someone in the middle dropped out, everybody would simultaneously rush for the empty spot."

Truly, a marcher's position could be a matter of life or death. On one memorable occasion an American prisoner was marching on the outside when he began to falter. He was obviously lurching, straying a few feet out from the main group, when a convoy of Japanese tanks happened to approach from the rear. The first tank operator deliberately swerved to run over him, and other tanks in the convoy followed suit, so that the American's body was squashed into the road like a free-fallen cartoon villain, his clothes pressed flat into the asphalt.

The march progressed from Orion to Pilar to Abucay and then funneled out of Bataan province. All along the winding route, the Filipino people showed their sympathies in countless ways. As devout Spanish Catholics intimately familiar with Passion plays and the pilgrimage traditions of the Penitentes, many of the Filipinos saw in the death march the quality of a tragic passage reminiscent of Christ's progress to Calvary through the Stations of the

Cross. In doorways and half-shuttered windows, women could be seen openly weeping. Peasants lined the sides of the roads, flashing V signs and offering bottles of water or cool moist rags. Little boys would toss dried mango or sugarcane candy at the staggering prisoners. A woman might emerge from the thickets with her arms full of ripe papayas or a whole cooked chicken. Sometimes the Japanese would allow the prisoners to accept these gifts of food, but usually they wouldn't. Often the guards would fly into a rage and attempt to kill any Filipino with the temerity to show such open allegiance toward the American forces.

The guards seemed to be of two minds on the question of how to treat the Filipino people. In truth, the Japanese had an enormous political quandary to sort out. On the one hand, the Filipinos had demonstrated their over-whelming fealty to the United States by fighting and dying alongside American soldiers for the previous four months. On the other hand, if the Japanese expected to occupy the Philippines with any measure of stability, they would have to win over popular support by granting wide amnesty and showing benevolence at every possible turn. General Homma, for one, espoused a policy of mercy toward the Filipinos, while others within the Japanese high command, including Colonel Masanobu Tsuji, advocated seizing total control of the populace through acts of terror and exact-ing immediate retribution for gestures of friendship to-ward the United States.

One afternoon Captain Bank came face to face with this latter sentiment. He was marching through a barrio when a pregnant Filipino woman appeared on the road and handed out cassava cakes for the prisoners to eat. The barefoot woman was young and sad-faced. Tears of sympathy pooled in her eyes. Having spotted this act of generosity, a Japanese guard grabbed the woman by the arm and forced her behind a tree. "I heard her plead for mercy," Bank said. "I couldn't believe what I was seeing. She was on the ground. He took his bayonet and gouged out her fetus right in front of her. We could hear her, screaming and screaming."

Bank resumed the march, his lips quivering in prayer.

— — — — —

At San Fernando, a sugar-mill town in Pampanga province, the men were led to the train depot and assembled into groups of one hundred alongside the narrow-gauge tracks. The boxcars had baked all day in the sun, so that vaporous heat now rose off the sheeny metal in thick waves. The guards threw open the doors of the cars and gestured with their bayonets for the prisoners to climb inside. Tommie Thomas was the first in line, which he now realized was a bad place to be. After surviving the false firing squad, Thomas had managed to get through five days of the march without great incident, other than sustaining a puncture wound from the quick jab of a bayonet. He felt as though he'd had a guardian angel watching over him. "I was well beyond what they thought our endurance was," he said. "Way, way, *way* beyond. I was so tired I couldn't move, couldn't even wiggle. Yet I'd take another step, and take another, and another. Something was driving me, something outside myself."

When the guards brought the group to the San Fernando station, he had imagined that the prisoners would take a passenger train to wherever they were going, and he thought that if he could get on early enough he might even find a seat. But once the string of tiny boxcars pulled up, he immediately saw his mistake. Somehow the guards expected one hundred men to fit into each one of these rolling cells. When Thomas climbed up inside, the steady pressure of boarding bodies shoved him farther and farther away from the door, into the stifling dead air. The car was not ventilated. It felt like a kiln.

The Japanese kept pushing and prodding, cramming more and more men inside. When it no longer seemed possible that any more could fit, the guards brought over an additional dozen or so, tamping them in with their rifle butts. Then, with a long hideous screech, the rusty doors slid shut behind them. In the pitch darkness, the men could hear the guards fastening the door with a padlock.

For a few minutes they just stood there, blinking. A terrific stench rose up, the body smells of a hundred men mingled in a close miasma. Most of them hadn't bathed in weeks. Their bodies were sour with encrusted sweat, gangrenous wounds, and the suppuration of tropical ulcers. Many of them had dysentery, and when they lost control, which was often, they had no option but to defecate where they stood. Soon the plywood floor was splattered with the blood-mucus diarrhea that is the classic symptom of the disease. Thomas recalled, "A guy next to me said, 'Sorry, fellows, I can't help it, I can't stand it, I've got cramps.' He was almost crying, begging. Then he started shitting all over everybody."

The train snapped forward and the journey began. It was 120 degrees Fahrenheit inside, maybe hotter. "I thought we were going to be roasted alive," Thomas said. He felt like he was suffocating. The ceiling was too low for a man of six foot four. He was stooped in his corner, listening to the moans and sibilances, the scraping and buckling sounds of the old train car, the sound of people vomiting. Men collapsed but had nowhere to fall. The living, the semiconscious, and the soon-to-be-dead all stood together in a press of diseased flesh.

Then the chills began. Thomas recognized instantly that he was having a malarial attack. His teeth clacked and rattled just like the train. His legs lost all strength, but the pressure of the other bodies kept him upright, pinned against the hot metal skin of the boxcar. He had cerebral malaria, the doctors would later ascertain—*Plasmodium falciparum,* the strain that made men go out of their heads and if left untreated often resulted in death. Shivering in the dark, hovering on the brink of awareness, Thomas seemed to lose track of time.

Finally, after several hours, the train came to a halt, and the door screaked open. "It was one of the sweetest sounds I've ever heard," Thomas said. Everyone tried to force his way out at once. Thomas pushed toward the daylight glare and leaped to the ground, sucking in the fresh air. Then he peered back into the gloom of the train car. There were about a dozen men, including the man who had been standing next to Thomas, who never came out. Sprawled in pools of excrement, they had stopped breathing.

— — —

Abie Abraham and his friend Arthur Houghtby emerged from their train into the bright heat of the day.

"Where are we?" Houghtby asked, disoriented and groggy.

"This is Capas," Abraham said. He was vaguely familiar with the town. It was located some twenty-five miles north of San Fernando in the hot plains of Tarlac province. The barrio was coated in the fine, powdery dust of the dry season. Off to the west, the green Zambales Mountains, dominated by the seething Mount Pinatubo, clawed at a hazy sky.

The Japanese led Abraham's group to an open space not far from the train station and detained the prisoners under the hot sun for more than an hour. The Americans came to call this form of torture "the sun treatment." Abraham's guard made no effort to find a shady spot. For many prisoners, already cooked by the train ride, this sun lashing was the final blow; by the dozens, the men began to drop from heat exhaustion.

Finally they were grouped into columns again and pointed west. The march still wasn't finished. They stumbled out of Capas on a narrow road lined with well-wishers. "Young girls threw us kisses," Abraham recalled, "and men working with their carabao in the fields turned and waved at us, some giving us the V-for-victory sign." The rural countryside was expansive, with faintly rolling hills covered in crisp dry grass. Containers of water had been left along the roadsides, but almost invariably the Japanese guards would kick them over before the prisoners could get a drink.

After a few hours of marching, the column crept to the brow of a gentle hill. There, spread before them in the dusty heat, was a vast encampment of some 600 acres surrounded by flimsy barbed wire. Scores of tattered nipa shacks slumbered in the glare, and thousands of people could be seen in the middle distance, moving about the pathways and thoroughfares. At the front gate the Japanese had built a tall tower of wooden struts from which they had festooned the Rising Sun—"the flaming red asshole," as the Americans called it. Before the war, Camp O'Donnell had been a training facility for the Philippine Army. It was designed to accommodate no more than 9,000 people. By the time Abie Abraham walked through the gates, however, O'Donnell's population had swelled to some 50,000 Filipino and American prisoners.

Abraham's group was brought into the parade ground, where they were lined up and made to stand at attention— more "sun treatment." The guards undertook a comprehensive shakedown of every prisoner. One by one, the men were relieved of any valuables or contraband items that had not already been taken during the march.

Then the camp commandant, Captain Yoshio Tsuneyoshi, stood on a box and, speaking through an interpreter, addressed the new arrivals. "You are the enemy!" he began. "You will *always* be the enemy! One hundred years from now, we will *still* be enemies!"

Captain Tsuneyoshi was a caricature of the bombastic prison warden. The Americans would call him "Little Hitler." A short, bowlegged, mustachioed man, he wore baggy pants and riding boots with spurs. A large samurai sword dangled at his side. He had grave, penetrating eyes, a bald pate, a scar on his right cheek, and a mole on his bottom lip. "He was one of the ugliest mortals I have ever seen," one prisoner later wrote. "He breathed the very essence of hate." Abraham described him as "bellowing, strutting, with an air of self-importance." Tsuneyoshi's initiation speech, which he gave with only slight variation to each group of newcomers, was a surreal diatribe of racism. Each time he spoke, he worked himself up into such a lather that he would spit uncontrollably into the air. Tsuneyoshi was obviously not a bright man. "The loose-lipped vacuity of his expression was that of an idiot," one prisoner observed. Prison camp duty was by no means a coveted post within the Imperial Army, and it can be assumed that abler officers were off on more pressing military assignments. But for the life-and-death power that Tsuneyoshi wielded over the camp, the Americans would have found him comical. He glared and gesticulated wildly. His speech went on and on:

Your domination of the Orient is gone forever! We will fight you and fight you and fight you for 100 years, until you have been destroyed. It is regrettable that we were unable to kill each of you on the battlefield. It is only through our generosity that you are alive at all. We do not consider you to be prisoners of war. You are members of an inferior race, and we will treat you as we see fit. Whether you live or die is of no concern to us. If you violate any of the rules, you will be shot immediately. Your country has forgotten your name. Your loved ones no longer weep for you. You are forever the enemy of Japan.

The harangue lasted about a half hour. Satisfied that he had made his point, Captain Tsuneyoshi stepped down from his box and swaggered off toward the headquarters shack that was perched on a knoll. Abraham and his group, having been officially welcomed to Camp O'Donnell, were led to their new barracks.

Camp O'Donnell was a temporary holding station, a brief detainment in the Americans' long passage to other circles of hell. Most prisoners were kept there for only about fifty days. Yet O'Donnell was, for many, the most horrific experience of the war. It was the place where all the seeds of hunger and disease sown on Bataan came to full fruition. Americans had not seen deprivational grotesqueries on such a vast scale since the days of Andersonville, the infamous Civil War death camp for Union soldiers in Georgia. One prisoner later wrote, "Hell is only a state of mind; O'Donnell was a place."

"I don't have the vocabulary to describe O'Donnell," said Bert Bank, "and I don't think anybody does." The camp was, as Thomas called it, "a putrid place." The sanitation was so appallingly bad, the stench so overwhelming, that the few Japanese who ventured inside the camp almost invariably wore surgical masks. The open slit trenches were breeding grounds for vermin—black flies, green blowflies, bluebottle flies, and intestinal parasites of every strain and stripe. The men were fed measly portions of whistleweed soup and lugao, a slop of watery rice that had a nauseating bluish tint and was often crunchy with maggots. The American side of the camp was equipped with only two water spigots to serve the 9,000 POWs now imprisoned there. Each barracks, originally designed to accommodate forty men, was crammed with more than a hundred. The double-decker sleeping bays were "rank with the smell of humanity gone sour," Abraham recalled. "At night, bedbugs by the millions crawled over us to steal the little flesh that still clung to our bones."

The death toll at Camp O'Donnell was catastrophic. One out of every ten prisoners who passed through

O'Donnell perished there. In two months, more than 1,500 Americans and some 15,000 Filipinos were buried in mass unmarked graves. "We constantly wondered who would be next," said Bank. "We couldn't keep up with our friends. The death toll was like a scoreboard that was constantly changing." With men dying at a rate of thirty or forty a day, the bodies began to stack up like cordwood. The burial details couldn't dispose of the corpses fast enough. "We worked like slaves, digging graves," Abraham wrote. "The days fell on us like a relentless hammer. We were wretched animals. Every day we walked among the dead, having no thoughts, no desires. There was no stopping the deaths. They went on and on like the waves of the ocean."

The critically ill invariably ended up in a place called the St. Peter's Ward, so named because patients consigned there were believed to have no chance of survival, and thus, in the grim triage of the camp, were offered no treatment. "It couldn't be called a hospital," one prison doctor later testified. "It was merely a place for men to go to die." By the hundreds, the diseased, half-naked prisoners were laid out on straw mats. Flies swarmed over their bodies. They were caked in their own night soil, and their pipe-stem arms and legs were covered with raw sores. To simplify the preparation of burial records, medics would scrawl the terminal patient's Army serial number across his chest with a tincture of iodine or gentian violet. When someone passed away, his clothes were removed (to be boiled and later recirculated among the living), and the body was stacked behind the ward to await burial.

O'Donnell was less a prison than it was an incubatorium for disease, a study in what happens when thousands of starving, ill men are brought together in close proximity in the tropics. Antique diseases that had long since been conquered by modern medicine rose out of the latrines for an encore performance. The vectors for contagion were too numerous to count. Pathogens spread from man to insect to beast to shit to man again. Starvation and vitamin deficiency lowered the immunological threshold for everyone, so that hundreds succumbed to diseases that wouldn't ordinarily have killed them. Principally, the patients were dying of malaria, dysentery, pellagra, acute dehydration, beriberi, or various sordid combinations thereof.

Yet in many cases the act of dying seemed to come by force of will. Every doctor saw it. A patient who was sick but not necessarily terminal would suddenly get an unmistakable look on his face—a million-mile stare, a crushing melancholy, as if to say, "I cannot bear another moment." He would simply give up. Within hours, sometimes within minutes, he'd be dead. The prisoners called it "give-up-itis." The doctors referred to it as "inanition," the absence of spirit. "Living was like holding on to a rope," said one medic. "All you had to do was let go and you were a goner."

One person who quickly developed the characteristic look was Sergeant Arthur Houghtby, Abie Abraham's close friend. The hike out of Bataan had been too much for him. "Look at Houghtby," a friend said to Abraham one day. "All he does is stare. He's in bad shape. I'm afraid he's not going to make it." A few days later, Abraham went to the ward to call on his friend. Houghtby's face was coated in a quivering mass of flies. They buried him later that day.

Burial, in fact, was the main focus and organizing principle of the camp. Anyone who was strong enough was expected to go out on the details. Two men would heave a bamboo pole with a blanket, tied at each end, that held the body. The pallbearers would walk over to the grave site at the edge of camp and unceremoniously slide the corpse out of the blanket into the hole. As they turned away, they'd hear the crack of one skull against another. Often they didn't have the strength to bury the corpses properly, and part of a hand or an arm would protrude from the soil, only to be eaten at night by scavenger birds and wild dogs.

When the monsoon rains came, the burials became particularly problematical, because the graves would fill with water, and the corpses would float to the top. "While one person threw on dirt, another would have to hold the bodies down with a long bamboo pole to keep them from bobbing up to the surface," recalled Bank. Sometimes the bodies would wash out of the graves entirely. Because the cemetery was located on a slight rise, the runoff would seep back toward the O'Donnell barracks. On the rainiest days, a steady rivulet of red-tinged water coursed through the center of camp.

The burial crews had to be especially careful when handling the bodies of those who had died from wet beriberi. The disease, a degenerative condition caused by thiamine deficiency, makes the feet, legs, hands, and testicles hideously swell up, elephantiasis-like, and, if left untreated, ultimately causes the victim to drown in his own pus. Some of the victims would become grotesquely swollen, assuming an unnatural corpulence of three hundred pounds or more, the skin cracked and oozing with a thin, yellowish serum. "We had to really struggle with them because they were so heavy," recalled Bank. "It was necessary to handle them with great care. If we didn't they would burst all over us."

The remainder of the deaths at O'Donnell could be attributed to human cruelty. On this score, Captain Tsuneyoshi proved true to his word. For various rule infractions, real or perceived, prisoners were beaten to death, shot, beheaded, bayoneted, or chained to poles and left to perish of thirst and exhaustion in the furnace heat of the afternoon. A particularly grisly method of dispatch was the "water treatment." The executioner would thread a hose down the victim's esophagus and turn on a spigot. As the water pressure increased, the man's abdomen would become distended. The guards would then jump on the victim until his intestines ruptured.

For some, the torture continued even after death. On one occasion, the Japanese affixed the decapitated head of an American Indian soldier to a long pole and paraded it around camp for several days. The display was intended as a deterrent to escape; the prisoner, purportedly, had been caught trying to break through the fence.

A week after his arrival at Camp O'Donnell, Tommie Thomas came within a hairsbreadth of sharing the American Indian's fate. On this day, Thomas was gripped by an attack of cerebral malaria. He raced out to the fence with the demented notion of busting loose. Lost in his paroxysms, he got himself hopelessly entangled in the barbed wire. When the fever broke and he shook off his delirium, several Americans were beckoning to him, whispering, "Come back, come back!" He had no recollection of how he'd gotten there, no memory of slipping past the no-man's-land to the outer fence. His face was doused in cool sweat. The barbed wire had sliced through his arms and legs. He turned and saw that the guards in the tower were nervously studying the situation. Perhaps they thought he was trying to escape. Perhaps they thought he was crazy—or feigning craziness. They pointed their rifles straight at him.

With their stares boring into his back, Thomas extricated himself from the razor ribbon and timidly crawled toward his barracks. Once again he had the strange sensation that a guardian angel was watching over him.

Chapter 4

A little past midnight, in the early-morning hours of Monday, January 29, 1945, the Rangers were stepping warily through a broad field of cogon, the ubiquitous weed of the Philippines. Cogon grass afforded terrific cover but it could also be a terrific nuisance. Each spike of coarse grass was as tall as a man and bore hundreds of silky hairs that made the Rangers' skin itch. Aside from its function as a thatching material, it was an agriculturally useless plant, inedible to humans and cattle alike. Still it grew everywhere in the archipelago, cropping up like a sharp-eyed opportunist wherever old-growth forest was felled. The only effective way to get rid of cogon was to burn it, and even now there were several brush fires smoldering somewhere in the distance, gauzing the night in an acrid haze.

As the Rangers were discovering, cogon could also make one a little paranoid, especially when you had to move through it at night. The trail twisted through the walls of grass, leaving the impression of a vast, wild maze spreading out for miles. The view was constantly checked by the vegetation. If they wanted to look anywhere, the Rangers had to look up at the powdering of stars and the fat moon dancing in and out of stray cumulus clouds. Their boots were soaked again after having forded the knee-deep Talavera River a few miles back, so that their collective footsteps made a soughing squish that was vaguely unsettling in the dark. When the breeze stirred, the individual pickets of grass shimmied and buzzed, throwing erratic moon shadows across the trail. The deeper thickets snapped with miscellaneous noises—buggy noises, reptilian noises. In the natural baffle of swaying weeds, it was hard to say which direction the sounds were coming from or how far away they were.

For the Rangers, raccoon-eyed from scant sleep, these chokes of cogon formed a spectral landscape. Anything could be out there, or so they could make themselves believe. A krait or a cobra. Cockroaches the size of mice. Feral dogs, wild boars. Or humans, the worst animal of all, if wearing an Imperial Army uniform and holding a rifle.

The guerrillas didn't like being out here any more than the Americans did. A lot of the Filipinos believed the cogon fields were haunted places at night, and the Rangers could tell some of them were a bit spooked. Living as they did in traditional agrarian villages without incandescent light, they followed nature's clock, rising with the sun and retiring to their houses soon after dusk, and they were wary of venturing into the fields at night. Their devout Spanish Catholicism coexisted with a smattering of older indigenous beliefs. Among other things, they believed in a certain demon called the aswang. An aswang was a person like anyone else during the day, but at night he shed his legs and sprouted wings and gadded around like a vampire, settling old scores and wreaking general havoc upon the land. In the country all around here, the nipa-and-bamboo dwellings were kept wide open and well ventilated during the day, yet in the evenings the Filipinos always shuttered their windows tight to keep these demons out. When aswangs were about, the last place you wanted to be was in an open field like this one.

The men clutched their rifles a little tighter and kept moving down the bolo-hacked trail. With their imaginations quickened, they took to playing a vigilance game. Dominoes, they called it. If anyone heard a suspicious noise, he hit the dirt, and everyone else followed suit. Dominoes was exhausting and a little comical to watch. After the first drop, the group paranoia was ratcheted up. It was contagious: The first guy would think he'd heard something, then everyone did. With a train of 200 men, all of this elaborate copycatting made for slow going. It could take an hour to cross a few thousand yards.

The Rangers had been playing dominoes for a half hour when suddenly something hurtled out of the sky at them—

Sssssss-flump.

The guys in the vanguard heard it the loudest. In an instant, they dropped to the ground and flipped off their safeties. Behind them, everyone else did the same. Whatever it was, it sounded large and heavy, like something with heft. It landed with a dull thud just ahead of them, somewhere in the cogon. In a flash of panic, the guys in the front thought it might have been a dud grenade or mortar shell.

The men waited, pointing their rifles at imaginary

targets that suggested themselves in the brush. Nothing. Just the sound of crickets and the wind sweeping through the grass.

A minute later, they all climbed to their feet and resumed the hike. Maybe they didn't hear anything. Maybe they *were* getting paranoid.

Then it happened again—

Flump.

Sssssssss-flump-flump.

Down the Rangers went, their minds racing. Somebody out there was lobbing something at them. They kept expecting an eruption from the bush, a banzai charge, a gleam of bayonets. Or perhaps it was just a rival band of Filipino guerrillas trying to scare Joson's men. Again everyone waited, squinting down rifle sights, palping their triggers.

Finally someone at the front broke the suspense, yelling back a perplexing report:

"Ain't nothing but birds."

"How's that?"

"Birds, I said."

"Excuse me?"

"Dead birds. There's a bunch of black birds up here. Dropped out of the sky. Looks like they died where they fell."

Once this bizarre news had sunk in, everybody erupted in laughter at the silly surrealism of it all. Up front, a group of the men crouched in the cogon to examine a few of the birds. They were still warm, their bodies unmolested. They hadn't been shot or wounded in any obvious way. The Rangers swapped theories: Had they collided with fighter planes? Had a thunderstorm sucked them into the upper atmosphere and hurled them back to earth? It was a mystery, one the Rangers had neither the time nor the inclination to solve now. Mucci glanced at his watch—2 A.M., past time to shove off.

He called out, "Company, march!" and led the column toward the dawn. From then on, the Filipinos were noticeably more nervous and sober-minded. The Rangers thought they could see the worry spreading over some of the guerrillas' faces. A falling bird was not a good omen. To them it was obvious: Aswang.

At daybreak, the long line of Rangers and guerrillas stopped to rest in the barrio of Balincarin. The rural village was just beginning to stir. The Rangers could hear chickens clucking, the cheerful natter of Filipinas busily cooking breakfast over woodstoves. A few scabby gamecocks pecked in the dirt, strutting the tight orbits of their chains. As with every village they'd passed near, the Balincarin dogs marched out to the edge of town to snarl at the Rangers, sending up an unholy racket.

"Will somebody shut up those mutts!" Mucci yelled.

Balincarin was five miles north of the POW camp, too close to the enemy for the Rangers' taste. Mucci worried that the dogs would send a signal to the Japanese that something was out of the ordinary. "From here on," Mucci said, "we've *got* to get the locals to muzzle every last dog in the area. The Japs will know something's up."

Soon the townsfolk emerged from their nipa shacks to hush the dogs. The people gathered around the Rangers, offering ripe papayas and the partially incubated duck eggs known as *balut*. Bare-breasted women, some of them nursing children, came up without a hint of shyness and mingled with the men. They smiled at the tall Americans, studying their unfamiliar uniforms and their strange-looking guns, saying, *"Magandang umaga! Salamat!* Long live America!"

Just a few weeks earlier, Balincarin had suffered a bloody reprisal from the Japanese Army, apparently because the barrio had been harboring guerrillas. A group of soldiers from the Japanese garrison in Cabanatuan City had stormed in with tanks and shot up the place, killing a substantial number of guerrillas and a few civilians as well. The people in Balincarin were uncomfortable talking about it, and it was unclear precisely how many had been murdered—Mucci later reported in an article in *The Saturday Evening Post* that as many as 100 people were killed in the vicinity, though other accounts put the number closer to twenty. When the subject came up, the villagers responded by smiling awkwardly and shaking their heads. All the Rangers were able to learn was that something horrible had recently happened there. The people of Balincarin were still obviously haunted by the tragedy and not so quietly nursing revenge.

Maybe this explained why they were so happy to see the Rangers. They'd been around Yanks before, of course, but these were a different breed from three years ago—bigger, it seemed, better armed, more confident, with a curious squash-yellow glow to their skin, the result of their daily intake of the new antimalarial, Atabrine. Over the past few weeks, the Filipinos had watched American planes vectoring overhead and they'd heard the welcome wrath of American artillery, yet this was their first look at flesh-and-blood

American troops since the days of Bataan, and it brought tears to their eyes. Their barrio, like so many others, had been ravaged by the Japanese. Yet the Emperor's Army was on the run now, and the people in Balincarin could sense by the swagger of these new Americans that it was only a matter of time.

If the villagers were excited to see Mucci's men, no one was the least bit surprised by their presence. The barrio already seemed to be well aware of the Rangers' mission. It was as though John the Baptist had passed through town several days earlier to herald their imminent arrival. Children, grandmothers, even the dogs appeared to know what was afoot.

Mucci was astonished and not a little miffed by this development. "So I guess the cat's out of the bag!" he snapped. The last thing a Ranger on assignment ever wanted was for his reputation to precede him. That this "top secret" mission was now common knowledge seemed to mock all their assiduous efforts at stealth. Mucci and Prince could only cross their fingers and pray the virus of common knowledge didn't spread to Japanese ears.

More than ever, they had to trust in the rock-bed loyalty of the local people. During the early days of the occupation, the Nueva Ecija countryside had certainly known its share of makapili—Japanese sympathizers—but now, with the tide so obviously turning in America's favor, the danger of collaborators seemed less likely. "I wasn't worried about informants," Prince later said. "I figured a quisling would have been pretty stupid by this point in the war, even if his sympathies *did* truly lie with the Japanese. They knew we'd taken Leyte. They knew we were taking Luzon. They could see the writing on the wall." It wasn't necessarily a question of informants, though; a breach might just as easily occur by accident. If a Japanese spy happened to be purposefully loitering around the rice granaries or the village market, one incautious remark among friends could precipitate disaster.

Mucci figured that if the Japanese got wind of the raid, by whatever means, they'd respond in one of two ways: Either their troops would try to ambush his men or, just as likely, the Japanese Army would simply hasten the timetable for a massacre at the camp, so that by the time the Rangers got there, the enemy would be long gone and the feared slaughter would have already been accomplished.

It was nerve-racking to think about all the nightmare contingencies that could conceivably arise from this gnawing problem of leaks. In the end, there wasn't much Mucci could do about it. He could muzzle the dogs, yet how could he expect to muzzle an entire province? This was the Philippines, after all. The villagers didn't love the Japanese, but they loved to talk. As a people, the Filipinos were famous for their garrulousness. They were the Irish of Asia, it was sometimes said—warm, openhearted, story-loving, with unslakable appetites for the latest rumor or fact. Throughout the Philippines there was a phenomenon known as the Bamboo Telegraph. News of every kind seemed to race across the countryside, if not at electric speed, then close to it. Not that the news was particularly accurate or nuanced, but for a drowsy corner of the Asian tropics largely lacking telephones or electric lines or even decent roads, it was mystifying how people deep in the provinces received word of important events so fast. The guerrillas had their own runners who plied the footpaths between barrios on foot or on the backs of ponies, disseminating details of one impending action or another. Even when the runners weren't running, though, the Bamboo Telegraph worked its magic, with every half-fact and whispered secret seemingly borne on the wind.

By now one could bet every village in this part of Nueva Ecija knew that the Rangers were planning to hit Cabanatuan that night. Already irritable from lack of sleep, Mucci had become extremely agitated by this—as if he needed one more wrinkle to worry over.

———————

The colonel had intended to keep marching another forty minutes to the village of Platero—the last barrio before Cabanatuan camp—but he could see his men needed a good rest, as did he. They would sit out the morning here. Footsore and frazzled, the Rangers lay down in the shadow of a decrepit school bus to unburden themselves of their loads and massage their calves. They'd been up twenty-four hours marching some twenty-five miles from the drop-off point at Guimba. After the encounter with the nose-diving birds earlier that morning, they'd hiked five miles to get here, crossing the muddy Morcan River and a second national highway, the Rizal Road. As with the first highway they had confronted, the Rizal Road was choked with Japanese convoys. The traffic soon thinned, however, and the Rangers were able to slink across, single file, without incident.

From Balincarin, the POW camp was only about an hour's march south. They were within striking distance.

The assault would begin at dusk. The flush of approaching combat was canceling, or at least masking, their physical fatigue. Sleep was what they needed most, even just a good catnap, but sleep seemed unthinkable now that battle jitters were taking hold—the gathering excitement, the thrum in the gut, the taste of metal on the tongue. Locals generously filled the Ranger canteens with artesian water and offered rice balls wrapped in waxy banana leaves. The Rangers bolted their breakfasts and talked high-spiritedly of the raid, wondering aloud what Mucci and Prince had planned for them.

A fierce sun had climbed over the Sierra Madre, sending early warning of another hot day on the Central Plain. By eight o'clock, the air was already torpid. The tropical sunlight bore down on them, a penetrating glare that seemed to have weight. Out in the fields, the glistening gray hulks of carabaos were hunched low in their wallows, creeping along through the muck. Because carabaos lacked efficient sweat glands, wallowing helped them keep cool while also affording a generous coating of mud to deter insects. With their great horned heads lunging forward on sturdy necks, they flared their ringed nostrils and stared impassively through the blast heat.

In the shadows cast by the old school bus, Captain Prince removed his boots and inspected his feet. It was worse than he feared. The jungle rot had left the skin on his ankles and feet as fragile as onion skin, and now they were raw with a half dozen blisters. Medallions of blood seeped through his socks. The blisters had smarted so intensely during the last few miles of the hike that he winced with every step. Prince wondered what he'd do if his blister problem got much worse. It was a potentially embarrassing situation for a company commander—to be this badly bunged up with something so banal as foot trouble.

So Prince didn't breathe a word about it to Mucci or anyone else. He figured he could certainly make it to the POW camp, as close as it was. The long marathon back to American lines, however, was iffier. By then he wondered whether he'd be just another gimp, as lame as the POWs he was supposed to be leading to safety. Gingerly, he slipped his socks and boots back on, keeping his secret to himself.

One of the Balincarin Filipinas approached Prince and offered him a rare treat: a chicken egg. Like everyone else, the captain had grown weary of canned and reconstituted Army food. He accepted the gift with profuse thanks but then wondered what to do with it. The egg was raw, and none of the Rangers had brought along stoves. Then the young Filipina solved his dilemma. "No, like this," she explained, delicately puncturing the end of the egg with a knife and handing it back to Prince. "See, you eat."

Prince's reaction was somewhere between a grimace and a grin. But being unfailingly polite, he was loath to offend local custom. Besides, he was hungry. So with a taut smile he tipped the scalped shell to his lips and sucked the yolk whole.

"Wonderful," he pronounced it, nodding appreciatively and wiping a viscous yellow trail from his chin.

Breakfast behind him, Prince broke out his map and began to sketch his ideas for the raid. With his M-1 lying in the grass beside him, he arranged a series of aerial photos of Cabanatuan that had been taken from a Piper Cub reconnaissance plane. Alternately tugging at his chin and swatting mosquitoes, he squinted to read the map's fine points in the broadening daylight. Beads of sweat rose on his forehead, occasionally spattering his notes.

No matter what else happens, he kept saying to himself, the crux of the enterprise, the linchpin, was absolute surprise. The significance couldn't be overstated. If we have it, Prince thought, then anything is possible. As he cross-checked the aerial photos against the map, however, one thing struck him loud and clear: The countryside surrounding the camp was as flat and expansive as Nebraska prairie. There appeared to be no trees or structures to hide behind, just a monochrome plate of grass. By the look of things, it would be a long, tense crawl, hundreds and hundreds of yards perhaps, before they reached the gate. They'd be exposed for the entire approach, like worms twisting on a sidewalk after a summer storm. Any Japanese guard up in the tower who was halfway vigilant could get a bead on them. Preserving the critical element of surprise, Prince now feared, would be trickier than he'd ever imagined.

For the young captain, the anxiety was mounting. The master plan Mucci had asked Prince to devise was supposed to cover every contingency, from the moment the first shot was fired to the moment the last prisoner stumbled out the front gate. Mucci would be in charge of getting them all to the edge of the compound, but Prince would take it from there. As the assault commander, he would oversee everything. With the help of his platoon leaders, he had to figure out how to apportion the manpower and the firepower, how to choreograph the event so that bullets flew in the right direction at the right time as hundreds of men ran this way and that through smoky darkness. While Mucci would be somewhere in the outlying grasslands watching the carefully designed fracas unfold through binoculars, Prince would be where the action was, having to make the split-second judgment calls. It was Mucci's show in the end, but the main act, the incursion itself, was Prince's special predicament to solve or bungle.

"I was very apprehensive," Prince later recalled. "Any commander's greatest fear is the fear of failure. It preys on you. You have to keep your focus. You have to consider all the things that could go wrong, but then you have to quickly banish them from your mind. If you think about them too long, you can't go forward—you're paralyzed."

Prince considered it an honor that Mucci placed so much faith in him, yet the pressure was immense, especially for someone so young. Captain Prince was twenty-five, just a few years out of Stanford, where he'd studied economics and history and served as his fraternity's president. (In college he had been close friends with the father of golf legend Tom Watson.) Yet Prince looked even younger than he was. He carried himself with a certain awkward youthfulness, as though he were still growing into his body. One Ranger remembered him as "fresh." He'd never seen combat before, not up close. Forty-eight hours previously, Prince had never heard of Cabanatuan. Now he was charged with liberating the place.

The window was uncomfortably tight. Just a few hours remained for Prince and Mucci to work out the details. As high as the stakes were, there was little in their training that had specifically prepared the men for this sort of endeavor. The Rangers were flying blind. "We couldn't rehearse this," Prince said. "Anything of this nature, you'd ordinarily want to practice it over and over for weeks in

155

advance. Get more information, build models, and discuss all the contingencies. Work out all the kinks. We didn't have time for any of that. It was now, or not."

Mucci thought the world of his C Company commander. "My wonderful Captain Prince," he called him. Prince, for his part, was mildly embarrassed by the colonel's attentions. "I don't know what he saw in me, really," Prince said. "But he liked me and I liked him. It was a personal thing. For some reason, he trusted me."

Prince had grown up in a middle-class Seattle family and had attended a high school where many of his classmates were Japanese-Americans. He'd spent his summers working in apple orchards, pruning trees, picking and sorting fruit according to the industry's curiously termed standards ("extra fancy, well-formed, or grossly misshapen"). In some ways, Prince seemed the direct opposite of the colonel. He wasn't gung-ho, he wasn't charismatic, he wasn't theatrical. He didn't radiate the conspicuous verve of a war hero. He had none of Mucci's athletic grace or strutting physicality. Prince was gangling of build, and his body language—cautious, tentative—failed to telegraph a martial sensibility. "If you were looking at him," recalled fellow Ranger Vance Shears, "you wouldn't even think he was a soldier." To some, Prince's instinctive sense of caution came off as aloofness, the reserve of a privileged college boy. As one man from F Company would later put it: "I wish I could have bought him for what he was worth and sold him for what he *thought* he was worth."

Most Rangers liked and greatly respected Prince, even if they didn't love him with the same abandon they reserved for Mucci. They saw that, in choosing the young captain to lead the assault, Mucci had made precisely the right call. In contrast to the mercurial colonel, Prince's assessments of things were always moderated, neither inflated with his own opinions nor lacquered with extraneous concerns. The young captain provided the sober ballast necessary to offset Mucci's fiery allure. As one Ranger later put it, if Mucci was the heart and soul of the operation, Prince was the brains.

"Mucci was good at sizing up an individual and he saw in Captain Prince something he didn't see in the others," said Alvie Robbins, who was in C Company. "At first, we didn't see what it was. When you have an officer as young as Prince was, you have a tendency to brush him off, especially when you're a group of rough and tough men like we were. Prince's personality sank in gradually. He carried himself in such a way that you had to respect him."

"He had a great mind and great composure," recalled Ranger Robert Anderson. "I never saw him irritated by anything. His name wasn't far off the mark—he was a prince of a fellow."

—————

More than anything else, what Mucci and Prince needed was hard information—the specs of the camp, accurate reports on the whereabouts and strength of the enemy, the precise location of every pillbox and guard tower on the premises, recommendations on the best routes of ingress and egress. They needed to know the size and style of the padlock on the front gate. They had to ascertain where every fence was, how tall, and composed of how many strands of barbed wire. Were there drainage ditches, ravines, or other features that could provide cover? Exactly how many

Americans were in there, and which barracks were they staying in? How many of them could walk and how many would require litters? Where were the power generators, the radios, the telephone and telegraph lines? On and on the list went. In the most copiously detailed sense, the Rangers had to understand what they were up against.

The vital information they needed, or at least the promise of it, came at last, in the form of Bill Nellist and Tom Rounsaville—two dusty, sweat-streaked, sun-scorched Alamo Scouts. The Alamo Scouts were a legendary unit of behind-the-lines intelligence gatherers that had been personally created by General Krueger earlier in the war. The Scouts had already racked up an incredible string of successful exploits elsewhere in the Pacific without losing a single man, including the flawless rescue of sixty-six Dutch POWs in the jungles of New Guinea. General Krueger and Horton White had dispatched two five-man squads of the Scouts ahead of the Rangers to undertake a thorough reconnaissance of the camp and to prepare an intelligence report for Mucci. Nellist and Rounsaville were the two squad leaders. Thrilled to see fresh American faces after two long days, the two men rushed to greet Mucci and Prince with exhausted smiles.

The good news was that all the Scouts had made the long overnight hike unscathed and apparently undetected, having crossed the same rivers and highways that the Rangers had crossed. Yesterday afternoon they arrived in the barrio of Platero, about two miles from Balincarin, and set up camp. Right now most of the Scouts were there, though a few were still nosing through the fields around the camp trying to learn what they could.

The bad news: The Scouts were nowhere close to

getting the goods. The recon report Mucci and Prince so urgently needed was still a work in progress. The Scouts had been working around the clock, carefully studying the perimeter of the camp. They'd made all kinds of preliminary sketches, and mapped out the likeliest escape routes across the Pampanga River. But the most salient pieces of information—such as how many tanks were parked inside, how many Japanese troops were there, and precisely where they were quartered—still remained question marks. They didn't even have a definitive layout of the camp.

"We can't get up close," Nellist explained. "It's flat as a pancake out there."

What little information the Alamo Scouts *were* able to glean was dismaying, to say the least. Day and night, the camp environs had been a nest of Imperial Army activity. The north-south road that ran directly in front of the main gate had seen a nearly uninterrupted flow of traffic— tanks, armored vehicles, transport trucks. "It looks like Main Street in Tokyo," Rounsaville said. "The place is thick with Japs." It was a confusing mishmash of movement. While some of the enemy vehicles appeared to be retreating to the north, others were hastening south to fortify the garrison at Cabanatuan City, where the Japanese were evidently preparing to take a stand against the advancing Sixth Army. Guerrilla reports indicated that as many as 7,000 Japanese troops were now assembled in Cabanatuan City. "And that's just four miles southwest of the camp, right along the road here," Nellist reminded the colonel as they hovered over Mucci's topo map.

"Seven thousand?" Mucci repeated the figure with obvious dismay spreading over his face.

To the northeast, Nellist and Rounsaville explained,

there loomed an even more immediate threat. Approximately two hundred Japanese soldiers were camped in a bamboo grove along the banks of the Cabu River. Their bivouac site was a mere mile away from the POW camp, easily within earshot of any shooting that would ensue during the night's sortie. They were elite Imperial Army troops—the Dokuho 359 Battalion under the command of Tomeo Oyabu—and they were well equipped with tanks and armored vehicles. Hearing this evening's fireworks, all they'd have to do is cross a wooden bridge spanning the Cabu River and speed a few hundred yards down the main road to the camp. It would be a bloodbath.

The final piece of the puzzle was the most crucial, and it was the piece the Alamo Scouts lacked: What exactly was the situation inside the enclosure? The Scouts had learned a few spotty details from guerrillas who nonchalantly snooped along the fence in civilian clothes, posing as farmers. There appeared to be about 70 armed guards staying inside the camp, and it was obvious that substantial numbers of transient Japanese troops were also sleeping there. How many was unclear, and the number fluctuated every night, but their best guess was around 100. At last count, four tanks had been seen entering the compound, as well as an assortment of other heavy vehicles, yet nobody was sure where they were housed.

This paucity of intelligence infuriated the colonel. He paced and brooded and fidgeted with his pipe. The raid was in peril. "We have to know more," he shouted. "A *lot* more." He stripped off his sunglasses to reveal bloodshot eyes seething with exasperated alarm.

"We can get it, sir," Lieutenant Nellist replied confidently. "We need more time."

"Don't *have* time," Mucci said, his jaw clenched. When it came to intelligence gathering, the Alamo Scouts were supposed to be the elite of the elite—Krueger's darlings, his eyes and ears—but so far Mucci was unimpressed. "Look," he said, "I don't care how you do it, just go back there and get the goods. We'll meet you this afternoon in Platero."

Chastened, Nellist and Rounsaville arrowed back to Platero to redouble their efforts.

⸻

Colonel Mucci, Captain Prince, and Captain Joson were gathered in a grove of trees with several noncoms, discussing various imponderables of the raid, when their confab was interrupted.

"Colonel Mucci?" a Filipino man called out in a soft voice.

The Rangers wheeled about to behold a guerrilla riding bareback on a tiny horse. His shoulders were crisscrossed with bandoliers of ammo, and he seemed perfectly at ease with the M-1 carbine that was strapped over his shoulder. He was small-statured and unprepossessing. Yet something about his presence, an air of steely competence, of quiet menace, made him vaguely intimidating.

"Captain Juan Pajota," he said with a crisp salute. Behind him was a force of several dozen guerrillas.

"Captain!" Mucci said, brightening just a little. "It's a pleasure to meet you."

Like his compatriot Eduardo Joson, Juan Pajota (pa-HO-ta) was a well-known Filipino guerrilla leader who had so tenaciously devoted himself to the resistance that the

Japanese had long ago put a price out on his head. Captain Pajota knew every inch of this neck of Nueva Ecija—knew it not only as an itinerant soldier and insurrectionary but as someone who had grown up there. His headquarters was over in Cabu, which lay just a few miles to the northeast of Cabanatuan City. His territory included Balincarin, Platero, and all the surrounding lands. The Cabanatuan POW camp was squarely in his backyard.

Pajota dismounted from his pony and shook hands with Mucci, Prince, and Joson. All told, Pajota could commit a guerrilla force of about 90 armed soldiers and another 160 unarmed men to help with logistics and aiding the prisoners. Most of Pajota's men were either in Platero or scattered about elsewhere in the region, awaiting his word.

Soon the Rangers fell back into a tense discussion of the raid, and Pajota was asked to contribute his thoughts on the matter.

"When do you intend to carry out the attack?" Pajota inquired.

Mucci and Prince were surprised by the question. "Tonight, at dusk," Mucci responded. "That's always been the plan."

After a long, awkward silence, Pajota said, "Sir, with all due respect, that is suicide."

Mucci was taken aback by Pajota's seeming effrontery. A little captain from the hinterlands questioning the soundness of a plan officially conceived and endorsed by the high command of the U.S. Sixth Army?

According to historian Forrest Johnson, Pajota quickly assured Mucci that it was the timing, not the plan itself, that was fatally flawed. "I'm sure you must know the enemy situation," Pajota said, and then proceeded to lay out nearly the same details that Nellist and Rounsaville had described earlier. Except that Pajota now supplied three disturbing new wrinkles: During the early-morning hours, he said, the force of 200 Japanese soldiers camping on the banks of the nearby Cabu River had swelled to more than 1,000. Instead of only 100 Japanese troops bivouacking inside the camp, new intelligence reports were indicating three times that number. Finally, Filipino spies in Cabanatuan City had received word that another large convoy of troops and heavy equipment would be pulling out early this evening and heading north toward Bongabon. If this report was correct, then tonight at dusk, when the raid was set to commence, the road directly in front of the camp's main gate would be thoroughly congested with Japanese traffic.

Thinking it manifest madness to undertake a prison bust in the midst of an enemy exodus, Pajota said calmly, "I think you should wait twenty-four hours."

Mucci and Prince studied each other and drank in the significance of everything Pajota had reported. "That," replied Mucci stubbornly, "is a decision I will make once we reach Platero and receive the latest report from the Alamo Scouts." Although Mucci was putting a bluff and resolute face on things, clearly Pajota's new details had rattled him, and the case for postponement was persuasive.

What made Pajota so compelling was his obviously intimate knowledge of the terrain. Throughout the resistance, the various guerrilla leaders of the Central Plain had cooperated with one another, but they could also be ferociously and jealously territorial. Joson, whose area of control lay farther to the northwest, had long enjoyed an amicable relationship with Pajota. Yet it was clear to all that, between the two, Pajota assumed the greater stature now that the raiding party had passed onto his turf. Joson and his 80 men had completed their initial task—to deliver the Rangers to Pajota's realm; the captain would take it from here. He knew all the mayors of all the barrios. He was familiar with the realities on the ground, every quirk of the carabao paths, every river bend. Whatever men or arms might need to be mustered, Pajota had the political wherewithal to make it happen.

Pajota was a stern-looking man of thirty years. He wore an old khaki uniform of the U.S. Army Forces of the Far East (USAFFE) with a .45 caliber automatic pistol at his side. He had a round, high-cheekboned face and a penetrating stare. His voice was grave, his English clipped and richly accented but quite fluent. Robert Lapham, the American guerrilla leader, recalled that Pajota was "quiet and sincere" but he had "a tough streak" in him. "He was a very unflamboyant guy with a natural bent for leadership. He was resourceful, organized, and extremely imaginative. He was from Nueva Ecija, and knew it like a book."

At the outbreak of the war, Pajota had been attached to the 91st Filipino Infantry and was trained, among other things, in electronic communications. Like many of his comrades, he'd been cut off from the Filipino-American forces during the retreat to Bataan. He'd spent the past three years perfecting his skills as a saboteur, a hit-and-run artist the Japanese could never catch. Early on he'd hooked up with Lapham and become one of his ablest officers, conducting countless sorties and ambushes, gradually building up a guerrilla force of 300 well-trained men answerable only to him.

There was no one more enthusiastic about raiding

Cabanatuan camp than Captain Juan Pajota. He was acquainted with the interior layout of the camp; as a soldier before the war, he once trained there and lived in a barracks on the premises. On several occasions before the invasion of Luzon, Pajota and Lapham had proposed liberating the American prisoners in a raid very similar to Mucci's current operation, but they'd never been able to secure approval from MacArthur's high command on Leyte. Though tantalized by the idea, MacArthur's people had then considered a raid to be premature, primarily because the guerrillas had never made a compelling case for where they could safely hide all those hundreds of sickly American prisoners following a jail break. "We could have attacked Cabanatuan successfully and gotten the prisoners out," Lapham later wrote in his memoirs. "But what then? Most of them would have to be carried out. Even if they'd been willing to join our guerrilla forces they would have been not an asset, but a heavy burden."

As the day wore on, Mucci, Prince, Joson, and Pajota remained huddled in Balincarin with their crimped and annotated maps sprawled in the grass. For hours and hours, they sat discussing every conceivable angle of the raid.

The conversation turned to the worrisome matter of transportation. What would they do with all the prisoners who couldn't walk? It was a problem Mucci had been stewing over ever since they left Guimba. Springing them was one thing; ferrying them those thirty miles back to American lines was something else again. Pajota explained that Cabanatuan camp was now essentially a hospital. Over the past few months, the Japanese had been systematically culling the able-bodied prisoners and shipping them to Japan. The Imperial Army had left behind the sickest and weakest of the lot. There were just over 500 remaining—most of them rife with disease, immobile, or semimobile.

"But I think I have an answer to that problem," Pajota offered, fetching immediate reactions.

"Yes?" Mucci said.

"Carabao."

The colonel was a little confused. "Carabao? Water buffalo?"

Pajota nodded enthusiastically. "I can send the word out to the barrios. We can have carabao carts waiting at the Pampanga River. Now that the rice harvest is over, the animals aren't being used. Each cart can carry about five or six prisoners."

The idea seemed laughable at first. The carabao, a notoriously sluggish beast of burden, was capable of galloping at a fleet two miles per hour, *maybe,* if ridden by a sinewy Filipino boy swatting the poor harrumphing behemoth with a green stalk of sugarcane. The beasts would be dragging rickety wooden carts with massive knotted wheels the size of dinner tables, their creaking wagon beds lined with rice straw. Pajota's plan seemed ludicrously low-tech. It was medieval transportation, glaringly out of step with the demands of a mechanized modern army. Yet the more Mucci thought about the idea, the more it struck him as irresistible. Moving at carabao speed, the return to the American lines would be a long, slow, deliberate plod, like a wilderness wandering in the Bible. The evacuation might look a little peculiar, but as long as the Filipinos could keep the beasts moving, the glacial cavalcade would eventually make it to safety.

It was settled—a hegira by buffalo cart. Pajota would

get the word out around Platero and the neighboring barrios and have the carabaos, wagons, and drivers at the ready. They'd be waiting en masse at the banks of the Pampanga River at eight o'clock that night.

━ ━·━·━ ━

A little after four o'clock in the afternoon, the Rangers packed up their belongings and marched out of Balincarin, heading straight for Platero, which lay a little more than two miles to the south. As they walked, Joson's guerrillas flanked the right side, Pajota's guerrillas flanked the left. Now they were a force of some 300 armed men fanning out over the rice fields. Despite Pajota's well-lodged caveats, everything remained set to begin at sunset that night—about three and a half hours hence.

Prince asked Pajota whether the dogs in Platero could be tied up and muzzled to keep the racket down. Pajota sent his messengers ahead to remedy the situation.

On the outskirts of Platero several Alamo Scouts were waiting for Mucci with bad news: Just as Pajota had warned, a large contingent of Japanese troops was pulling out of Cabanatuan City. Now, hundreds—possibly thousands—of Imperial Army soldiers were marching northeast on the main highway, heading directly for the prison camp.

Hearing that, Mucci made his decision instantly. Pajota was right: Continuing on would be suicidal, a head-on collision. The attack had to be delayed. As Mucci later told the *New York Times*, "There was nothing we could do against that force."

Mucci ordered his communications man to call in the

news to Sixth Army headquarters. The Rangers were supposed to break radio silence only in the most exigent circumstances, but these circumstances certainly qualified. The radio operator transmitted the encoded message: "New developments. Twenty-four-hour delay."

After a few long minutes, the radioman got the truncated reply—"Message acknowledged"—and the men stumbled toward Platero, immensely relieved by their late-breaking extension.

Chapter 5

However lowly and humble our present position, we are fortunate in being assembled here alive and more or less physically fit. I desire to impress upon you that we are operating under a strictly absolute power. There is only one interpretation, and that is the Japanese interpretation. The Japanese make all decisions. From their orders, once formally issued, there is no appeal. Ours is a state of complete subjugation. Your duty therefore is to obey. Not only for your sake, but for the welfare of the entire personnel of the camp, I know that you will obey . . .

from a circular distributed by Colonel
Curtis Beecher, the American commanding officer
at Cabanatuan camp

Each morning the sun snapped on like a heat lamp as it rose over the Sierra Madre, striking the landscape with blunt force. Nothing had changed from the day before: the wooden water tower soaring above the ground haze, the warrens of thatch and stamped mud spread out like a dirty quilt over the land, the happy ducks bobbing in the Japanese pond by the front gate, the guards performing their calisthenics, the lumpy mounds in the field marking the American graves.

Another day, refusing to veer from the seamless sameness of days, another sunrise in a thousand sunrises at Cabanatuan. Geckos were draped all about the barracks, sated from the night's mosquitoes, occasionally calling out in their distinctive two-note chirp that the prisoners swore sounded like "Fuck you! Fuck you!" Abie Abraham sat on his bunk, waiting for the residuum of the dream to dissipate, the nightmare he'd been having, over and over, since he first arrived at the camp. He dreamt that skeletons were dancing around his bed. "They beckoned and grinned and leered at me," he recalled. Abraham would shout back at them, "I am human!" but the skulls wouldn't listen. Then he would glance up from his bed and see his own face rotting away. "I too was a skull, grinning and leering with the others, a skeleton rattling in the wind."

The forms issued from the grass buildings. Stove fires roared beneath immense cauldrons of bubbling starch. The men visited the latrines and then at 5:45 lined up for the day's first roll call. The trappers checked their traps—rat traps, dog traps—to see if the night had brought extra protein. Then everyone who was able-bodied streamed to the mess halls for a ladleful of glutinous rice.

With his back to the sun and his mess tin set upon the ground, Abraham squatted low on his haunches, fanning flies with his left hand while eating breakfast with his right. Tanned by dirt and sun, like all the others, his body was clad in a G-string and sandals fashioned from hand-carved slats of wood. His hair was cropped close to discourage the lice. He had mild cases of malaria and beriberi. He'd lost forty pounds. But he was, relatively speaking, in fair condition, decidedly *not* ready to join the dance of the skulls above his bed.

The Japanese authorities brought them here in June 1942. After 1,500 Americans had perished at O'Donnell, it had become obvious to the Japanese that they needed another cantonment—a place that was less crudely equipped and geographically better suited to accommodate large numbers of long-term prisoners. They chose Cabanatuan, a prewar Philippine Army installation which the Japanese considerably expanded. The camp was named after nearby Cabanatuan City, a bustling regional capital of 50,000 people that was set in the province of Nueva Ecija, some sixty miles east of Camp O'Donnell. Cabanatuan was the centerpiece; all other camps in the Philippines served as satellites. The Japanese used it as a reservoir, a holding station for slave labor. They were constantly shuffling prisoners around. Whenever they conjured up a new work project—a bridge or an airfield that needed repair—they'd draft men from Cabanatuan. Some details were shipped off to Taiwan or Mindanao, Manchuria or Palawan. In the end, Cabanatuan would become the largest continuously running prisoner-of-war camp in the Philippines, and the largest American POW camp ever established on foreign soil. As many as 9,000 Americans would pass through Cabanatuan's gates. Nearly one-third of those would end up buried beneath the ashen clay just beyond the camp fence.

When the Americans from O'Donnell began trickling into Cabanatuan in June, they were greeted by thousands of their compatriots, veterans from Corregidor. The Rock had surrendered in May. The Japanese had sent the American nurses off to a civilian internment camp and then had paraded General Wainwright's shell-shocked men through the streets of Manila as trophies of war before bringing most of them to Cabanatuan to set up housekeeping. Although they too had been mistreated, the Corregidor men were truly shocked by their brethren from Bataan. Comparatively, the Bataan defenders were in abominable condition. The siege, the march, and the septic squalor of O'Donnell had taken a cumulative toll. "These Corregidor folks were cleaner, brighter, better fed," said Bert Bank. "When we arrived that first day, they looked at us like we were the living dead."

Cabanatuan in the first few months was but a continuation of O'Donnell. Essentially, it was an extermination camp—extermination not in the Nazi sense of the word, not according to a cold master plan, but through a kind of malign neglect. The first commandant of the camp, Shigeji Mori, a calm, impenetrable man in his late fifties who was said to have run a bicycle shop in Manila before the war, seemed either unaware of or uninterested in the death rate. In some ways he was the direct opposite of Captain Tsuneyoshi, the rabid American-hater at Camp O'Donnell. Mori had a dignified facade, an air of quiet precision. He wore black-rimmed glasses and kept his clothes immaculate. His neat black hair was filamented in gray along his temples, and he spoke in a carefully modulated voice. He usually used an interpreter, although he spoke tolerably good English. Colonel Mori was neither stupid nor baldly mean-spirited, but he seemed impervious to the horror that he left in his wake. He once remarked, "The prisoners are sick because they need more exercise."

For reasons that were never apparent, basic medicines that could have readily saved legions of lives, medicines like quinine, emetine, and sulfa tablets, were never made available. Five hundred and three men died at Cabanatuan in June, another 786 in July. As summer dragged into fall, the toll began to level off. The graveyard details buried tens instead of fifties each week. Finally, on December 15, 1942, Cabanatuan reached a gratifying benchmark: its first "zero-death day."

The camp began to organize itself. Those American prisoners who had engineering predilections took charge. They dug irrigation ditches and septic systems. They spiked the latrines with larvacidal substances like copper sulfate, unslaked lime, and creosote. They staged bug-killing contests and found ways to flyproof the garbage pits. They declared a jihad on lice and other ectoparasites, boiling their clothes, cutting their hair, and airing out their sleeping mats in the bright sun.

As bleak as the circumstances were, any hope of survival dictated that there be some semblance of a society at Cabanatuan, and as in all societies, there was a discernible structure, with elaborate grapevines for disseminating goods and information. Cabanatuan became, in many ways, a tropical enclave of America. A baseball diamond was laid out. The main thoroughfares took on familiar names—Broadway, Fifth Avenue, Main Street. The camp's prime meeting ground became known as Times Square. A "morale program" was instituted, which included Bible studies, horseshoes, and Ping-Pong matches. The prisoners formed a camp library and filled it with

3,000 titles that were assembled from God only knew where—dog-eared copies of Twain, Dickens, Poe, and Pearl S. Buck. The books, which first had to pass the Japanese censors, were kept in states of partial repair with strips of canvas, old rags, and rice paste.

During their free hours, the prisoners at Cabanatuan did what Americans do instinctively—they formed little groups and clans and held spontaneous meetings all about the camp. The Knights of Pythias gathered once a week, as did the Knights of Columbus, the Masons, and the Elks. Texans, Iowans, and New Mexicans got together. The camp had a musical band—"the Cabanatuan Cats"— and a troop of amateur actors put on skits and revues whenever they could muster the energy. There were fierce chess matches, with pieces whittled from carabao horn and gnarled scraps of narra wood. Abie Abraham became instrumental in establishing the Carabao Wallow, a "cafe" where prisoners gathered beneath coconut-oil lamps to play bridge and pinochle and drink ersatz coffee made from chunks of charred rice steeped in hot water. In what was facetiously called "the University of the Far East," the better-educated officers lectured enlisted men in history, French, and biology. Astronomy was the most popular class of all. Lying on their backs beneath the Southern Cross, students followed the course of the stars and planets, bathed themselves in meteor showers, and took their minds off this world by contemplating others.

Abie Abraham poignantly described the passage of days:

"I held time in my hands. I lived minute to minute, and each seemed an eternity. There came a point when I didn't consider myself as being held in a prison camp. I began to look at the inside of prison camp as my home. I would try to insulate myself from my former life. Then something inside me would burst, like a dam. I became flooded with thoughts and feelings, memories of my wife and daughters. I thought about my hometown of Lyndora, Pennsylvania. Why was I in love with this place when it never did a thing for me? Sometimes I would look up from whatever I was doing, and I would understand nothing of what was going on around me. Is it really me rotting here in this bright Philippine sunshine? Is there nothing left of what I was before?"

In the middle of the camp, a group of Navy men from Corregidor erected a post from which they hung a rusty metal triangle. It looked something like the traditional dinner chimes found on ranches and farms back home, though larger and cruder. Every half hour the designated timekeeper would go out with a stovepipe in his hand and give the contraption a set number of dings in accordance with an old Navy custom called "sounding the watch." The system was a little intricate until one got used to it. Far from dulcet, the tone of the ring was hard and sharp, a metallic sound punctuating the day with seriousness. The Cabanatuan prisoners came to like it, though, for segmenting the blur of chronology, for the sense of orderliness it brought. To some, it sounded like the proud, clear voice of duty.

When the Navy men first proposed the bell system and secured Japanese approval for it, they entered into the timekeeping business with great solemnity and fanfare. Broadcasting the passage of time became a kind of sacrament for them. There was no pressing need for a public clock in an open-air camp where each day was calibrated by nature's whistle, with everyone rising with the sun and retiring with the coming of darkness. Yet like a faithful band of druids, the Corregidor men built a little life around the bells. For them the ritual was a way of keeping a quaint Navy tradition alive in a hostile climate dominated on one side by the Japanese and on the other by the philistine culture of the U.S. Army.

Wherever they might be in the camp, whatever they might be doing, the prisoners could hear the bells, every half hour, day and night. As weeks became months and months became years, the men no longer consciously registered the clanging of time, but it was never far away from their minds. The bell was their day's metronome, the sonic measure of their confinement.

Albuquerque in time for turkey
Kalamazoo by close of forty-two
On the sea by forty-three
Mother's door in forty-four
Back alive in forty-five
Out of the sticks in forty-six
Golden Gate in forty-eight

———————

After breakfast, the men lined up for the day's details. Prisoners held jobs in the pumphouse, the powerhouse, the garage, the poultry farm. They worked as cooks, typists, cobblers, tailors, grass cutters. Some would spend the day burying bodies at the camp cemetery, known as Bone Hill. Some would head in the direction of the airstrip for eight hours of leveling and raking. The lucky ones would get to leave the premises for the day, riding with their guards on stake trucks into the cool Sierra Madre to cut wood, or venturing into the markets of Cabanatuan City to purchase rice and other staples.

The largest and least desirable of all the Cabanatuan details was the Farm. Each day, crews marched out the gate and into the fields to stoop over the long rows of camote sweet potatoes and mongo beans. Eight hundred acres baked in the sun. Everything was done manually. They would haul water in buckets because there was no irrigation system. They would haul human excrement in buckets because there was no other fertilizer. Practically everyone slaved on the Farm at some point.

By and large the guards on the Farm, like the guards everywhere at Cabanatuan, were none too swift. The cream of the Imperial Army was off fighting somewhere, and these were the dregs and misfits, the out-to-pastures and the callow youths. Many were Koreans or Taiwanese, pressed into service and left to sulk in a thankless post. The Americans had their own names for the guards. There were Liver Lips, Web Foot, Charlie Chaplin. There were Little Speedo, Beetle Brain, Simon Legree. Eleanor was bucktoothed and widely thought to resemble the First Lady. "Many Many" always demanded to see the Americans bowing their heads—not just a few, but "many many."

On the Farm, prisoners were usually watched over by the universally hated guard they called Air Raid. Air Raid was strong, thick, and dense, with the eyes of an eagle.

Although they were starving they were not allowed to harvest the fruits or vegetables for themselves, only the pigweeds, whistleweeds, and camote greens. If they slipped a root or a pod of beans into their personal gunnysacks, Air Raid would come down on them with his pickax handle, which the men called a "vitamin stick" for its mysterious ability to energize and motivate. Air Raid was a sadist, the worst of the lot. For sport, Air Raid liked to pit the Americans against one another, mano a mano, and make them slap each other silly. He was dead serious about these slapping bouts. The fight was supposed to go on until one of the two Americans couldn't get up. The blows had to be honest, loud, and convincing, or else he'd clobber the unwilling contestants with his club.

There was another especially mean guard on the Farm known as Donald Duck. During his spluttery piques of rage, the prisoners thought he sounded a bit like the cartoon character, and the name was cemented.

"Who is Do-noo Duck?" he demanded to know one day, overhearing the Americans.

"He's a famous Hollywood movie star!" they explained.

"Does he make much money?"

"Millions."

More than satisfied with the answer, Donald Duck beamed with pride. "From now on," he insisted, "you address me as Do-noo Duck."

One evening the prisoners and the guards were assembled together in the camp's central clearing to watch a movie. The entertainment committee decided to show a cartoon short before the main feature. For the first time Donald Duck saw himself quacking on the screen. "The next day," one chronicler recalled with supreme understatement, "the prisoners under his jurisdiction had a rough time."

The men on the Farm could only hope to end up with one of the better guards, like Big Speedo, who was demanding but fair. He had been known to strike down other Japanese guards who were cruel to Americans. Big Speedo was sober-minded, conscientious, a former cop from Osaka. He followed the rules and had no tolerance for predation.

With Big Speedo, the Farm detailers could talk and joke among themselves, so long as they got their work done. To pass the long hot hours in the fields, the Americans might sing one of their camp songs:

> *We'll all be back by Christmas Day*
> *We'll see the lights of Old Broadway*
> *Until then a song of cheer will pay*
> *Happy days will come again*
> *Frisco lies just o'er the hill*
> *The U.S.A. will be there still*
> *With what it takes to fill the bill*
> *When sailing day draws near*

— — — — —

The tedium was excruciating—the monotony, the starchy sameness. The mental torpor wasn't merely caused by vitamin dearth—it inhered in the long spool of undifferentiated days. "Rice brains," they called their dull-witted condition. Three years dragged on without plot. The prime of their lives floated away, unaccounted for. Henry Lee, in one of his poems, wrote of the "bitter

179

penace, living day to day, and watching the years unfold unused and slow, the youth starved in the breast." There was day and night. Rainy season and dry. The Navy chimes went off. Each evening the same strains of "Kimigayo," the Japanese national anthem, blared through the tinny loudspeaker. Each day had its little notches and markings. The trick was filling the long gaps in between.

While at their work, they daydreamed through the flats of midmorning, through the doldrums of the forenoon, and on until lunch. The prisoners played games in their own heads. They pursued insipid discussions based upon the flimsiest of facts—one prisoner recalled a long and heated conversation he once had with a fellow on the question of whether a possum's penis has two heads.

Tommie Thomas became an imaginary construction worker back in Grand Rapids. Having been virtually homeless as a kid growing up there, he decided it was time to build himself a house, the exact house he wanted to build in Grand Rapids one day, to live in. Nothing fancy, a bedroom, a stoop, a couple of dormers in the attic. Brick by brick, he built it up from its cement foundation. Sometimes he couldn't quite remember where he'd knocked off during the last session. He never cheated, though. That was part of the hard, sad fun of it. He had to get it right, down to the last brick, no corner-cutting, no skipping ahead. There were rules to the exercise, methods in the madness of boredom.

Sometimes, if he didn't have work duty, Thomas liked to go over to Section 8, the medical ward for the mentally disturbed, and crouch beneath the window. There was a guy in there who would "broadcast" baseball games from time to time. The Cubs would be playing the Giants, and this poor baseball-obsessed lunatic made the play-by-play sound so realistic it was astonishing. There might as well have been a radio blaring. People would get so caught up in it they'd forget it wasn't real. The announcer would go on relaying the game, oblivious to the rapt audience growing beneath his window. Late arrivals would whisper, "What inning is it?"

Most of the time, they dreamt about food. Even in months of relative plenty, they were food-obsessed. They never tired of the subject. Next to food, women didn't stand a chance. Sex was a distant memory, a vaguely amusing problem not germane to the subject. The subject was ice cream. Georgia peaches. Strawberry rhubarb pie. Asparagus with hollandaise. If they ever made it home, they would surround themselves with food. They would start restaurants. They would get a deep freeze and fill it to the top. They would pool their money and buy a grocery store and never come out. Some people fixated on exceedingly narrow bands in the culinary spectrum, and their cravings drove them nearly insane. "When I was in there all those years, mostly what I thought about was cheese," said Robert Body, a private from Detroit who had been a 31st Infantry machine gunner on Bataan. "I never ate cheese in my goddamn life, but when I got in there, that's all I could think about."

Over time, the prisoners perfected the sport of gastrosadomasochism. At night the men would swap recipes for dishes that were ludicrously, obscenely rich—chocolate syrup on mashed potatoes, molasses and whipped cream over a whole stick of butter. They would torment each other with elaborate recitations of the meals they were going to prepare. They'd be lying on their bunks in the dark, and without preface or provocation, someone would say, in a tone of perverse glee: *Bacon, lettuce, and tomato sandwich!* Everyone would writhe and groan. A few minutes would pass, and someone would break the silence: *New England clam chowder!* On and on it would go until they finally became sated and drifted off to miserable sleep.

———————

One day in December 1942, an unfamiliar sound erupted from the camp, a sound the men hadn't heard in many months. Near the front gate, a group of prisoners sent up an immense whoop of joy. It was bright and infectious, "an unnatural shout," as Dr. Hibbs recalled, spreading outward as though a canister of laughing gas had been released. Everyone else streamed toward the gate to learn the source of this mirthful commotion. Men were hooting, giddy with excitement. From the bed of a large truck, Japanese guards were unloading boxes into the arms of Americans.

"Red Cross! Christmas packages! They didn't forget!"

Nearly everyone would remember this day of Christmas manna in December 1942. Each prisoner would recall precisely where he was and what he was doing when the packages came. Their psychic effect was incalculably powerful. "The celebration went on for days," Dr. Hibbs wrote. "The morale soared and the death rate tumbled. The truly unbelievable had happened. Not hundreds of planes and thousands of ships but food—good old life-saving stuff—was placed in our hands."

The American Red Cross Standard Package Number 8 weighed only nine pounds and was not much bigger than a shoe box. The Japanese guards had already opened and selectively pilfered the contents, yet for the most part the parcels were intact. They contained a few tins of sardines and corned beef, small supplies of instant coffee and cocoa, an eight-ounce package of cheese, a sixteen-ounce package of dried prunes, some hardtack biscuits, Eagle condensed milk, oleomargarine, and smoking tobacco. These might not seem like the sort of items that would warrant such an outpouring of emotion. But the arrival of these Red Cross packages underscored just how hungry the prisoners had become—hungry not merely for food but for any contact with the outside world. It was impossible to exaggerate how deeply they longed for tastes and echoes of home, for American ways of doing things, for familiar-looking labels and brand names. Up until then, they had received no word whatsoever from the United States of America, although they had been allowed to send censored postcards to their relatives back home. The sense of abandonment they'd felt on Bataan had only intensified during captivity. Many prisoners had come to think of themselves as forgotten maroons. They wondered whether America even knew of the existence of this frowzy prison, seven thousand miles from San Francisco. With these packages came proof that somebody in Washington—or in Geneva, or wherever—knew they were alive.

There was a ritualistic quality to the way the Red Cross packages were disseminated and opened and used. Most tried to savor the contents, making them last for months. They discovered little tricks. They found that if they boiled a can of condensed milk in water, the contents would turn to caramel custard. Men traded the individual foodstuffs in much the same way that adolescent boys traded baseball cards. Each item had value in and of itself, but it could also be a bargaining chip for other things. Many prisoners used Red Cross items as barter for medicines that could be bought on the black market. A prisoner had to survey himself and prioritize his deficiencies, playing wants against needs, luxuries against essentials. Anyone who nursed too strong a desire for any one thing had to be extremely careful—his craving could skew the delicate calculus, sometimes fatally.

For all too many, an addiction to tobacco led straight to the grave. The Red Cross cigarettes were the hottest commodity of all. Cigarettes took one's thoughts off the immediate environment. They seemed temporarily to focus fuzzy minds while dulling the razor edges of hunger. Mostly, they provided something to dicker with during the long boring interstices of the day. "A lot of guys gave their life to cigarettes," Bob Body said. "They'd smoke anything they could get. The Red Cross cigarettes were the best. But it got to where some of these guys would smoke weeds, leaves, even banana peels."

Body vividly remembered his first encounter with a doomed fiend. "There was this one guy right across the aisle from me," he said. "He had traded all his food for smokes. He wouldn't eat, and we all knew he was dying. I sat watching him this one night. He was in real bad shape. He said, 'I gotta have a cigarette.' I had one, so I took it over and I gave it to him. He never finished it. He died with it in his hand."

Body reached over and removed the cigarette from the

184

man's hand and snuffed it out. Then he found himself doing something he never imagined he would do. He'd seen the same scenario around camp time and time again. Men who had an inkling that someone was about to die would get a certain anticipatory look on their faces. They'd hover and stare, just like vultures, waiting for the death rattle. Around camp these opportunists were known as "grave robbers." That night Bob Body became one. "I went over to the dead guy's bunk," he said, "and I rifled through his stuff. I took his uniform and his pair of boots. I took his food. Because I figured *he* wasn't going to need it. I adopted a dog-eat-dog attitude right there. From then on, I more or less spent all my time scrounging for Bob."

Even before the war, most of the prisoners had been well accustomed to the art of scraping by. The majority of them had grown up on small farms and ranches during the depths of the Great Depression. They knew discipline and self-reliance. They were field hands and shade-tree mechanics, men who were crafty with their fingers. They understood how to scrimp and barter and improvise. They grew up hunting, fishing, tinkering with tractors and old cars. From early boyhood most of them could tend their own gardens and were expert at butchering and dressing animals, using every scrap of the carcass.

Cabanatuan took this generational tendency toward self-reliance and gave it a desperate edge. The prisoners were forced to locate extra calories through ingenuity and vigilance and, sometimes, ruthlessness. They hoarded and stole, they committed small treacheries of survival. In memos and speeches, Colonel Curtis Beecher, the American camp commander, talked incessantly about one for all and all for one. He exhorted the men to stick together. He urged the few to think about the welfare of the many. And while everyone appreciated the larger import of Beecher's sentiment, few people lived strictly by the communitarian message from day to day. The camp was too large and too obviously threadbare for the men to trust in a common largesse. Every prisoner understood that fundamentally, he was on his own.

Yet to operate on one's own, to go completely solo, seldom proved a successful strategy. There were a few hard misanthropes who managed to do it, but they were the exceptions. Typically a prisoner would team up with two or three others. Like Dickensian pickpockets, they found it best to work in small cooperative packs, triangulating each other's efforts, scrounging as a unit for stray morsels of food or information. They watched out for each other. When a surprise windfall came one man's way, he'd share it with the others. When one fell ill, the others brought him medicine and sustenance. Later in captivity, when the Japanese allowed the prisoners to tend small gardens of their own—"quan gardens," they were called—members of a group would take turns through the night guarding the ripening vegetables from midnight poachers.

Cabanatuan was marked by various larger clans and cleavages. There was Army versus Navy, officer versus enlisted man, Texan versus everyone else. There were a few dozen members of other nationalities living in the camp—British, Dutch, Norwegian. Yet while such affiliations mattered, the core unit of daily life at Cabanatuan was one's immediate survival group. Three or four men seemed to be the ideal number for these functional brotherhoods. Any group larger than five tended to be too cumbersome. (Besides, as Bob Body put it, "you never wanted to have too many attachments, because you were always afraid your friends were either going to leave on some work detail—or die.")

Yet a prisoner almost invariably grew attached to the others in his survival group. Depending so completely upon one another as they did, the bonds in these little cliques often grew extraordinarily close. The steadfastness of some friendships was legendary. Stories circulated about a certain pair of friends who'd grown so intimate that when one died unexpectedly, the grief-stricken side-kick followed suit a few days later, as though by force of will. The most poignant story involved two loyal friends in camp who'd both lost their teeth. Somehow or other, one of them acquired a set of dentures. The two men developed a routine at mealtimes. When the first man finished eating, he removed his dentures, rinsed them, and then handed them over so his friend could eat.

———

The little survival clans that flourished at Cabanatuan not only scrounged for food, they stalked it. They became small-time trappers and hunters. No animals were safe. Any cat, snake, or frog that strayed into the camp's midst was quickly eaten. In a slightly perverse employment of his professional training, Herbert Ott, the camp veterinarian, was put to work designing "humane" dog traps— and then commissioned with overseeing the butchering of the snared canines for mess-hall stews. Ducks were similarly doomed. Primarily for ornamental purposes, the Japanese kept a flock of ducks on a small man-made pond that had been dug by the front gate. Although their wings were clipped, they had a mysterious habit of vanishing during the night. Unbeknownst to the guards, the Americans had made a fine art out of duck theft. They called it "gorking."

Dr. Hibbs helped perfect the technique. The prisoners had access to the pond through a short drainage culvert that crossed under the fence and was sealed with wire meshing. The Japanese guardhouse was only twenty yards away, so they had to be extremely discreet. The bird robbers would crouch in the ditch beside the culvert and pull back the mesh. Then with a stick they'd drop a fishing line into the culvert. The line was set with a hook and baited with a few kernels of corn. On the other side of the culvert, the duck would spy the corn and gobble it down. "Timing was vital," Hibbs explained. "We waited until the kernel reached its voice box. With a sudden jerk the bird was 'gorked.' It couldn't make a sound, so the guards never heard its quacks of alarm." The Japanese lost half of their flock of forty waterfowl before they formally accused the Americans. Hibbs recalled, "Mystified by the modus operandi, yet sure who the culprits were, the guards ordered us to stop doing whatever it was we were doing."

Sometimes, instead of having to pursue food, the food came to the prisoners. One night Tommie Thomas was asleep beneath his mosquito net when he awoke with a strange sensation. "I lay very still," he recalled. "I felt a gentle nibbling on my big toe." Eventually Thomas realized what it was. Twisting in his sleep, he had worked his foot outside of the mosquito net, and now a rat was steadily gnawing on his toenail. Cabanatuan was crawling with rats, and for some reason they found human toenails to their liking. The same thing had happened to other POWs in his barracks. Thomas subdued his initial instinct to jerk his foot away—he had been told that some of the local rats were rabid. Instead, without budging, he hissed for help in the dark until one of his bunkmates heard him. "It's Tommie," he whispered. "Um . . . I think there's a rat attached to my toe."

A couple of other prisoners rose from their sleep and studied the situation. "Let's club the son of a bitch!" one of them interjected, sotto voce.

"Don't scare him!" Thomas said. "He'll bite me."

The men stood around discussing the mode of attack, figuring the various angles. In a shaft of moonlight, they could see the rat, still sawing away on Thomas' nail, oblivious to their whispers.

They decided to have one prisoner make a loud clomping noise from across the room, hoping that the distant racket might surprise the rat without making it panic, causing the rodent to raise its head in curiosity, briefly interrupting its integumentary feast. The rat responded according to plan, and when it did, Thomas jerked his foot away and two other prisoners promptly smashed the rat with bamboo clubs. The next day the conspirators reported the deceased rodent to the camp authorities and were awarded a tin of tobacco (the standard per-carcass prize in a rat-killing contest then in progress). Rats were one item Thomas could not bring himself to eat, but that night he enjoyed the tobacco while his friends prepared a private stew.

A few lucky animals were considered sacrosanct, however. Geckos, for example, were left alone because they ate mosquitoes. And the marines had a bulldog mongrel named Soochow who became the camp mascot. Soochow had traveled with the marines all the way from Shanghai to Corregidor, and through convoluted means had wound up at Cabanatuan. The mutt was spoiled rotten. In inverse proportion to the surrounding misery, the marines doted on him and pampered him like royalty. During camp musicals and plays, the marines would proudly lead the dog to the front row and set him up on a special VIP pillow (everyone else sat on the bare ground). No prisoner, no matter how hungry he might be, ever laid a finger on Soochow—it was a given that the marines would visit a swift vengeance on anyone who tried.

One prisoner had adopted a monkey as a pet. Everyone knew the monkey was strictly off-limits—it was this man's darling possession. But, in truth, nobody liked the hyperactive primate; it was always chattering and fidgeting, and it was known to bite. So the monkey was marked. Everywhere it scurried, prisoners eyed it with evil intent, waiting for just the right moment to snatch it. The person who bagged it, in the end, was Bob Body. "I crept up on that monkey one day when his owner was at the latrines," he said, "and I cut his throat. I skinned him and boiled him in a pot. I figured, if it's going to help take me home, I'm going to eat it. If the guy had ever found out who did it, I think he would have killed me. I done a lot of things I'm not proud of, and that was one of them. Stealing, hoarding, scheming. When I went to bed at night, I was working on tomorrow."

The Japanese camp authorities were firm believers in mass punishment. If one person stole an egg from the poultry farm, the entire poultry farm detail went on half-rations. If one person sabotaged a piece of equipment on the airstrip, everyone suffered. In matters of discipline and reward, Colonel Mori preferred to rule the camp as a single organism. To an extreme degree, the welfare of the one and the many rose and fell together. It was a managerial philosophy predicated on certain social hallmarks of Japanese culture, and typical of the Japanese Army at that time. This same rule of mass punishment applied to escapes. Colonel Mori grouped the prisoners at Cabanatuan into units of ten. These ten were generally prisoners who slept close to one another in the same barracks and often worked on the same detail. The men were supposed to get together frequently and discuss the futility of escape. They were supposed to "meditate" on the subject with great "earnestness and sincerity." These decimal units came to be referred to as "shooting squads" or, more commonly, "blood brothers." At all times, each prisoner was keenly attentive to the whereabouts of his nine brothers, and for good reason. If a single American attempted to break out, all nine of his comrades would be executed along with the culprit.

The deterrent was highly successful. Very few people even considered escape, let alone attempted it. Most of the escapes were undertaken by people who were out of their heads with malaria, or out of their heads for some other reason. They almost invariably ended up getting caught—and promptly shot. Camp memories are a little fuzzy on the subject, but it is generally agreed that while many prisoners were executed either singly or in small groups, the blood-brothers concept was carried out only twice.

One of the occasions was in June 1942 on a bridge-repairing detail that had left the premises of Cabanatuan. During the night a prisoner escaped. In the morning the guards flew into an apoplectic rage. The nine men in the escapee's shooting squad were forced to dig a large hole and stand at the edge to await execution. As it happened, there were two actual siblings in the work crew, the Betts brothers. Edwin Betts, the older of the Betts boys, was forced to watch as his younger brother, Ross, lined up with the condemned. Then the nine were all shot. Their bodies crumpled in the common grave. Edwin Betts returned to his work.

Prisoners were shot on a number of other occasions without invoking the blood-brothers rule. Sometimes they were shot with clear provocation, and sometimes they weren't. On the morning of August 11, 1944, Second Lieutenant Robert Huffcut was working in a small private garden that he was allowed to keep by the side of the camp. Huffcut's patch happened to be located close to the fence, but he had been openly tending it for months with full approval of the guards. Suddenly, however, the guard known as Liver Lips, who was standing in the southwest sentry tower, took offense at Huffcut's presence. On this day, Huffcut was stooped over, quietly picking eggplants. Liver Lips drew a bead on him and fired without warning. Huffcut was struck in the arm. He cried out for help. Tommie Thomas, who knew Huffcut well, was standing twenty yards away. He and several other Americans ran out and implored the guard to stop. Liver Lips leveled his rifle again and shot Huffcut in the head. He staggered and fell, his body throbbing on the ground.

"It was a cold-blooded murder," Thomas said. "Absolutely uncalled for. Liver Lips wouldn't even let us pick

Bob up. He had that rifle pointed at us. The American commander had to go to the Japanese commander and seek approval for us to retrieve the body. By the time we got over there with a litter, Bob was dead." The prisoners huddled in their barracks. Within minutes, the whole camp was seething. Everyone had hated Liver Lips for years. People seriously discussed plans for how they would set upon him and kill him. But the next day, Liver Lips was transferred out. "They got rid of him for his own good. They knew the Americans were seeking revenge."

Later in the day, the official pronouncement came from Japanese headquarters: Huffcut was too close to the fence. He was shot for trying to escape.

Being a doctor at Cabanatuan was a daunting and horrible challenge, but it was never dull. The "medicines" at the camp's disposal were scarcely more than placebos and folk remedies. In the hospital for the critically ill, known as Zero Ward, the doctors labored with improvised equipment and conducted operations with nothing more than what was termed vocal anesthetic ("It won't hurt much"). They constantly experimented and guessed their way through procedures. They concocted dysentery palliatives from guava leaves, cornstarch, and charcoal made from charred coconut shells. They cleaned out wounds with maggots. Dentists filled cavities with melted-down fifty-cent pieces, crafted dentures from carabao teeth, and performed oral surgery with a crude drill powered by foot pedal. Dr. Ralph Hibbs, who spent most of his time at Cabanatuan in charge of the tuberculosis ward, built his own

Rube Goldberg pneumatic contraption for collapsing lungs.

Once the immediate crisis of mortality began to dissipate in the fall of 1942, once dysentery and malaria and other causes of mass death were brought under a modicum of control, a whole new crop of ailments emerged. Often they were not illnesses exactly, but odd concatenations of symptoms and syndromes without clear identity. Over time the camp increasingly became a kind of freak show of medical exotica. "The whole place was a pathological museum," said Dr. Ralph Hibbs. "Most doctors would never see such cases in their entire life." Never before had physicians encountered such graphic and strange illustrations of the effects of long-term vitamin and mineral deprivation. The Cabanatuan doctors found themselves peering into the abyss of human physiology. Starvation had worked its way down to the biochemical substratum, down to the level of enzymes and amino acids, down into the cells of the brain. The human body, it seemed, was full of trapdoors and trick connections that were now slowly revealing themselves. The doctors entertained uncomfortable questions: What organs are the first to play out when a certain mineral is withheld? At what point during the process of nutritional strangulation does the body, and even the personality, begin to disintegrate and fray? With the last phantom residues of nutrition burning away, the prisoners came up against the margins of their own chemistry.

People lost their voices. People lost their hair. They lost eyes, they lost hearing, they lost the signal of their peripheral nerves. Their teeth fell out. Their skin fell off. They developed strange ringing in their ears. Rank metallic tastes soured the backs of their tongues. Their fingernails grew brittle and developed strange textured bands that, like growth rings in trees, reflected times of relative plenty or abject dearth.

Scurvy, pellagra, rickets—these were the ordinary ailments, and they were all experienced early on. The advanced cases of beriberi from which so many men suffered were largely attributable to the polished rice that the Japanese insisted on feeding the prisoners; the highly milled rice was devoid of the outer husk or "pericarp," which was the only part of the grain that contained vitamin B, which the men so desperately needed. In a world already overburdened with grotesque distinctions, the prisoners came to realize that there were *two* kinds of beriberi, wet and dry, and that an individual could have both kinds at the same time.

Wet was the more dramatic and hideous variety—it was the form of the disease that caused extremities to swell up to often drastic proportions. Yet dry beriberi could be just as painful and debilitating. It made the nerve endings of the feet throb and ache with a kind of hot electric tingling. Prisoners by the score would stay up much of the night, lying on their backs, kneading and rubbing their feet with their legs in the air. Like thousands of others, Bert Bank suffered peripheral neuropathy on his soles that never went away, and his feet throbbed so intensely that he had to cut open his shoes. Those afflicted with dry beriberi walked with a strange, birdlike gait (known as the Cabanatuan Shuffle): They wildly flung out their hands with each mincing step in an instinctive reflex to balance themselves while also absorbing some of gravity's shock.

One night after dinner hundreds of prisoners simultaneously came down with the same peculiar ailment. The affliction had but one symptom: Their necks turned to rubber. They couldn't hold up their heads. They had to brace their chins with their hands. It was a bizarre spectacle to see literally hundreds of men walking around the compound with their heads drooping uncontrollably like rag dolls. Both Bert Bank and Tommie Thomas experienced the strange curse. After a few hours the malady went away just as quickly as it had arrived. "We called it 'limber neck,' " said Bert Bank. "It was a weird thing. I mean it hit nearly everybody in camp. The Japanese got frightened 'cause they thought it was some contagious disease that was going to affect them too." At first Dr. Hibbs feared the worst, that the condition was the onset of a form of encephalitis. The following day everyone who'd experienced the syndrome was fine until just after dinner. Then, as though a transformer switch had been thrown, people's necks drooped again. Eventually, by trial and error, the doctors figured out that the paralysis was caused by a neurotoxin in the rancid fish heads that had been served several nights in a row with the evening's rice. Hibbs recalled, "The fish heads were salted down in large rattan pots with their eyes staring at us, the poorly preserved mess shipped to us without refrigeration. The association was fixed. Our encephalitis epidemic was over."

Another strange ailment that developed at Cabanatuan was gynecomastia. The malady afflicted hundreds, if not thousands, to lesser or greater degrees. The precise cause was unclear, but the symptoms were unmistakable: Men sprouted breasts, and in a few cases their nipples expressed a thin, clear fluid. The mammary tissues swelled not with the bloated unsightliness of beriberi edema but with a shapely femininity. It was widely said that the chests of the men afflicted typically looked like those of fifteen-year-old girls. Hard, disk-shaped tumors developed beneath the nipples. Although gynecomastia was neither contagious nor permanently harmful, it caused much discomfort, not to mention embarrassment.

John Cook, a Bataan Army medic from the Texas hill country who served in the Zero Ward mess hall at Cabanatuan, remembered the gynecomastia cases well. "They didn't have anything to put on, not even a T-shirt," Cook said. "They were running around with their breasts hanging out like a pubescent girl's. It got pretty bad. The next thing you know some people were saying, 'Honey, aren't *you* getting big! Say, come here! Let's go out on a walk tonight! You come see me!'"

Some of the men were so uncomfortable with their condition that they actually had their breasts surgically reduced. "I'll tell you it was the first time I'd ever seen a male mastectomy," said Cook. "They did it to keep from getting raped by some of the other men in camp, the perverts and the queens. I would say that in '43 and early '44 there were at least a dozen mastectomies performed at Cabanatuan."

━ ━ ━ ━ ━

On October 26, 1942, Bert Bank realized he was going blind. That day he was working on the Farm. He was supposed to be pulling thistles and weeds, but he couldn't see what he was doing, and he kept yanking out the vegetable plants instead. A guard swooped down upon him wielding a club, but before he struck the first blow, he realized something was wrong with this prisoner. The look in Bank's eyes gave it away. His stare was dull and unfocused. He clearly couldn't tell what he was doing. "Everything was a blur," Bank remembered. "I could distinguish day from night but I couldn't see my hand in front of my face." Bank's world was fast closing in on him. In a few weeks, he was almost totally blind.

Scores of men at Cabanatuan were in the same predicament. The blindness was caused by vitamin deficiency. At first the Japanese either didn't understand the problem or thought the prisoners were faking; on a number of occasions the guards beat these prisoners senseless for various infractions before the reality of their impairment finally sank in. Growing tired of these miscellaneous assaults, a number of men took to hanging little placards around their necks—BLIND PRISONER, PLEASE DO NOT HIT—and requested indoor details that demanded little in the way of visual acuity. Bank, for his part, left the Farm and spent his workdays twisting hemp threads into rope.

A young Japanese guard took pity on Bank. His name was Hirota, an eighteen-year-old kid from Kobe who had worked in the Bureau of Statistics before the war. Hirota seemed more intelligent than many of the other guards, and he was a perfect gentleman. Bank never saw him strike a single prisoner. He would save scraps of food for Bank, or give him cigarettes, which he could then barter for food. Hirota spoke a little English and always loved to brush up on his skills. The two would spend hours talking about their hometowns, about the war, about what they hoped to do with their lives once the fighting was over.

One day he produced a map of the United States, and Bank, after much squinting, was able to show Hirota his home state of Alabama. He invited Hirota to come visit him in Tuscaloosa. "I don't know how it happened that we became such friends," Bank said. "Maybe it was because I was so obviously blind, fumbling around the camp. Hirota-san could see that I needed help. But he was kind to me, and decent. I'll never forget him."

———————

In the fall of 1942, a diphtheria epidemic raged through Cabanatuan, killing more than a hundred men. Diphtheria is an especially virulent and horrific disease caused by a bacillus, *Corynebacterium diphtheriae*. The Filipinos called it by its more descriptive Spanish name, *garrotillo*, "the strangler." It typically strikes, with rapid onset, in the throat. The tonsils become sore, a strident, phlegmy cough develops, and the tissues swell dramatically, producing the eerie telltale symptom known as "bull neck." Inside the throat, a layer of mucus called a "shaggy gray membrane" steadily covers the air passage until the afflicted gradually suffocates. If the victim does not choke, he may die of cardiac arrest. As the bacillus spreads over the palate and pharynx, it produces a potent toxin that enters the bloodstream and causes paralysis of the heart and other vital organs. Classically considered a children's disease, diphtheria opportunistically emerged at Cabanatuan only because the men's immunological resistance was already weakened by starvation and other diseases. Diphtheria is easily treated by an antitoxin, which, of course, the camp doctors did not possess. Once it reaches an advanced stage without treatment, diphtheria is almost always fatal.

One day Tommie Thomas noticed that he was having

difficulty swallowing. He was already in the hospital, struggling to recover from malaria. He had lost nearly 100 pounds since the start of the war; he was so skinny that he could place his hands around his waist and, with only slight pressure, touch fingertip to fingertip. A physician on his ward, a Dr. Comstock, examined Thomas' throat and then sought a second opinion from another doctor. "What do you think?" Comstock asked. They both agreed. Thomas had diphtheria.

He would have to be quarantined. The diphtheria patients were housed next to Zero Ward in a kind of annex building that was called Zero-Zero Ward. "It was generally assumed that the numbers on the wards indicated the chance of survival," said Thomas. "There wasn't much they could do without serum. I had been told that diphtheria brought a slow, painful, and agonizing death. I felt lonely and helpless. I never was this scared on Bataan. Other POWs looked at me not knowing what to say."

The Zero-Zero Ward was a desperate place filled with raspy, labored breathing. Men lay around spitting mucus into Pet evaporated milk cans. "It was a dreadful sound hearing the men trying to cough that junk up," Thomas recalled. "When they couldn't, they slowly choked to death. We tried to encourage each other, but that only helped so much." Lying next to Thomas was another diphtheria patient named Armando Trujillo, from New Mexico. Everybody called him "Chief" because he was a Pueblo Indian. Trujillo had coughed with such violence that he'd torn away his palate, and when he talked he seemed to slur and muffle his words.

The diphtheria epidemic spread so rapidly that Dr. Willard Watrous, who was in charge of the ward, was eventually able to persuade the Japanese to send for anti-toxin (Colonel Mori recognized that the contagion could easily spread to his guards). Two days later the serum arrived and shots were immediately dispensed. When they worked their way down to Thomas and Trujillo, the doctors realized with some alarm that they had only one shot left. Thomas was next in line to receive the serum.

"Which one of us is worse off?" Thomas asked.

"Armando is," the doctor replied soberly.

"Then give it to Chief."

Trujillo mumbled his thanks while the doctors inserted the needle. Thomas felt good about his decision. Clearly Trujillo was in dire straits. "I hadn't known Chief very long," he said, "but you become pretty close in those circumstances."

The doctors told Thomas they were trying to procure more serum. "You'll receive the first shot," they assured him.

That night Thomas' diphtheria worsened. The mucus was steadily building. "It got to where I could hardly swallow," Thomas said. He coughed and coughed into his spit can. Trujillo, who was already noticeably improved, stayed up with Thomas, encouraging him, keeping him from suffocating in his sleep.

In the morning, Thomas felt remarkably strong. He told the doctors that he'd had a bad night but now it seemed as though his throat was clear. The doctors examined him and were stunned. The shaggy membrane was gone. Dr. Watrous was called in, and he confirmed it. Thomas was far from healthy, but his diphtheria never returned.

Thomas could only call his recovery a miracle. More

serum arrived two days later; had he not rallied so dramatically there still was a chance that Thomas would have survived long enough to receive a lifesaving shot. Still, he could not shake the feeling that his reversal without antitoxin was related to his passing the shot on to his buddy Trujillo. There had been numerous cases of miraculous recoveries in the wards of Cabanatuan, and these stories were the subject of endless theological speculation. Thomas, who was not a deeply religious man at the time, did not know what to make of all this, but he was, like Trujillo, most grateful to be alive.

"When I came through that diphtheria," Thomas recalled, "I knew that if anyone was going to walk out of that prison camp it was going to be me. I had made it this far, and as long as the Lord was willing, I was going to make it the rest of the way."

—·—·—·—

Every day brought the prisoners some sort of reminder that they were living under the dominion of a culture that they truly did not understand. Unable to anticipate the changing whims of the Japanese command, many simply chalked up their odd experiences to the "inscrutable Orient." Often their encounters were so bizarre as to be comical. One day Colonel Mori lined up a large group of Americans and calmly demanded: "All millionaires step forward!" The Americans looked from side to side, grinning discreetly, assuming at first that this must be some sort of joke, then realizing that Mori was stone serious. A few awkward minutes passed. When no one stepped forward, Mori seemed quite surprised, then disappointed, as though his flight of fancy—whatever it was—had been abruptly grounded by this unforeseen response from the Americans. Mori delicately pushed his glasses off his nose and turned back to his headquarters. The assembly was dismissed.

On another occasion, the Japanese made each prisoner at Cabanatuan write an essay detailing his "most horrible experience" during the war. The prisoners dutifully turned in these compulsory essays, but a few days later the papers all came back. "These are not satisfactory!" the guard explained. "Do over!" So the entire camp sat down again, redoubling their efforts, retelling their grimmest war stories. Everyone was delighted to do so because the exercise necessitated missing yet another day of work. A few days later, the essays came back again, only this time they were *graded*. The stories were marked with an A, B, or C (a C simply meant "no good"). The guards declined to elucidate either the purpose or the grading criteria of the essays, and the prisoners were completely mystified. As a prize, the 356 authors of A-winning stories received two slices of fried sweet potato and a lemon wedge.

One day the Japanese demanded an assembly of all the American Indians at Cabanatuan. They were to meet in the camp's central clearing at an appointed hour. (The camp census included a surprisingly large number of Apache, Navajo, Hopi, and Pueblo Indians because one of the major outfits on Bataan, the 200th Coast Artillery, had been formed from the ranks of the New Mexico National Guard.) Once they were lined up, approximately fifty in all, a Japanese doctor appeared. Slowly, he went down the line of Indians, raising their arms and carefully smelling their armpits. The doctor asked each subject to precisely estimate the amount of Native American blood he had. The doctor's assistant stood nearby, taking notes on a clipboard. The doctor would sniff and the assistant would record the data, following a finely calibrated odor scale. "I almost cracked up," said Dr. Hibbs, who watched the whole affair. "What would they think of next? The game ended with us still in the dark. So ended the great research project."

———————

Rumormongering was an assiduously practiced sport around camp. The rumors spread even faster than disease. At times it seemed that Cabanatuan was composed of 50 percent pathological liars and 50 percent naifs who'd believe anything. People made stuff up for the fun of it— just to see what would happen, just to track the stories and marvel at how they would warp and twist and evolve. It was not a malicious tendency, however. Very seldom were rumors hatched that prisoners didn't want to hear. If the rumors preyed on people's hopes, they were themselves a reflection of hope. They were spread in the spirit of certain universal understandings, the main one being that prisoners of war are not interested in the truth.

A few: The Russians had landed on the Japanese island of Honshu and were advancing toward Tokyo. When the prisoners returned home, Washington would give each enlisted man a new Ford, each company-grade officer a new Buick, and each field-grade officer a new Packard. The Australian government was formally offering every Bataan defender a farmhouse and 100 acres, in gratitude to the Americans for their having stymied the Japanese push to the south.

Rumors like these were generated on a daily basis. They came from both within and without. Prisoners who went on work details outside the camp were able to glean various developments and incidental facts from local Filipinos, but the veracity quotient was seldom dependable. Many of the rumors came in over the airwaves, for Cabanatuan had at least one clandestine shortwave radio. It was built by a virtual genius named Homer Hutchison, a former mining engineer. Most of the time, the radio was hidden beneath the library, but this was known only to a select few. It was a jury-rigged contraption fashioned from a toothpaste tube, an old truck battery, and a crude crystal. Hutchison improvised many of the parts and cannibalized others from Japanese radios that American technicians had been asked to repair. A few choice components were smuggled into camp at his behest. Finally, he assembled the receiver and cleverly housed it inside a false-bottomed canteen.

Hutchison was able to pick up KGEI out of San Francisco, a station that relentlessly broadcast the American viewpoint on the war, with considerable Army propaganda. KGEI also played music, and it was on Hutchison's radio that a number of listeners first heard a young singer with the unfamiliar name of Frank Sinatra. Even though few people actually heard the radio and its very existence was practically a rumor in itself, Hutchison's brainchild worked wonders for camp morale. For the first time the prisoners were able to gather news reports about American successes on Guadalcanal, New Guinea, and elsewhere in the Pacific. The KGEI accounts contradicted the stories the Japanese guards were telling them— namely, that Imperial forces had invaded Oregon, that

Germany had defeated Britain, that Tojo would ride his horse down Pennsylvania Avenue come spring. The radio corrected a lot of rumors, but it also created new ones, in part because the broadcasts were slanted and in part because the stories drastically changed as prisoners told and retold them around camp. "Cagey says . . . ," a prisoner would whisper, and the listener's ears pricked up for the latest from KGEI. By the time the story made the rounds, it was often unrecognizable from the original version.

———————

Sometime in 1943, the Japanese guards developed a bad problem with gonorrhea. On their nights off they would occasionally go whoring in Cabanatuan City and come back with the clap. Once the disease was contracted, the Japanese seemed at a loss for what to do. For some reason they felt uncomfortable approaching their own doctors, and they apparently feared that their immediate superiors would punish them severely. Informally, singly or in small groups, they approached the Americans. The guards wanted to obtain sulfa drugs. Even though the Americans had no sulfa drugs, they were quite willing to oblige their captors, for a price.

Almost overnight, a cottage industry was formed. A group of entrepreneurial-minded pranksters decided to moonlight as pharmacologists, manufacturing fake sulfa pills at five dollars a tablet. Each pill was handmade, with great effort expended to achieve realism. They were stamped out with a hollow bullet casing and slow-baked in an adobe oven so that they had a slight burnish. The principal ingredients were Dr. Lyons mint-flavored tooth powder, pulverized grains of raw rice, and water. The perpetrators used a hand-whittled letter attached to the tip of a carabao horn to engrave the pills with a "W" for Winthrop, the pharmaceutical company that produced the real thing. (The responsible parties, however, preferred to say the "W" actually stood for "Witchcraft.")

Ralph Hibbs, who as a doctor was intimately familiar with the Winthrop pills, thought the counterfeits were "beautiful gems," indistinguishable from the originals. They even bore the signature groove down the center to facilitate breaking the pills into two pieces. Either the guards sought additional medicine elsewhere or the pills actually worked, demonstrating once again the baroque powers of the placebo effect. For the prisoners, steeped in three years of unexpressed rage, such acts of vengefulness were both therapeutic and impossible to resist, even though the penalty for defiance, as the American commander constantly warned them, might be their own death.

Do not oppose, insult, or offend the Japanese. Control your temper. Avoid all profanity in your official dealings. Bear in mind Article 60 of Camp Rules and Regulations: "For any violations of Regulations the death penalty may be inflicted." These words are unconditional. They mean just what they say; do not doubt them, do not test them; put your shoulder to the wheel and do your best.

The American commander,
Colonel Curtis Beecher

Chapter 6

Platero was a pleasantly run-down village of a few dozen thatched huts perched on knobby legs of lumber and set among rice fields near the alluvial plain of the Pampanga River. The barrio was scarcely different from any of the others the Rangers had passed through except for one detail: The POW camp lay two miles away, a half hour's hike at best. But for the haze and the thick brush growing along the river, the villagers in Platero could have made out the guard towers of the stockade directly to the south.

Because of its proximity to the target, Mucci had decided to make Platero the Ranger staging area and bivouac site. Here he would establish his headquarters and the communications people would set up the field radio equipment. Here Dr. James Fisher, the battalion surgeon, would fashion a triage hospital to perform emergency surgeries in the probable event of injuries. And should the Rangers succeed in springing the POWs, Platero would serve as their first rest stop on the way to freedom. Though it was a speck of a place with little room or food to spare, the village would instantly double its population: The U.S. Rangers were moving in.

Reaching the edge of Platero in the failing light of the late afternoon, Mucci and Prince were pleased to learn that the village dogs had been silenced, just as Pajota had promised. They were tied up in shuttered nipa shacks and animal hutches made of bamboo, their snouts twined shut with straw rope. The barking problem was solved, but as soon as the vanguard entered the town, the train of Rangers abruptly came to a halt. Something was amiss: loud voices, exchanges, a big commotion. The column inched forward a few feet, then halted again.

Captain Prince nervously craned his neck to learn what the delay was. He heard something strange, a chorus singing softly in the twilight. The tune was hard to make out at first, but then Prince caught it—"God Bless America," the familiar stanzas rendered in thickly accented English, the melody charmingly curdled with the occasional stale note. At the entrance to the town a few dozen teenage girls dressed in white gowns were singing in sad, sweet voices. It was like a hastily arranged beauty pageant. The local school principal had gone door to door recruiting the prettiest young women from Platero and the surrounding countryside. Some of the girls slipped garlands of fresh sampaguita flowers over the Rangers' heads and offered welcoming kisses.

Behind this cordon of singers, the village bustled with the sounds of cooking and preparation. The town was planning a feast. People were slaughtering their chickens and cows, building fires, stirring vats of stew. The villagers had prepared a classic Filipino fiesta, with all the gaiety and spare-no-cost lavishness, everyone brimming with a warmth that would almost seem cloying if it wasn't so obviously sincere. Many of the Rangers welled with tears. That the people of Platero were throwing this kind of a reception in the midst of war's misfortunes made their generosity all the more stirring.

Colonel Mucci was as touched as everyone else by this welcoming ceremony, but he was also understandably paranoid about the noise. He kept darting nervous glances south, in the direction of the camp. It was hard to join in the spirit of the party when phalanxes of the Emperor's Army were now on the move a few miles away. Mucci told Joson and Pajota to have their men form a tight circle around the village to guard against Japanese ambush. He smiled awkwardly as one of the ladies hung a lei around his neck. "I told them they might sing if they would do it very softly," Mucci said. "Then we all joined in, and there in the semidarkness, very low, we sang 'God Bless the Philippines.'"

The Filipinos' feast was magnificent under the circumstances—rice and camote sweet potatoes, fresh papaya, whole chickens wrapped in banana leaves and baked in the coals. They poured glasses of lambanog, a stout coconut wine. The hungry Rangers sat around fires scattered about the barrio and fell into spirited conversations with the locals. Occasionally little kids would timidly reach out and touch the Rangers to see what an American felt like.

The locals smoked spindly cigarettes rolled in old newspaper and talked about the war, about the Japanese, about MacArthur. They seemed to love MacArthur especially, loved his imperial style, his swagger-stick grandiloquence. They responded to his biblical cadences and did not seem to be put off, as so many American soldiers were, by his incorrigible fixation on the vertical pronoun. For the Filipinos, steeped in the stark passions of Spanish Catholicism, his pronouncements sounded something like the judgments of God.

Of course, they despised the Japanese with a countervailing passion. There had been collaborators out here in the rice country, but not many—and most of them had simply gone along with the new dispensation to protect their families and their livelihoods. At the start of the war, the Japanese thought they could easily win over the countryside with their "Asia for the Asiatics" rhetoric. They declared: *We've come to free you from the bonds of Western colonialism. Join us in a new day.* But the new shibboleths sounded phony to even the most unsophisticated Filipinos; almost laughably so.

It didn't help that the Japanese military police, the Kempei Tai, had sent any number of provincial villagers off to dungeons in Manila. Nor that pimp contractors for the Emperor's Army had come and drafted pretty Filipino girls, often under false pretenses, to serve as "comfort women" in crab-infested bordellos over in New Guinea or the Solomon Islands.

These were a few of the flagrant cases, but the people's impression of the Japanese was mostly informed by the smaller daily indignities, not the least of which was the problem of slapping. Japanese soldiers were prodigious slappers. They slapped to discipline, to scare, to convey a point. It seemed to be a primary method of communication, even among themselves. Early on, after the fall of Bataan and Corregidor, a Japanese officer would come into a village like Platero on what might loosely be termed a courtesy call, and even though his apparent aim was to win over the people and convince them of Japan's

211

goodwill, within a few minutes he would slap somebody. Perhaps he'd have provocation, and perhaps he wouldn't, but the slap clashed fundamentally with a basic rule of Filipino etiquette. "One of the worst ways to insult a Filipino is to slap him in the face," said Robert Lapham, the American guerrilla leader who presided over the Nueva Ecija area. "You do that to a Filipino and you have a deadly enemy for life." In a war full of dying and atrocity, it seemed like a small thing but it wasn't. The Japanese had no idea what sort of virulent reaction this set up in the ordinarily peace-loving Filipinos, how they seethed and boiled with a pride that was mixed with just enough Spanish machismo to leave them dreaming, day in and day out, of sweet revenge.

After dinner, the mayor of Cabanatuan City showed up and produced a bottle of Johnnie Walker Black. "It was good prewar scotch," Mucci recalled. "We passed it around so that a lot of the boys could get a little sip, just a taste." The colonel then struck up a conversation with the mayor and, despite his hospitality, gradually began to have his doubts about the man. "I was pretty suspicious of him," Mucci later wrote, "because he had been mayor all through the Jap occupation." Mucci felt something was wrong. He wondered if there was even the remotest possibility that this man was a collaborator, a makapili. The colonel didn't take any chances. He thanked the mayor for the whiskey and then, with apologies, explained that the Rangers were placing him under house arrest with an armed guard to watch him at all times. It was just a precaution, Mucci assured him, and the good mayor would be allowed to return to Cabanatuan once the mission was over.

As the night wore on, the Rangers dispersed into smaller groups, each one following a different Filipino host to his home for the night. A few of the luckier Rangers were invited inside the shacks to sleep on real beds, but most were quartered in barns and toolsheds and lice-infested stables strewn all about the barrio. Mucci instructed his men to sleep with their boots on in case something happened and they all had to react quickly during the night. Pitched among rice sacks, their rifles set in the straw beside them, the haggard Rangers dozed off to the night bugs and, for some, the sour breath of a carabao tethered in the next stall.

––·––·––

While the Rangers slept, the Alamo Scouts were crouched in the shadows a little over a mile to the south, watching as the long column of Japanese vehicles trundled past the camp on the highway. The Scouts rotated their watch through the night, and periodically one of them would run back to Platero and report to Mucci. The sobering moonlight vigil graphically validated the colonel's decision to postpone the raid. All evening the Japanese kept coming—tanks, trucks, and thousands of foot soldiers—a stanchless stream of men and matériel hastening toward Bongabon and points north. The retreating Japanese, determined to avoid lethal American air attacks, had become nocturnal creatures, sitting out the day's glare burrowed in jungles and bamboo thickets or under whatever air cover might present itself.

Among other things, the Scouts were watching for any warning signs of an imminent massacre. Disposing of 500

Americans would be a chore for the Japanese, and the guards would probably need to enlist some of the Imperial Army soldiers to help with the task of mass execution and burial. There were some troops inside the enclosure—precisely how many was unclear—but it seemed likely that the guards would need to recruit even more men to carry out their grisly task. Yet these transient Japanese soldiers on the highway appeared uninterested in the camp. They had more urgent appointments in northern Luzon, where General Yamashita had other strategic purposes in mind for them. The Scouts were relieved to see that the front gate of the camp remained shut through the night.

By dawn the flow of traffic finally ran dry, and the road was clear again. The Emperor's Army had passed with the night.

It was now the morning of Tuesday, January 30, and the Scouts had a series of complex and difficult tasks to carry out. Within a few hours they absolutely had to supply all the reconnaissance data Mucci and Prince so desperately needed in order to finish planning the raid, which was scheduled for dusk. Gleaning these details would not be any easier than it had been twenty-four hours earlier. The transient Japanese troops from Cabanatuan City may have moved on, but there were still some 75 armed guards inside the compound and perhaps 200 or 300 soldiers staying in the camp barracks. The compound was fortified with pillboxes and guard towers manned by machine gunners. The terrain was an agoraphobe's nightmare—flat, dry savanna unfurling in all directions.

The Scouts were able to assemble certain nuggets of information based on the observations of Filipino guerrillas, who could easily don straw hats and civilian garb and skirt around the edges of camp in the natural guise of the rice peasants they actually were. Pajota's intelligence aide, Lieutenant Tombo, had his men snooping around all over the place, taking measurements, pacing off distances, counting Japanese. Tombo even recruited a little kid to ride on a carabao and take mental note of everything he could see as his beast plodded around the barbed-wire perimeter. But there was still vital intelligence missing, and by the forenoon the Scouts were beginning to despair of their chances of gathering any of it.

Then Lieutenant Bill Nellist had a thought. If the Scouts couldn't draw up close to the camp, then perhaps they could at least find a higher vantage point. Earlier in the day Nellist had spotted a lone nipa shack standing out in the rice fields to the north of the compound. The one-room shack, which appeared to be abandoned, was situated just a few hundred yards from the camp and was conveniently aligned with the main gate—almost dead-on, in fact. Since it was constructed on stilts, the shack promised just enough elevation to enable the Scouts to peer down into the camp enclosure. It didn't seem like much, but out there on the griddle of grass, every vertical inch could discernibly improve the sight lines.

Getting over to the shack was the problem. They'd surely be spotted and shot if they hoofed it all the way over there in their Scout uniforms. So Nellist asked a Filipino runner to go fetch two broad-brimmed buri hats and some farmer clothes; they were going to disguise themselves as locals. It was decided that Private Rufo Vaquilar, an Alamo Scout who happened to be a Filipino-American, would accompany Nellist to the shack. Soon the runner materialized with farmer "costumes," and the two Scouts quickly pulled on their new clothes and hats. Nellist eased his M-1 rifle down his pant leg with the barrel pointing toward the ground. He'd have to lurch over there as though he were wearing a knee splint. The limp would look suspicious, but at least his weapon would be concealed from the tower guards.

Then Nellist and Vaquilar shoved off. They walked down the highway for a few hundred yards then emerged onto the broad field right in front of the camp. Taking slightly different paths about 100 yards apart from each other, they slowly shambled over to the nipa hut—in full view of the Japanese sentries every step they took. "We just sauntered up to the shack pretending like we were looking at the rice plants," Nellist would later say. Nervously, the two Scouts scrambled up an old bamboo ladder into the stifling heat of the shack. They felt sure their little ruse must have attracted notice among the guards. Nellist and Vaquilar lay on the slatted bamboo floor for a few interminable minutes, hyperventilating, listening anxiously for the report of a long-range rifle or the shout of approaching Japanese. There was an old rocking chair by the open window. Nellist extricated his M-1 from his pant leg and crept over to the chair. Staying low, he sat down and stole a glimpse of the prison stockade. To his relief, nothing seemed untoward. The camp was quiet. The Japanese must have bought the disguise.

Encouraged, Lieutenant Nellist peered out the window again, this time taking the full measure of things. A smile soon spread over his face. The vantage was even more commanding than he'd expected. The entire camp was spread out before him, a puzzle waiting to be solved. He and Vaquilar could see prisoners ambling about the compound and could even count the guards up in the towers. He could discern the general logic of the place, the relationships among the various buildings, the layout of the paths and service roads. Details the Scouts had only been guessing at were now apparent to him, as if he were perched on a ladder grasping the design of an English hedge maze that, at ground level, had seemed inscrutable.

Bill Nellist was a hawk-eyed rustic in his late twenties who'd grown up hunting and fishing in the ferny rain forests of northern California's Humboldt County, not far from the coastal town of Eureka. A lean, patient, wry-witted man, he had the easy confidence of someone who'd spent most of his life outdoors, in deep stands of redwood and Douglas fir, with a gun in his hands. Nellist had taken his natural love of hunting and tracking and applied it to the U.S. Army. People who knew him back in Eureka called him a "white Indian." He loved to lose himself in the nuances of terrain, inferring the movements of animals and men from the faintest spoor. Nellist was also said to be the best marksman of all the Alamo Scouts. Before the war, he'd been the "rifle champion" of the California National Guard. Like most great shots, he was adept at estimating distances using nothing more than the sights of his rifle. He placed his M-1 on the windowsill and pointed the barrel toward the camp.

From his pocket, Nellist produced a large photograph of Cabanatuan camp that had been taken from an Army surveillance aircraft. He began to compare the particulars of the photograph against the details that now lay before him. Then, steadily shifting his gaze between the photograph and his rifle's sight, he was able to triangulate his estimates and arrive at accurate distances between all the camp's major features. He sketched out his own map of the compound, and then took copious notes on every conceivable feature—distances and elevations, what the buildings were constructed of, where the fences were, where the power lines and telephone wires ran. By meshing these new details with the ones the Scouts and Filipino guerrillas had already gathered, Nellist was finally getting the full portrait.

The enclosure was set out in a vast rectangle, about 800 yards deep and 600 yards across, the grounds cleanly bisected by a dirt road that ran straight as a ruler from the main gate to the rear of the compound. If one were standing at the gate, facing south into the camp, the American prison barracks would all be off to the immediate left of this central road, while most of the Japanese were quartered in buildings to the right. The main entrance was a cumbersome, double-gated construction of lumber and barbed wire, about eight feet tall. The two big gates could swing in or out like enormous flippers, but now they were closed together and fastened with a single padlock. There were three guard towers and two pillboxes, and the perimeter of the compound was secured with a succession of three ten-foot-tall barbed-wire fences. A fourth barbed-wire fence marked the boundary of the American section. The firmly packed terrain inside the compound was cross-hatched with deep irrigation ditches. Overall, the grounds were almost perfectly flat except for a slight rise in the rear, where several more Japanese barracks were located.

Finally there was the question of armored vehicles. Nellist and Vaquilar couldn't spot any tanks parked out in the open but it was obvious where they were stored—in a large metal shed located just off the central thoroughfare approximately 300 yards from the front gate. The cavernous shed, whose galvanized-metal sheathing glared in the bright midday sun, was the only structure large enough to serve as a garage. After the raid started, this was where Captain Prince would want to direct the bazooka team. Nellist circled and boldly marked the building on his diagram.

With all these details noted, Nellist felt confident that the Scouts now had the goods Mucci and Prince needed. The next question was how to get the recon report back to Platero. Then the answer presented itself.

At about one-thirty in the afternoon, Nellist and Vaquilar glanced out the rear window and caught a suspicious movement in the grass. "Looks like we have visitors," Nellist said with a grin. Three Alamo Scouts—Franklin Fox, Harold Hard, and Gilbert Cox—were on their bellies out in the grass, slowly creeping up on the shack. They'd taken a much safer and more circuitous route to get here, doubling all the way back to the Pampanga River and then slinking up from the rear. The three Scouts had come to check up on Nellist and Vaquilar, who'd been quietly holed up in the shack for nearly two hours. Nellist and his comrades would later recount the particulars of their meeting to historian Forrest Johnson.

"You think this is a convention?" Nellist said once the three Scouts had pulled themselves up into the cramped shack. "Where's the rest of the guys?"

"We're spread all over the place," Fox replied.

"Here," Nellist said, handing over his completed recon report. "Make yourself useful. Get this back to Colonel Mucci before he blows a fuse. Get lost now—this place is too damned crowded."

The abandoned nipa shack afforded such an ideal crow's nest for surveillance that Bill Nellist and Rufo Vaquilar decided to remain there all day. Nellist figured someone ought to keep an eye on things, and besides, having two more men clamber down from the shack in daylight hours was risky. With too much coming and going, the Japanese would eventually become suspicious. So he and Vaquilar intended to hide out until the attack was nearly underway and then leap into the fields at dusk to join the Rangers and other Scouts as they crept toward the prison.

That, at least, was Nellist's plan. But around four o'-clock, the two Scouts were rattled by an unexpected development. Vaquilar spotted it first.

"Look at this, Bill," he said, pointing out the open window. "What's *she* doing over there?"

A few hundred yards off, a lone Filipino woman was ambling down the road directly in front of the camp.

"Don't know," Nellist said, bewildered. "I thought Pajota had ordered all civilians to keep clear of the highway."

The lady walked right up to the front gate and began to engage in what appeared to be an animated discussion with one of the Japanese guards in the tower, as though she knew him personally. After a few minutes of conversation, the guard reached down and offered her something—payment, it seemed. Whatever it was, she slipped it in her pocket and then promptly resumed her walk across the front of the camp along the highway.

The more they considered it, the more squirrelly it seemed. They didn't understand why this woman would be on such friendly terms with the Japanese. Their worries mounted. Could she be an informant? Was the all-important secrecy of the mission compromised? "I just knew that she was telling them that American soldiers were on the way," Nellist explained to military writer William McRaven. "It scared the hell out of me. I thought the whole thing was going down the drain right there."

Vaquilar had to know for himself. "I'll go to the gate," he proposed. "If the Japs are tipped off, the place will be full of action." Since he was a Filipino-American in authentic barrio disguise, Vaquilar reasoned, the guards would simply think he was another civilian.

Nellist didn't like the sound of it, but he too was deeply curious to learn what, if anything, this Filipino lady had set in motion. "I can't cover you," Nellist warned. "If they go for you, I can't shoot. It'll blow the mission."

Vaquilar said he understood that, but he was going anyway. Armed with two automatic pistols, he hopped down into the field. He tacked far to the right before intersecting with the highway. Then he turned left and walked along the shoulders of the road, heading straight for the camp. Nellist remained in the shack and studied Vaquilar's every movement. Instinctively, he clutched his M-1 even though he knew he couldn't use it.

When Vaquilar reached the front gate, he glanced at the guard standing in the tower and tipped his buri hat. The guard nodded back, impassively, and then scowled.

In the nipa shack, Nellist held his breath, his heart pounding.

As he strolled down the road, Vaquilar casually peered into the camp for signs of commotion, anything that might look out of the ordinary. He kept walking along the road until he passed from the guard's line of vision. Then he crossed the road and angled back to the shack, a roundabout hike that took about fifteen minutes.

"I don't know what she said," Vaquilar said once he crawled up, "but everything seems normal in there."

Nellist was somewhat encouraged by the news, but his fears were not entirely allayed. He thought there was still a possibility that the woman was indeed an informant, that even now the Japanese officers were assessing this major new development back in their quarters, quietly making plans to sabotage the Rangers with a surprise counterattack. Nellist sat in silence and anxiously scanned the camp, his M-1 propped on the windowsill.

In the village of Platero, two miles to the north, Colonel Mucci and Prince received Nellist's intelligence report with enormous relief. It was two-thirty in the afternoon of January 30—late, almost too late. Finally, the Rangers could set to work in earnest.

Mucci and Prince had been up since dawn, huddled together in a village house, buzzing with plans that sprang from hollow facts, from knowledge they didn't possess, from a map still swimming with hypotheticals. They anxiously realized that nearly everything they had conjured was predicated upon fragments of supposition. And yet, one way or another, they were going through with the raid at dusk. Over breakfast, through the morning, and over lunch, Prince had sat sketching ideas in his notebook, while Mucci paced and stewed and sucked his pipe with increasing petulance. They couldn't imagine what had happened to Lieutenant Nellist and his Scouts. The report was supposed to arrive no later than noon.

When Prince dug into the Nellist report, however, it

became clear that whatever the Scouts had been doing across the river, they hadn't been loitering. Prince was astounded at the depth of detail. All the crucial points Mucci had asked for—and numerous ones he hadn't even considered—were there. Given what Prince already knew about the terrain, it was hard to fathom how the Scouts had been able to gather such rich particularity. The report may have taken a little longer than they would have liked, but this was impeccable recon work, accomplished against great odds.

With this fresh information in hand, the master plan quickly took shape in Prince's mind. All day he'd been thinking about it and discussing it with the various platoon leaders, but it hadn't all crystallized for him until now. He sketched it out as a diagram in his notebook, and at three o'clock he submitted the plan to Mucci.

It didn't take long for the colonel to sign off on it. Mucci suggested a few tweaks of his own and then at four o'clock he summoned all the noncommissioned officers and guerrilla leaders to meet on the outskirts of the village. Mucci's earlier concern about Filipino eavesdroppers had diminished somewhat, as Platero had become almost a ghost town. Most of the locals had cleared out of the place, on the order of Captain Pajota. A few hours earlier, he had called for the evacuation not only of Platero but of several other barrios in the immediate vicinity of the camp to minimize civilian bloodshed should the Japanese retaliate. Now most of the women, the children, and the elderly had moved out and were quietly making for the safety of the Sierra Madre foothills.

Only able-bodied men remained. Some of them were full-fledged guerrillas under Pajota's direct command, while others were noncombatants recruited to perform such logistical tasks as collecting food or commandeering carabao and wagons from the surrounding countryside. Pajota had thought of everything, it seemed. He had lieutenants fanning out in all directions, gathering last-minute intelligence, cutting phone lines, setting explosives. He even dispatched a young woman to walk up to the main gate and speak to the Japanese guards, ostensibly to sell them fresh garden vegetables but actually to take detailed notes on the layout of the front of the camp. (This was the woman Nellist and Vaquilar had spotted, with so much alarm, earlier in the day, fearing she might be an informant.) Crafty, stubborn, quietly intense, Pajota had so many little subplots working, it was difficult to keep track of them all. Here on his own turf, the seasoned guerrilla captain was used to working independently, and he kept Mucci, Prince, and the Alamo Scouts only partially informed of his various sideline operations. All across Nueva Ecija, in groups of twos and threes, his agents were inconspicuously setting the stage for the night's firestorm.

With the sun dropping fast, the time had come to make all the individual assignments. The Rangers were to set out at five o'clock, in one hour's time, and now the men were preoccupied with the private reveries and ritualistic tics of imminent combat—checking sidearms, filling bandoliers, synchronizing watches. Beneath a clump of shade trees, the various noncoms and platoon leaders huddled with their weapons, waiting intently to hear what Mucci and Prince had in mind.

Captain Prince's master plan was intricate. As he elaborated the details, he clutched a stick and scratched out diagrams in the soft dirt.

At Mucci's signal, the Rangers would clear out of Platero and march south toward the camp, flanked by Pajota's 200 men on one side and Joson's 80 men on the other. Just before reaching the Pampanga River, the two guerrilla groups would break off from the Rangers. Pajota's forces would bear sharply to the left. Their task would be to set up a massive roadblock on the highway, about a mile northeast of the camp, near the Cabu River bridge. Precisely at 7:40, they were to destroy the bridge with land mines which Pajota's explosives experts would have already set among the span's log pylons. Just across the river, more than 1,000 Imperial Army soldiers would still be bivouacked down in the bamboo thickets. Should they charge toward the POW camp upon hearing the Ranger fire, Pajota's 200 guerrillas would be there, waiting in ambush, reinforced with a bazooka to hold any Japanese tanks at bay. Lining themselves across the road and facing the bridge in a classic open "V," Pajota's guerrillas would proceed to cut down the enemy with enfilading fire.

Captain Joson's job would be the mirror opposite of Pajota's. He and his forces would peel off toward the right and erect another roadblock on the highway, this one just south of the camp, to stop any Japanese troops that might hasten from Cabanatuan City. Here, the Japanese threat was less imminent (since Cabanatuan was four miles away) but potentially far greater than for Pajota's men at the Cabu River bridge, as there were said to be as many as 8,000 of Yamashita's best soldiers stationed in the city.

Joson, too, would have bazookas and land mines at his disposal, but if Japanese forces were to get early notice of the raid and attack en masse, his men might soon be overwhelmed.

This part of the plan was exceedingly risky, but Pajota and Joson, working in tandem, had to seal off a solid mile of the road and hold it long enough for the Rangers to attack the camp, remove the prisoners, and then cross back over, melting safely into the rice paddies in the deepening night. The two Filipino forces were to function as a synchronized pair of shutoff valves in a great water main, temporarily blocking the flow in both directions so the Rangers could go in and do their extraction work with little worry of a surprise surge in the pipe.

For the Rangers, reaching the camp would pose a much more immediate problem. For the last mile beyond the Pampanga, on the bald plain, they had to crawl on their stomachs in the hope of escaping detection. As they approached the highway, the thirty members of F Company would then break left from Prince's larger group, sneak around to the back of the camp, and creep along a dry ravine that was, they hoped, deep enough to conceal them from Japanese sentinels. The F Company men would position themselves to fire on the rearguard towers and pillboxes, as well as on the Japanese barracks, which were believed to house several hundred transient soldiers. F Company would fire first, just as the sun was setting—at about 7:30. This opening salvo would serve as the cue for Prince's C Company to leap across the road and kill the guards in the towers while simultaneously storming the main gate.

Once the gate was breached, a first wave of men would race down the camp's central thoroughfare, pivot right, and then riddle the Japanese side with a merciless barrage of automatic fire from tommy guns and BARs. Then the bazooka team would penetrate deeper into the compound, destroying the metal shed where the Scouts believed the tanks were parked. Japanese resistance quelled, a final wave of men would push in with wire cutters and free the prisoners, with a reserve of Rangers and Alamo Scouts waiting at the front gate to escort the escapees to the Pampanga River, where carabao and civilian-driven oxcarts would be waiting.

Captain Prince would direct the traffic and oversee the action while standing at the threshold of the main gate. As the stream of exiting POWs trickled off, he would personally go in to inspect each barracks to make sure every last prisoner had been removed. Once satisfied, he would fire a red flare high over the camp—the signal to all participants that the assault was over. After the column of Rangers and POWs had successfully crossed the Pampanga, Prince would fire a second red flare, this one a sign to both guerrilla groups to commence their withdrawals.

Then the hardest part: At the river, the Rangers and POWs would embark on their thirty-mile trudge north toward American lines, passing through Platero on the way, with the guerrillas serving as rear guard. It promised to be a long, slow trek of moonlight marching, but by dawn they should be scot-free, in the Sixth Army's embrace.

———————

This was the essence of Prince's design for the raid. In the pitch dark, with so much thunderous gunfire and scurrying back and forth, it might appear to be a melee, but every moment would be carefully choreographed, with the major action of the raid taking no more than thirty minutes. "Organized confusion" was how Prince described it. "We wanted all hell to break loose," he said, "but to break loose precisely on our terms." The captain was confident of the broad strokes, but what concerned him was the high level of coordination that the plan required. It was a sustained and intensive collaboration involving so many disparate groups—Rangers, Scouts, two separate guerrilla organizations, Filipino civilians, POWs, not to mention the lowly, shambling water buffalo. All told, the raid would employ a cast of nearly 1,000 characters, every one of whom had to do his job and do it correctly or else the mission hung in jeopardy. The individual tasks seemed straightforward enough, but taken as a whole the operation had to unfold as an intricate progression, each action building on the success of the previous one, each stage driving ineluctably toward the next, like tricky, interlocking patterns of tipping dominoes. With such precise coordination necessary to bring it off, Prince sorely wished there were time for a dress rehearsal, but that was, he knew, an impossible luxury.

"It was such a complex group of people, none of whom had had any real dealings with one another before, not on such a scale," Prince said. "The main thing that made it conceivable to think we could succeed was that we were in friendly territory, with friendly people. Trying to do that somewhere else, I don't think you could even come close."

Prince and Mucci would give the platoon leaders wide latitude in assigning the teams and ordering specific tasks to be performed by their subordinate enlisted men. Of all the different components of the plan, what worried the platoon leaders most was the approach itself: That long, slow crawl to the gate gave off a faint whiff of suicide. The Japanese would still have ample light to see the Rangers as they wriggled to their final positions in the fields. How could the men expect to escape the notice of the guards?

Here, Captain Pajota spoke up. Over the past few weeks, he said, his guerrillas had noticed something interesting. It appeared that the Japanese guards at the camp were unusually agitated by the specter of American planes flying overhead. The planes would roar into view. Even the sputter of innocuous little Piper Cubs would set off a panicked reaction, and the guards would excitedly scour the skies. Why not call in a few American planes to buzz the camp in the last moments leading up to the raid, purely as a diversion? It might distract the Japanese sentries just long enough for the Rangers to sneak into their positions. Instead of looking down, the guards would be looking up.

"No shooting, no bombs," Pajota reportedly said. "Just a flyover."

Mucci instantly liked the sound of it. As with Pajota's suggestion of using carabao carts, the idea was novel, even a little odd, yet at the same time compellingly simple: Air cover not as a defense but as a decoy, a gaze averter. The aircraft would just be up there, looping and droning and turning, flummoxing the guards, commanding their attention. It might at least buy the Rangers more time. Mucci felt it was well worth breaking radio silence to request that Sixth Army headquarters scramble a plane. The mighty U.S. Army was not always known for its lightning reflexes, however, and at this late hour it seemed unlikely that a plane and pilot could be assigned in time to do any good. Still, Mucci thought it was worth a try. He had the radio operator call in the request.

Hovering over the many doubts and contingencies Mucci had to grapple with, one outcome seemed certain: With an assignment as perilous as this, there were bound to be casualties. Mucci made sure Dr. Jimmy Fisher was well prepared. Fisher spent the better part of the day turning the one-room schoolhouse of Platero into a makeshift hospital. Fisher had befriended a local Filipino doctor, Carlos Layug, who agreed to help conduct surgeries, dress wounds, and do whatever else was needed. Trained in Manila before the war, thirty-seven-year-old Layug was an experienced Army physician from the Bataan battlefields—a survivor of the Death March, in fact—and he'd spent the past three years serving as the surgeon for Captain Pajota's forces. During those years, he had encountered just about every sort of trauma and malady the war could throw at a young doctor, and he'd learned to work miracles with scant supplies, rudimentary equipment, and no pay. When Layug treated patients he was usually accompanied by his wife, Julita, who was also a surgeon, every bit as competent and resourceful as he. Dr. Fisher had spent the previous night in the Layugs' home and had made a deep impression on them. Fisher was plainly troubled by the extreme poverty he encountered in the Philippines, and he went out of his way to share his expertise and medicines. Ten days before the mission, for example, he had delivered a Filipino baby near the Ranger headquarters. He became the newborn's godfather. Julita Layug later wrote, "In a short period of time, we grew to love Captain Fisher. Of all the [American] officers who came

230

through Platero. I was touched by his solicitude for the welfare of the poor guerrillas, promising them medicine, equipment, and everything. How kind, democratic, and likable he was."

By midafternoon, with a bit of jury-rigging and the generous donations of locals, Fisher and the Layugs had completed their metamorphosis of the school. They'd pulled together teachers' desks to function as operating tables. They'd collected dozens of spare bed linens and hung blankets over the windows to keep out the bluebottle flies and the glare. The "hospital" was as ready as it was ever going to be, the packets of morphine and gauze and syringes arrayed on side tables, containers of plasma carefully stockpiled, scalpels sparkling in the guttering light of coconut-oil lamps.

Dr. Fisher decided he would personally participate in the raid, crawling along with everyone else to the very threshold of the prison. This was a bit unorthodox. Many other battalion surgeons would have chosen to stay at the hospital and wait for the medics to bring casualties in. Mucci didn't like it at all. "You're crazy, Jimmy," Mucci told him. "This is a raid. We can't have you in there." Mucci argued that Fisher's skills were far too important to risk on the line, that an injured surgeon wouldn't be of much use to the company in its hour of greatest need.

But the doctor turned Mucci's argument on its head. Fisher thought he should go along precisely *because* this was such a dangerous mission. He felt strongly that he'd be needed right from the start, at the gate, in situ. Moreover, Fisher doubted whether his small team of four medical corpsmen could handle the job if casualties mounted. He felt his expertise might be crucial in helping to stabilize patients and save lives outside the compound. There was also the question of the POWs themselves. "You've got five hundred prisoners in there, many of them are terribly ill and might require special medical attention from the outset," Fisher told Mucci. Then, too, Fisher contended, Dr. Layug and his wife were more than qualified to stay in Platero and staff the hospital while he was out in the field.

Fisher was persuasive, and ultimately Mucci relented. The young surgeon's stubbornness on this point reflected something of his character. Ever since he joined the Rangers in New Guinea, he'd consistently been the kind of soft-spoken, self-deprecating doctor who expected to be treated the same as everyone else, to march the same marches, to venture out on the same patrols, to get himself into the same physical shape as his Ranger comrades. He hated the pretentiousness typical of so many Army surgeons and always insisted that even the greenest of enlisted men address him, simply, as "Dr. Jimmy." Perhaps it was, in part, his way of compensating for his Harvard medical education and his privileged upbringing as the son of the popular Vermont writer and educator Dorothy Canfield Fisher, one of the charter committee members of the Book-of-the-Month Club. Captain Fisher, who had traveled widely throughout Europe and Russia and who spoke fluent French, keenly wanted to show that despite the sophistication of his background, he was one of the guys.

Fisher's father had bravely driven an ambulance in France during World War I, and Dr. Fisher wanted to embrace the same sort of risks and challenges his dad had assumed in the line of duty. He was a restless adventurer who had hiked through the Alps and loved to tramp in the mountains around his home in Arlington, Vermont. But he wasn't foolhardy, nor was he swayed by misguided ideas about the romance of being close to the action. Certainly he was no vicarious warrior. If anything, his spiritual background urged him to take a dim view of combat. A son of New England Quaker stock, he graduated from a Quaker prep school in New York and the Quaker college of Swarthmore just outside of Philadelphia, which produced more than its share of conscientious objectors. At Swarthmore, Fisher promptly dropped out of his fraternity upon learning that its national bylaws formally discouraged the acceptance of Jews. With his strong egalitarian sense, Dr. Fisher simply took for granted that it was his responsibility to go along wherever the Rangers went, and he had no reason to think this assignment was any different.

With five o'clock fast approaching, Dr. Fisher hurriedly pulled together a rucksack of emergency medical supplies and waited for Colonel Mucci's signal to march.

Chapter 7

The prisoners of Cabanatuan, though desperately impoverished, were not completely lacking in sources of outside help. Over time an extensive underground developed, a network of brave civilians, philanthropists, and priests, most of them headquartered in Manila, who regularly smuggled goods into the camp in direct violation of Japanese orders. Whether they operated as part of the Philippine resistance or strictly out of humanitarian interests, these men and women took immense and sometimes suicidal risks to save hundreds, if not thousands, of lives inside the camp. There was an American woman living in Manila named Margaret Utinsky, who was astonishingly successful at raising money and spiriting all manner of essentials—from rice to shoes to sulfa drugs—into the camp. There were generous Filipinos, including Ralph Hibbs' girlfriend Pilar Campos, who worked out elaborate schemes for slipping food to the American work details that ventured outside the camp each day. There was a German Catholic priest in Manila named Father Heinz

Buttenbruck who, presumably because of his nationality, was allowed to enter Cabanatuan camp to perform various ecclesiastical duties. Since the Japanese guards conducted frequent searches, Father Buttenbruck seldom smuggled in goods on his person, but he was said to have a photographic memory, and he brought in and out scores of personal messages during his weekly visits—messages that proved invaluable to the workings of the underground.

The most fascinating of all of Cabanatuan's clandestine enterprises, however, was the one operated by a mysterious woman known to the prisoners only as "High Pockets." During the occupation, High Pockets ran a popular Manila cabaret, Club Tsubaki, where Japanese officers liked to congregate. Club Tsubaki was located near the waterfront, at the corner of San Luis and Mabini streets in the Ermita section, just outside the old walled city. From the front door of the club, one could look back and see the vast piers and wharf installations along Manila Bay, where the Japanese warships and transports docked for repairs and where Imperial Army and Navy quartermasters resupplied their stores for the fierce battles that were being waged throughout the Pacific. After Corregidor fell to General Homma, the Japanese made Manila Bay a crucial stopping point between Japan and the various war fronts—Guadalcanal, the Solomons, New Guinea. The newly arrived Japanese officers could walk right off the planked piers and into Club Tsubaki for an evening of drinks, dancing, and female companionship.

Club Tsubaki featured floor shows every night. The club billed itself as the ultra-exclusive nightspot for the occupation elite—"only the best people," its business card discreetly stated. (*Tsubaki* is the Nipponese word for camellia, a flower that in Japan is regarded as delicate and rare.) Patrons would be greeted at the door by the club's owner, a glamorous, thirty-three-year-old woman who claimed to be a Filipina of Italian extraction named Dorothy Clara Fuentes. She would be dressed in a white evening gown with a plunging neckline and a slit halfway up her thigh. Her olive skin would glitter with jewels. She would bow very slowly and, with an expansive gesture, she would say, *"Kombanwa."* Then she would escort her guests arm in arm through the cream-colored bar, past the dancing stage with its curtains of lavender satin, to the rattan settees along the back wall. Fuentes would set up each party with a suggestively dressed hostess, who was theirs for the night. The hostesses would pour the Japanese drinks, stroke their hair, light their cigarettes, and keep up a constant chirp of flatteries in a mangled polyglot of English, Japanese, Spanish, and Tagalog.

Club Tsubaki was not a brothel, but some of the club's hostesses were rumored to make sidebar arrangements for select patrons after hours. The space had been a dance studio before the war, and Fuentes had carpenters convert the upstairs rooms into apartments for herself and a few of her favorite dancing girls. Club Tsubaki had a fully stocked bar that specialized in tropical cocktails of various iridescent hues. Food could be ordered in from Chan's, a popular Chinese restaurant around the corner. The Filipino waiters, wearing white dress shoes and immaculate sharkskin suits, never let a glass go dry.

The floor shows lasted far into the night, with accompaniment provided by a five-piece orchestra of Filipino players whose tastes ran in the direction of twangy Hawaiian jazz. Each night the dance troupe performed beneath the spotlights wearing little more than gold satin G-strings, coconut shells, and bright headdresses fashioned from turkey feathers. Fuentes encouraged her dancers to vamp it up as much as possible while still keeping the operation within the bounds of good taste. There were fan dances and feather dances, rice-planting dances and Moro dances. One of the girls would appear onstage and sing a set of traditional Japanese songs. The club favorite, however, was the Siamese temple dance, a sultry piece that started slow but ended in raucous abandon, with the mostly naked women gyrating off the stage and circulating among the clientele. The Japanese officers were mesmerized. "As the tempo increased," Fuentes later wrote, "our visitors, open-mouthed and attentive, sprang from the shadows and joined the mad dance."

Now and then throughout these entertainments, Madame Tsubaki herself would climb the stage and sing a few of her signature torch songs. Fuentes may not have been destined for Broadway or Hollywood, but she was a natural chanteuse. She had a willowy figure with lustrous black hair and penciled brows that arched with precision. Onstage, her face was radiant, but her eyes were dark and dreamy and seemed to brim with sorrow. When she sang, she usually changed into a clinging, halter-necked evening gown. Her lounge voice was husky, and she slinked about the club with all the camp gestures and come-hitherisms of the trade, "coo[ing] in my most saccharine tones," as she later fondly recalled.

After her set, she would cuddle up beside the club's most prominent guest and give him all the attention he could stand. She would light him another cigarette, pour him another drink, and then, in a coquettish voice, she would begin to ask questions: *Will you come tomorrow night? When do you leave Manila? Which one of those ships out there is yours? What are you carrying in such a big boat? Where will you go next?*

Eventually Fuentes would excuse herself with a Mona Lisa smile and a demurral—"I don't know a thing about that war stuff"—and drift on to other tables, and other questions. At the end of the evening Madame Tsubaki would escort her clients to the door and bow low in gratitude. Fastening the dead bolt, she'd hustle upstairs to her apartment and count the night's take. While her memory was still fresh, she would jot down everything the Japanese officers had told her that might be of military significance. She'd promptly hand her code-written note to a Filipino runner waiting in the alley at the club's back door. The runner, in turn, would deliver the message to American guerrillas operating in the hills of Bataan, who would then relay relevant details, via shortwave radio, to General MacArthur's strategic headquarters in Australia or New Guinea. Her notes, dashed off in a nearly illegible scrawl, would always close with the recognizable sign-off:

Yours in war,
High Pockets

Clara Fuentes was not a Philippine national nor was she of Italian extraction, and she wasn't actually named Clara Fuentes. Her real name was Claire Phillips, and she was an American by birth, hailing from Portland, Oregon. The press would later call her "America's Mata Hari." Gleaning information from soused Japanese officers was only part of her M.O. as an American insurgent and spy. Her nightclub served as a clearinghouse for information, contraband goods, and all manner of sub rosa activities. The hostesses at Club Tsubaki were all dedicated to the resistance movement; some of them took Japanese-language classes during the day in order to converse intelligibly with their customers at night. Phillips used the proceeds from Club Tsubaki to purchase food and medicines that were smuggled into Cabanatuan camp on a routine basis. On one occasion, she was responsible for collecting more than 10,000 quinine tablets, which were surreptitiously slipped into Cabanatuan, saving hundreds of lives. Deriving her code name from her habit of stashing secret letters inside her brassiere, High Pockets risked her safety each week tracking the flow of messages in and out of Cabanatuan. Inside Cabanatuan, the name High Pockets became a legend, although few were aware of her actual identity. In their minds, she was a rumored-to-exist saint, or perhaps a group of saints, from whom life-sustaining gifts flowed each week. Many prisoners referred to her as "the Angel."

Claire Phillips was the kind of person who seemed to drift against the grain of events, her life shaped by a series of near-misses and contretemps. She arrived in Manila in September 1941, an inauspicious time when every American who could was hurriedly clearing out of the place. War loomed, but she was either unwilling or unable to see it. Restlessly unhappy with her staid life in Portland and looking for a new adventure after a recent divorce, she was taken with the idea that Manila would be a fine place for her to develop a career as a torch singer. Show business was in her blood. She'd dropped out of high school to tour with a tent show, and in her twenties had traveled widely with American theatrical stock companies. Almost immediately she found a job singing at a popular club called the Alcazar. One night after a performance she met an American sergeant from the 31st Infantry, a radioman named John Phillips. They fell for each other, and the romance developed quickly. They danced with several thousand other couples at the famous Santa Ana cabaret, on the dance floor touted to be the largest in the world. They spent nights drinking gin at the newly opened Jai Alai Club and watching the Basque ballplayers fiendishly swatting their wicker paddles for the betting crowds. Afterward she and "Phil," as all his friends called him, would wander through the old Spanish precincts of the Intramuros, strolling the desolate streets dimmed by the test blackouts. When they reached her apartment, they'd lie together in the darkness listening to the ghostly whine of the air-raid sirens.

By early December, Claire and Phil were talking openly of marriage. When the initial Japanese attacks came on December 8, however, they were forced to put their plans on hold. Not knowing what else to do, Claire joined the growing civilian exodus to Bataan. Throughout the month of December, she lived with various Filipino friends on the peninsula, staying as close as possible to her fiancé's unit. On Christmas Eve, Phil and Claire were married by a local Catholic priest. There seems to have been some question about the legality of the nuptials; Claire had apparently failed to have her previous marriage formally annulled. Although the paperwork was in disarray, the priest made allowances for the chaotic circumstances of war and pronounced the couple man and wife. Sergeant Phillips unexpectedly had to return to duty the next morning, spoiling the Christmas feast the newlyweds had begun to prepare. In the weeks that followed she tried to keep close to her husband in the hope of seeing him from time to time, but in the pandemonium of the siege, they lost all contact. When the surrender came on April 9, she still hadn't located Phil.

Shortly thereafter she hooked up with John Boone, an American soldier who had, like her husband, been in the 31st Infantry. Having refused to surrender, Boone was arming a band of insurrectionaries and heading into the hills to wage guerrilla war on the Japanese. Boone convinced her to join the resistance by going to Manila and setting up an espionage ring that would forward to the guerrillas intelligence reports on Japanese troop and ship movements. Phillips lay half naked in a cane field for days to darken her skin so she might more easily pass as a native. Then she returned to Manila, obtained phony papers from a friend in the Italian consulate, and established her new identity as Dorothy Clara Fuentes.

John Boone may have nudged Phillips in the direction of espionage, but the bold idea of starting an officers' club for the Japanese was hers alone. She joined forces with a Filipina dancer named Fely Corcuera, who knew a bit of Japanese and had already developed a following among Imperial Army officers while dancing at another nightclub in town. Club Tsubaki opened its doors in October 1942 to rave reviews in the Japanese-controlled press. At the close of her first week, Claire Phillips aka Clara Fuentes aka Dorothy Fuentes aka Madame Tsubaki aka High Pockets could scarcely believe how well the ruse appeared to be working. Although she spoke not a word of Italian and looked only vaguely Mediterranean at best, none of her clients seemed to question her identity. "I had to remind myself," she said, "how thin the ice was I was skating on."

High Pockets' regular customers at Club Tsubaki included many of the most powerful Japanese men who passed through the Philippines. There were generals, admirals, submarine captains, doctors, merchant marine skippers, and zaibatsu businessmen. There was Colonel Saito, "rotund head" of the Department of Propaganda. There was a mining company president named Hochima, a movie star named Kawazu, a symphony conductor named Ichikawa, and a young scion of the powerful Mitsui family. Early on, some of her customers balked at her high cover charges and drink prices. "It is necessary to pay to be exclusive," she would tell them, and this seemed to placate them. Phillips found most of the pseudo-amorous discussions around the bar to be little more than "nauseating prattle—you rike me? I *rove* you!" but it was astonishing how often the banter seemed to do the trick. After the hostesses had warmed up the guests, Phillips or her assistant, Fely Corcuera, would "cajole the alcohol-be-fuddled men into talking about troop movements, and the conditions of the roads and bridges."

During the daytime the club saw a constant flow of activity—as runners, suppliers, and relief workers came and went. Usually these operatives were disguised as telephone repairmen, peddlers, bottle collectors, and meter readers from the utility company. High Pockets kept up a brisk correspondence with John Boone's guerrilla organization. All the operatives had code names—Morning Glory, Papaya, Compadre—and all the notes were written in a trun-

242

cated argot. If the information High Pockets had sent him was especially helpful, Boone would write back, "Beans delicious." If the news was stale, he'd jot down, "Cabbage spoiled on arrival." The messengers had to be extremely cautious, for if they were caught by the Kempei Tai, the Japanese military police, they would face torture and possibly death. One runner slipped his notes into a special pair of double-soled shoes. Others would make an incision in the center banana of a bunch, tuck the message inside, and fasten the skin back into place.

Much of the information that High Pockets was able to glean from her customers didn't amount to anything of strategic importance, but occasionally she'd stumble upon something of vital significance. One night a naval captain entered the club and soon became quite drunk and voluble. He told Phillips that he had just arrived from Bougainville with many troops. "They are all wounded?" Phillips inquired, as she had seen the ship docked in the harbor earlier that day with conspicuous Red Cross markings on its hull. The skipper laughed loudly and replied, "No, they are all first-rate troops. It is not really a hospital ship." Phillips forwarded this tidbit to Boone posthaste, for "it seemed to me rather important that we know the Japanese use hospital ships for troop transport."

One of High Pockets' customers was the commander of a submarine flotilla. He had taken a fancy to Madame Tsubaki and insisted that she perform a certain provocative fan dance that he had once seen, years earlier, in San Francisco. He told her that he had to leave for the Solomon Islands in two days. "You return tomorrow night," Phillips promised, "and I'll do the dance." Hurriedly, she sent word to Boone relating the flotilla's departure date and destination. Then she and Fely stayed up most of the night sewing a pair of flesh-colored tights and making fans from split bamboo and tissue paper. The next night the commander showed up for his special "bon voyage party," with forty Navy officers in tow. High Pockets performed the fan dance beneath a prurient red spotlight. Phillips later wrote, "The commander and his forty guests almost lost their eyesight straining to determine whether I was nude behind the fans." High Pockets' intelligence reached Boone and, ultimately, USAFFE headquarters in Australia, and most of the flotilla was eventually sunk. Several months later, an officer returned to the club and informed Madame Tsubaki that he was one of the few survivors. As he drank to the memory of his comrades, Phillips and her dancing girls "all shed a few crocodile tears."

Another Navy officer, this one an aircraft carrier captain named Arita, took a special interest in High Pockets' partner, Fely Corcuera. Captain Arita came night after night to see her perform and to sit close with her on the rattan settees. "Arita was a fine chap," Phillips wrote. "He told us of his home and family in Japan, how he would be glad when the war was over, so he could join them." One day Captain Arita announced that regrettably he was leaving in a few days, and Phillips decided to throw him a farewell bash. At the party Fely asked the captain where she could write to him. Arita, who was not a drinker, freely explained that he was sailing first to Singapore and then to Rabaul. Phillips promptly relayed this information to the guerrillas and wept when Arita departed, for she realized she was "sending him to his doom."

Sometime in late October 1942, Father Buttenbruck, the German Catholic priest who helped the resistance in Manila, sat Phillips down in his study and soberly shared with her a piece of news that he'd learned on a recent trip to Cabanatuan. Her husband, whom she had not heard from since Christmas Day, had fallen seriously ill during the march from Bataan. In July, wasted by malaria and malnutrition, he had died. John Phillips now lay buried in a mass grave at Cabanatuan.

In the depths of her grief, Phillips received a secret missive from a prisoner at Cabanatuan, Chaplain Frank Tiffany. The note consoled her on the death of her husband and explained in greater detail the circumstances of his passing. Chaplain Tiffany ended his note in a beseeching tone. He wrote, "But I beg of you not to forget the ones that are left. They are dying by the hundreds." A new thought took root in her mind. Up until then, Phillips had envisioned using her club primarily as a focal point for espionage activities. With Chaplain Tiffany's note, she recognized that Cabanatuan's needs were far more pressing. In this way, she found herself drawn into the desperate world of the camp and its newly established smuggling rings. As Phillips put it, she would work "on both sides of the ledger"—making money off the Japanese and using it to buy food and medicine for the Americans. It was a Robin Hood scheme.

From October 1942 through the spring of 1944, Phillips sent clothes, medicine, hospital equipment, literature, radio components, and a considerable amount of money into Cabanatuan. She was instrumental in printing up a periodic tabloid sheet detailing the latest war developments—an underground source of news that worked wonders for camp morale. Members of High Pockets' organization unraveled bedspreads and reknit the thread into socks. They scoured the pharmacies and hospitals of Manila collecting tens of thousands of quinine tablets. With money raised from the nightclub, her operatives would go to the local markets and buy massive quantities of native calamansi oranges, which they would boil with sugar to produce a fruit concentrate rich in vitamin C. The "life-giving juice," as she called it, was bottled in demijohns and smuggled into Cabanatuan to counteract the advanced scurvy then widespread among the camp population. One of her main smuggling conduits at the camp was a young Filipina named Naomi Flores (aka "Looter"), who lived near Cabanatuan and who had secured a Japanese license as a peanut vendor. Other smugglers found that certain guards could be induced to look the other way with gifts of watches, pens, or cameras, so High Pockets spent a portion of her club proceeds purchasing bribery trinkets on the Manila black market.

Hundreds of letters trickled in and out of Cabanatuan through her organization. High Pockets regularly corresponded not only with the chaplains who were responsible for distributing the smuggled goods but also with individual prisoners, some of them old friends of John Phillips, who wanted to relay their gratitude for her benevolence.

Dear Friend,
So you are Phil's wife. Your letter was a God-send. I had begun to think that we in here were the Forgotten Men. Thanks for the money. I sure can use it. I'll be known from here on as Sky Pilot.

Dear High Pockets:

Yes, I'm the same Gentry you knew. I met you at
Louise's apartment a few times . . . I heard several men
here talking about an angel named High Pockets
sending things in. I never dreamed you were the angel.
I got shoes . . . with part of the money you sent. Been
barefooted for the past year. . . . I got bananas with the
rest . . . I'll try to repay you someday, somehow. God
bless you. Gent.

Hello High Pockets:

When I got your letter I came to life again. Gee, it's
good to know someone like you. You deserve more
gold medals than all of us in here together. You've
done more for the boys' morale in here than you'll
ever know. Some of them are flat on their backs and I
wish you could have seen the looks of gratitude. In
answer to your question about John's grave . . . don't
worry, Pal. When it's all over you and I will come back
here and get John.

Chaplain Tiffany (aka "Everlasting") wrote High Pockets frequently. On one occasion Tiffany urged her to write
a "cheer-up note" to a hospital patient named Yeager, who
was critically ill. Tiffany's next correspondence acknowledged Yeager's receipt of her note.

We read the letter you wrote Yeager all over the
hospital area and everyone got a big laugh. It sure
cheered the men up. I had to do the reading as Yeager
is almost blind. I bought eggs, milk, and fruit for him
with the money you sent. Yeager says to tell you he

would like some candy. The quinine arrived okay. We can make use of all you send. I hate to be begging all the time, but I do need shorts for my church services. I am ashamed to stand in front of the men looking so ragged.

God bless you, Everlasting

In a subsequent letter, Tiffany followed up on Yeager's status.

Yeager got the candy and enjoyed it very much. He insisted I take one piece. He died the day after your candy and letter arrived. (It wasn't the candy I'm sure.) I know you worked hard to save him, but it was just not meant to be.

As the months slipped by, Claire Phillips became ever more keenly aware that she was pushing her luck beyond all reason. Her operation had grown large and multitentacled, and even though she had exercised extreme caution at every turn, it was impossible for her to ignore her deepening peril. Running Club Tsubaki proved to be a nightly high-wire act; the stress of her work caused her physical and mental health to deteriorate. On one occasion a Japanese officer who had spent time in Rome quizzed her on her knowledge of several popular Italian songs, and she caused titters of suspicion when she came up dreadfully short. On another occasion, a powerful Japanese businessman ransacked her club after she refused his numerous advances. Eventually, the perpetual anxieties of her espionage work got the better of her. One day during a meeting with some of her operatives, she collapsed on the floor in excruciating pain. A Filipino physician, who was a personal friend and a member of the resistance, removed six inches of her ulcerated intestine. The procedure was successful but she contracted a nearly fatal case of tetanus from the operation, developing a dangerously high fever and the characteristic lockjaw. Antitetanus serum was temporarily unavailable in Manila, so a friend at the Bureau of Animal Industry manufactured a veterinarian version of the antitoxin in time to save her life.

Phillips recovered and resumed her work, but her fears only intensified. With all the projects she had simmering between Manila and Cabanatuan, Phillips knew that eventually the Kempei Tai was sure to catch a scent. She was pretty sure her phone had been tapped—on more than one occasion she had heard "the unmistakable sound of a throat being cleared." If the military police intercepted just one of her runners, her whole operation could unravel. Too many tracks led to Club Tsubaki, too many players drifted in and out. "We were all in it too deep to think about quitting," Phillips wrote. "But I was worried about how many people were 'in the know.' I had to rely on a sixth sense."

On one notable occasion her quickened intuition may have saved her life. One day a Filipino boy arrived at her back door with a formally worded note from a "Captain Bagley," soliciting help for his guerrillas in the hills. Phillips was immediately suspicious. She'd never heard of Captain Bagley, nor had she ever seen the Filipino runner before. Quickly studying the letter while the boy stood waiting at the door, she decided on the spot that it was specious.

Phillips made a great show of indignation. "I am an Italian!" she shouted. "I'm not interested in the least in Americans."

She dismissed the young messenger with much histrionics and then had a club employee tail him. Across Luneta Park, the boy was seen conferring with four military policemen. Phillips waited in dread for the early-morning knock on her door, but none came. The Kempei Tai must have accepted her reaction to the boy's phony message, but it was now abundantly clear that Club Tsubaki was under surveillance. "More and more," she later told an American magazine, "I feared the net would envelop me."

On May 23, 1944, it finally did. That morning the military police burst through Club Tsubaki's door and apprehended Phillips in her housecoat and slippers. "Where are your papers, Madame Tsubaki?" one of the agents shrieked, shoving a revolver into her ribs. "You are a spy!"

The men blindfolded her and led her across town to the Kempei Tai headquarters. The interrogation was led by an intelligence officer who spoke solid English. "We know everything," he began, then added, with an incisive lilt, *"High Pockets."*

It shocked Phillips to hear her code name on Japanese lips. She realized that the Kempei Tai had intercepted a message. "But to whom?" she wondered. "Boone? If so, I was as good as dead."

The officer began reading a note she had written to "Everlasting" (Chaplain Tiffany) and at once she understood the origin of the dragnet. Clearly a Filipino runner had been apprehended at Cabanatuan.

"Who is Cal?" her inquisitor demanded.

Phillips explained that "cal" was an abbreviation for

250

calamansi, the small citrus fruits she'd been sending into the camp as a concentrate. In the letter, Phillips had mentioned that she was running low on demijohn containers.

"And who is Mr. Demi John! We are no fools! Cal, John—these are American names!" The inquisitor was certain these two were American guerrillas to whom High Pockets was connected, and there was no convincing him otherwise.

A pair of goons broke into the room and assaulted Phillips, hitting and kicking her until she lay bleeding on the floor. "Please—do you have an English dictionary?" gasped Phillips, who, still blindfolded, was now fumbling for her chair. "Look it up, demijohn is in there!"

The guards stripped her and tied her to a bench. She felt something forced into her mouth, a cold nozzle of some kind. She heard the metallic creak of a spigot and then a stream of water gushed from the tube's opening, at great pressure. This was the "water treatment" about which she'd heard so many horror stories. Her throat and lungs flooded, and she began to drown.

Phillips passed out. When she came to, the guards were pressing lit cigarettes along the inside of her thighs. "Answer who is Cal!"

High Pockets spluttered a few feeble words about oranges, but the inquisitor furiously interrupted, "So I see you want more water!" The hose was again inserted into Phillips' mouth. "Then the water poured in," she wrote, "and I died all over again."

Once more Phillips revived, and still she refused to acknowledge her connections to American guerrillas. Frustrated with their inability to break her, the guards transferred Phillips to the dungeons of Fort Santiago, the old Spanish citadel built along the banks of the Pasig close to where the river empties into Manila Bay. Santiago was famous for the diabolical design of its basement torture chambers, which, as a result of a network of pipes and grates connected to the river, became fully flooded with the brackish water at high tide. Fortunately Phillips was given a room higher up in the stone complex. For three months she languished in solitary confinement inside a dark cell, awaiting her sentence.

— — — — —

After the Kempei Tai captured High Pockets, its agents then went to work identifying her contacts within Cabanatuan. Most of these contacts were camp chaplains, and although they usually used code names in their letters to Phillips, not all of them did. Without yet realizing it, these men were in mortal danger.

In a world of perpetual suffering, the chaplains played an exceedingly important role in the life of the camp. Theology was an immediate, and intensely practical, matter. The mysteries of survival often condensed down to spiritual mysteries. The prisoners saw daily evidence of the spirit world, felt the constant beckoning tug of dead comrades beseeching them to join the ghostly ranks. The men saw the way some individuals kept their faith even through their moments of deepest anguish, while others seemed to give up easily and will themselves to go, almost as though surrendering the spirit were a disease in and of itself.

Cabanatuan's chaplains constantly found themselves in the midst of the most profound life-and-death questions. As mediators, as maintainers of morale, as defenders of a guttering flame, they were presented with a nearly impossible task. Favoring scriptural themes taken from Job, the Babylonian Captivity, and the trials of Christ, the chaplains wrote their sermons in tiny, cramped letters on the backs of can labels. Every day they had to explain the unexplainable. They were the ones who were supposed to have the answers.

In truth, not all of the chaplains were admired. Some acted as though they were too good for the muck and despair of prison camp and appeared to display an almost Pharisaic aloofness. Others looked distressingly well fed. One of the universally respected men of the cloth, however, was a former regimental chaplain of the 31st Infantry named Robert Preston Taylor. Chaplain Taylor was among the core group of ministers with whom High Pockets corresponded. She had briefly met him on Bataan before the surrender. Her husband had known him well and had great admiration for him. Texan by birth, Baptist by denomination, Taylor was tall and thin and gangling, even in times of plenty. His skin was fair and splotchy. He had a crust of bristly red hair and ruddy cheeks, and he spoke softly in the piney woods dialect of East Texas. He was well educated, having received a bachelor's degree from Baylor University and both a masters and a Ph.D. in theology. Yet Taylor was extremely unassuming, one of twelve children of a rural family from the flat tornado country due east of Dallas, not far from the Louisiana border. His parents were poor farmers, so poor that when he was a teenager, Taylor trapped furs to put himself through school. Tommie Thomas, who once served as his chaplain's assistant, described Taylor as "common as an old shoe. You'd never have known he was a chaplain if he didn't have his insignia on."

When Taylor was preaching, however, he seemed to undergo a personality transformation. As he became entranced with the spirit, the fervor rose in his voice and he flailed about as though he were wrestling with Satan himself. Ralph Hibbs fondly recalled Taylor's great expenditures of energy. "With some consistency," Hibbs said, "the Japanese decided to give our chaplains half-ration because 'they just talk and no work.' This generally might have been true, but if you ever saw redheaded Bob Taylor grapple with the devil in a Sunday morning arena, you'd give him a ration and a half."

Whether in battle or in captivity, Taylor was known for instinctively placing himself at the point of maximum danger. On Bataan, where he served on the front lines, Taylor won the Silver Star for taking immense risks carrying wounded soldiers from the battlefield. Shortly before the surrender, Taylor had ventured out to find a group of his comrades who had become separated from the rest of their unit. He succeeded in finding them, but then the group became surrounded by the enemy. For the better part of a week they hid in the jungles, wounded and starving, forced to wage isolated battles with the advancing Japanese troops in order to survive. In Fort Worth, Texas, his wife, Ione, received a report that he was "unaccounted for" and presumed dead. At Cabanatuan, he worked in the most hopeless place of all, the Zero Ward, ministering to the terminally ill, risking his own life by living in daily exposure to contagious diseases. It was said that Chaplain Taylor was the only man at Cabanatuan to whom you could give a glass of powdered milk intended for the sick and know with perfect assurance that it would reach the hospital untouched. In the ward, he was remembered for turning prayer into an athletic act. Taylor conducted last rites and burial ceremonies by the hundreds if not the thousands. He played a pivotal role in securing medicines and supplies for his ward while helping doctors make some of the toughest triage calls. "He was a huge influence on the camp," said Tommie Thomas. "Everyone knew him and respected him. Wherever people were most in need, that's where you'd find him."

In one of her letters to the camp, High Pockets had asked Chaplain Taylor if there was anything he'd like to have—something special, just for his own personal use. "I said, 'I don't need anything,'" he later told an oral historian. "Then on second thought, I said, 'Well, if she can get her hands on a Greek New Testament, send me one.' I had studied Greek and I thought I could refresh myself. Of all the things to request in a prison camp!"

One day in April 1944, the Kempei Tai apprehended one of High Pockets' runners and found a Greek New Testament with an inscription that said, "To Chap Bob from High Pockets." The Japanese quickly figured out that Chap Bob was Robert Preston Taylor, and Captain Suzuki, the camp commandant at the time, called him in for interrogation. Soon the guards had rounded up a dozen other prisoners they viewed as ringleaders, most of whom were also chaplains. Commandant Suzuki was certain that the chaplains had direct ties to the guerrillas and was determined to torture them until they revealed the names of their contacts. Chaplain Alfred Oliver was beaten so ruthlessly that his neck was broken. A prominent camp doctor, Colonel Schwartz, was held so long without water and food that he hovered on the verge of death; several of his doctor colleagues succeeded in releasing Schwartz on the specious grounds that he was suffering from acute appendicitis; then they staged an "appendectomy," going to the trouble of making a superficial abdominal incision without anesthesia in order to convince the Japanese guards of the procedure's authenticity. "The Japanese never requested to see the surgical specimen," Dr. Hibbs recalled. "Much to our amazement, Colonel Schwartz was allowed to return to his own quarters."

Chaplain Taylor faced the longest and most grueling ordeal of all. He was thrown into the "heat box," a tiny bamboo cell designed to "sweat the truth out." There he stayed locked up in solitary confinement for the summer of 1944. Unable to stand up or stretch out, he spent his entire sentence in an awkward squatting posture. Without exercise, the flesh of his legs withered away and he developed grotesque sores from sitting on hard bamboo. "The worst part," Taylor said, "was not knowing whether it would ever end." In the daytime he was able to read in the narrow shafts of light that shot through the slats of his cell. He worked his way through five readings of the Bible. Someone slipped him a copy of Dostoevsky's *The House of the Dead,* in which he encountered with great interest the famous passage: "The degree to which a society is civilized can be judged by entering its prisons."

During his ninth week of solitary, Taylor's dysentery got the better of him and he lapsed into a coma. American prison doctors who were allowed to visit Taylor thought he had died and succeeded in securing permission to remove the chaplain's body for burial. When they gained entrance to the heat box, the doctors realized he was faintly breathing. They quietly moved Taylor to the hospital, without disclosing to the Japanese authorities that he was actually alive. For the following week, the camp held a vigil as Taylor drifted in and out of consciousness. Everyone in camp recalled how steadfastly he had prayed for the condemned men of Zero Ward; now the tables had turned, and the camp was praying for him. "Hundreds of men milled around outside the hospital ward, waiting for word about Taylor," the chaplain's biographer would recount. "Most of them had been in the hospital at one time or another and knew how faithfully the chaplains were trying to help the sick. More than any other person in the prison, he had encouraged others to hope. Now it was their turn to reciprocate."

At last, one morning in mid-September, Taylor opened his eyes. Within a week he was seen hobbling around the hospital grounds with a hand-carved bamboo cane. Some of the more religiously inclined prisoners thought Taylor's recovery was a miracle. In what was perhaps a corollary miracle, Commandant Suzuki stepped down that very week and was replaced by a new official who was more lenient and unaware of the history of the Kempei Tai dragnet. The whole matter was dropped.

On the morning of September 24, just a few weeks after Chaplain Taylor was released from the heat box, the camp was aroused by an unforgettable noise. "We heard a tremendous droning coming over the mountains," Taylor recalled. "Then, suddenly, aircraft came streaking right over us, dozens and dozens of American planes." The reaction within the camp was electric. The planes were Navy

257

Hellcats orginating from Admiral Bull Halsey's aircraft carriers, which were then steaming in the Philippine Sea not far from Leyte Gulf. Taylor watched the planes with astonished glee as they sped past Cabanatuan and swarmed off in all directions over the Central Plain, seeking out targets. Later, the men could sense the trembling detonations of distant bombs. In succeeding days, more planes were spotted in the skies, and it seemed to the men that the tide was dramatically turning in their favor. "The flyover was a great morale builder," Taylor said. "We thought, well, it's going to be over in just a week or two." Henry Lee, the lieutenant from California who had written so many poems during his stay at Cabanatuan, spoke eloquently of the men's returning sense of hope.

> *And still we have faith—faith in your might*
> *In each bright weapon in the far-flung fight*
> *And in the blood of weary men*
> *Who take the coral beaches back again*

The high hopes in the camp were abruptly dashed on October 7 when the Japanese authorities announced that a large contingent of prisoners—some 1,600 in all—was to be shipped to Japan. Cabanatuan would become little more than a hospital; only the sickest would stay behind. With MacArthur's return imminent, the new policy of the Imperial Army was becoming clear: As the Japanese pulled back to the home islands, they planned to drag along all prisoners healthy enough to work so as to prevent them from falling into American hands. The Japanese intended to use them as slave laborers, putting them to work in munitions factories, mines, mills, foundries, and shipyards across Japan and Manchuria. Over the past few months, the Japanese had been systematically siphoning off Cabanatuan's population, sending large details of men to Manila to await the next available ship. The camp census had steadily drained from a peak of 8,000 men to slightly more than 2,000. Boatload after boatload of prisoners had left the Philippines in unmarked transport ships, aiming north for Japan through the warm blue expanse of the South China Sea.

Because the Americans were fast winning control of the skies and seas, this latest shipment of 1,600 prisoners would be the final exodus, the last boat out. A few prisoners actually *wanted* to go—they figured anyplace was preferable to Cabanatuan, and they clung to the vague hope that they'd eat better in Japan. But most of the men dreaded the notion of leaving the Philippines with liberation seemingly so close at hand, and they greatly feared the long odyssey through submarine-infested waters.

Among the 1,600 chosen to go were Colonel Curtis Beecher, the American commander of the camp, and Lieutenant Henry Lee, who would carefully wrap his notebook of poems in six layers of canvas and bury it beneath the camp library in the hope that someone would find it after the war. From the days of the Bataan battle, Lee had displayed a remarkably stoic, and sometimes fatalistic, attitude about his chances of survival. In one of his last letters home to his family, he had written:

Dear Mother, Dad and Frances:
My prayer each night is that God will send you, who are suffering so much more than I am, His strength and peace. During the first few days of war I also

259

prayed for personal protection from physical harm, but now I see *that* is something for which I have no right to ask, and I pray now that I may be given strength to bear whatever I must bear . . . Life and my family have been good to me—and have given me everything I have ever really wanted, and should anything ever happen to me here it will not be like closing a book in the middle as it would have been had I been killed in the first days of the war. For in the last two months I have done a lifetime of living, and have been a part of one of the most unselfish cooperative efforts that has ever been made by any group of individuals.

Chaplain Robert Taylor, reasonably well recovered from his stay in solitary, was also selected to make the journey to Japan. Taylor viewed the trip with intense trepidation. "We all suspected," he later said, "that the possibilities of successfully making the sea voyage were remote."

Since being sick was the only way a person could avoid going to Japan, nearly everyone at Cabanatuan suddenly developed acute ailments of one kind or another. The Japanese wouldn't simply take a "sick" prisoner at his word, however; they required proof. Among other things, they made all the prisoners submit stool samples to check for the presence of amebic dysentery. Anyone who tested positive had a better chance of being passed over. Inevitably, a few entrepreneurial-minded dysenterics began selling their "hot stools" to healthy fellow prisoners—for a steep price. In this way, scores of the relatively hale and hearty won reprieves from the impending voyage.

Robert Body was one of them. "I tried every method I could think of to avoid going to Japan," he said. "I told a friend of mine, 'Jeez, I'm gonna have to go. I'm on the shipping list.' He said, 'Give me the specimen can, I'll get you a positive.' And he did. I turned it in to the lab and got myself waived. So I stayed and somebody else's name got put on the list."

Finally the shipping list was solidified. The 1,600 men were trucked to Manila and kept for two months in a sour national prison known as Bilibid. On the morning of December 13, they were herded through the walled city and taken to Pier 7, where a great Japanese passenger ship was docked. On the side of the boat was the designation *Oryoku Maru. (Maru* is a common designation on Japanese vessels; thought to derive from an ancient word for "circle," it conveys the hope that through all its voyages the ship will return safely to harbor.) Taylor brightened when he saw the vessel. A former luxury liner that had been built around 1930 and turned into a troop transport during the war, the 7,300-ton ship was in good condition and seemingly well equipped. Perhaps, he thought, the voyage to Japan wouldn't be as uncomfortable as he'd feared.

For a short while he imagined that the prisoners were to ride in the ship's first- and second-class quarters. Then a group of approximately 2,000 Japanese nationals approached the pier, many of them with their wives and children in tow. These well-dressed, slightly anxious-looking civilians were clearly intended to be the *Oryoku Maru's* first-class passengers. They were the professionals who'd been running the country during the occupation—engineers, merchants, diplomats, accountants, and clerical workers. Now, before it was too late, they were scrambling

261

home. The Japanese families smiled vaguely as they filed by with their bags, trying not to register their disgust at the prisoners' wretched presence. As the distinguished passengers stepped on board, the ship's captain bowed deeply and escorted the various parties to their berths.

Waiting on the hot pier for the Japanese to complete their boarding, Chaplain Taylor looked out over the calm waters of Manila Bay and felt a sharp frisson of dread: The American planes had turned the harbor into a marine graveyard. The vast crescent of blue was littered with wrecked warships and transports. Manny Lawton, a prisoner from South Carolina who was a good friend of Bert Bank, remembered the "bomb-blasted, rusting hulks, some listing heavily, some upright with water washing over their decks, others identifiable only by smokeless stacks reaching helplessly toward the sky." The scene's devastation set up a complicated range of feelings in the men, for while they were heartened to see the toll American planes had lately been taking on Japanese shipping, they understood that the *Oryoku Maru* could be next. "With disturbed hearts," recalled Taylor, "the men milled around restlessly on the dock, as though it were the night before an execution."

The prisoners started boarding the vessel around three o'clock. "The Japanese were very anxious to get us aboard in a hurry and get us out of there," wrote Taylor, "because they knew that the American planes would be back." The guards prodded them up the gangplank and across the wooden deck and then emphatically gestured toward the hatch leading to the ship's hold. One by one the 1,600 men descended the narrow stairway into the blackened cargo spaces below. It soon became apparent that there was insufficient room to accommodate the legions of men, but the guards continued packing the prisoners in, hurrying them along with sharp, hissing reprimands, swatting them with brooms.

Inside the ill-ventilated hold, the air was stifling and stale, and the temperature quickly grew infernal from the collective heat of the prisoners. The sweaty bodies were pressed tightly against one another, and still more men came wedging in. On the sunny side of the ship the metal skin of the hull was too hot to touch. The anonymous depths of the hold were so dark that a man could not recognize his best friend standing next to him. A single beam of milky sunlight slanted in from the hatch's small aperture. "The heat was indescribable, unbearable," said Taylor. "We perspired profusely and became gripped by a gnawing thirst." Bodies steamed. Some men licked the sides of the hold, hoping to find beads of condensation. Within minutes, the close environment became life-threatening. Soon the prisoners were gasping for air and passing out from lack of oxygen. A great cry of panic rose up from the hold, the screams and moans of suffocating men.

The Japanese interpreter on deck peered down into the hatch. He was a particularly cruel and small-spirited man known to the prisoners only as Mr. Wada. "You are disturbing the Japanese passengers!" Wada shouted. "If you don't shut up, I will be forced to close the hatch cover."

This quieted the prisoners for a few minutes. They felt the great engines of the *Oryoku Maru* rumble to a start. The ship weighed anchor and slipped away from the docks in a convoy of other ships. The prisoners had hoped that the ship's movement would breathe fresh air into the hold, but it didn't. Soon the screams of panic rose up again.

Wada returned. True to his word, he fastened the hatch cover. The hold went pitch black. The men could not believe it. This time they erupted with shrieks of abject despair, pushing and shoving in pandemonium. From the din, a single voice emerged. A man named Frank Bridget climbed high on the stairway and shouted down at the teeming masses in a clear, resolute voice. "Gentlemen," he said, "we're in this thing together and if any of us want to live we're going to have to work as one." Bridget struck just the right cool note at just the right time, and the hysteria abated. "Keep your wits about you," he urged. "If we panic, we're only going to use up more precious breaths of oxygen. Now listen—we're all going to calm down, every one of us."

Bridget was not a high-ranking officer, nor was he especially well liked or admired. Prior to this day, he had been known as a nervous, intense, overeager guy who wore jodhpurs and generally rubbed people the wrong way. But this day he rose to the occasion in a remarkable act of poise and resolve. Manny Lawton, who had positively hated Bridget before, remembered his display of natural leadership with awesome gratitude. "Sometimes people rise to greatness," Lawton told an oral historian, "and you never can predict who will. Bridget was waiting in the wings, and he took responsibility. I don't know where he found the calmness. He saved us with his voice."

"Now hear this!" Bridget yelled. "The men in the far corners are suffocating! Take off your shirts and hats and fan the air toward them." The men responded and the improvement was almost instantaneous.

Bridget then climbed all the way up the stairs and cracked open the hatch cover, shouting to Wada, "I'm coming up to speak with you. I'm telling you, Wada-san, I'm coming up." Wada vaguely knew Bridget from their days in camp and respected him as someone who played by the rules. Bridget explained the situation down in the hold and told Wada that people were dying of suffocation. With the same firm clarity in his voice, he beseeched Wada for buckets of water and asked that the hatch cover be kept open. He requested permission to gather up those who had passed out and to bring them up on deck so they might revive themselves in the fresh air. Remarkably, Wada agreed to all of Bridget's requests.

"You may bring four at a time," Wada told Bridget. "Any who attempt to escape will be shot."

The unconscious men were hauled over the heads of the prisoners and handed up the stairway, where they were laid out on the wooden planking. The ship was puttering slowly south out of the bay, with the jumbled steeples and parapets of Manila receding in the background, and the wrinkled mountains of Bataan rising dimly off to starboard in the fading light of the day.

The *Oryoku Maru* was nearing the tip of Mariveles when the sun sank. All through the night, the ship motored slowly around the Bataan Peninsula. In the pitch black, the men became crazy with fear. They shrieked gibberish, they cried and clawed at each other in claustrophobic hysteria. "No one could sleep because we could feel men constantly butting around in the dark," recalled Manny Lawton. "They didn't know what they were looking for or what they thought they could do, but they couldn't just sit there in that floating dungeon." Some were so crazed with thirst that they drank their own urine. Others turned into human vampires, biting their fellows in the dark and sucking their blood to "satisfy their lust for liquid," as Lawton put it. Men had murder on their minds. Throughout the hold were the sounds of strangulation, of men turning on one another in madness and bashing each other with their canteens. Only when the thin rays of morning came were the men able to learn what had happened in the crowded pit.

Fifty men had died of heat prostration, bad air, and human malice. "It was a nightmare of darkness and suffocation," Taylor recalled. "We had suffered the torments of perdition, the worst night of our lives."

--- --- ---

At approximately eight-thirty that morning, December 14, airplanes appeared in the skies. The *Oryoku Maru* hadn't made it very far in the night, having only rounded the tip of Mariveles and worked its way up the serrated west coast of Bataan. The ship's antiaircraft gunners began firing, and all prisoners scurried belowdecks. The men could hear the planes diving toward the ship followed by the staccato rattle of their machine gun strafing. Hot .50 caliber bullets angled into the open hatch and ricocheted through the hold, wounding several prisoners. The men heard bombs dropping all around them, exploding in the water, destroying other ships in the convoy. The planes kept circling back for more strafing runs. Frank Bridget sat on the top step of the stairway and surveyed the battle in the skies, narrating to the men below as though he were a radio announcer. "A flight of Navy planes headed this way. Two peeling off to attack a freighter . . . several burning ships in view."

Perhaps it was Bridget's influence, but the men remained

remarkably calm as they listened intently to the sounds of the planes hectoring the ship. Some even cheered the planes on, momentarily forgetting that the pilots' success was their own doom. "The prisoners were soldiers to the very end," Taylor recalled. "As the guns were strafing the decks of that ship, the men were yelling, 'Give 'em heck, pour it on!' And here we were right down under it." No one seemed to panic at the prospect of being sunk. "We were prepared for the ship to explode and destroy us all," Taylor said. "We had processed ourselves to accept whatever comes."

Bridget continued his narration. "Here comes another one, boys, he's getting closer . . . closer . . . *duck.*"

A bomb smashed into the water nearby, blasting a jagged hole in the side of the *Oryoku Maru* just above the waterline, instantly opening a vent of bright, fresh air in the hold. Then the men felt a terrific concussion off the stern of the ship. It was not a direct hit, but the rudder was damaged irreparably, and the crippled *Oryoku Maru* ran aground at a place called Olongapo Point, in Subic Bay. The planes vanished in the afternoon glare, and in their absence, the men could hear the wails of the Japanese passengers above. The strafing had chewed up the decks and severely damaged the staterooms and sleeping berths. Hundreds of Japanese were dead or wounded, many of them women and children. American doctors were summoned from the hold to treat the injured. All through the night the men could hear the sounds of the Japanese passengers being off-loaded from the ship and ferried to shore in lifeboats.

The next morning, December 15, Mr. Wada poked his head into the hatch and told the prisoners to prepare themselves for leaving the ship. They would all be swimming to shore, which was only about five hundred yards away. While they were organizing themselves into groups, they heard the dread sound of Navy dive-bombers speeding over the Bataan Peninsula, barreling down toward them. On their second pass, the planes dropped a string of bombs and scored a direct hit on the aft hold of the ship, where Chaplain Taylor happened to be stowed. Taylor and the group of ten men for whom he was responsible all hit the floor in a cluster. The explosion blasted off the stern of the *Oryoku Maru* and ignited a fire in the hold. Some two hundred men died instantly.

"After the impact of the explosion," Taylor remembered, "a hail of falling debris and planks rained down on us. Then there was a moment of complete silence, not a scream or a moan, when everything seemed to be over." Semiconscious, Taylor struggled to his feet and inspected his wounds. He'd taken a piece of shrapnel in his hip and one in his wrist that left his hand numb. He looked around and saw that only one other prisoner from his immediate group of ten was moving. The other eight were dead.

While doctors tended to the wounded, a long, panicked procession of prisoners issued from the smoky hold. On deck, Wada shouted orders while the guards nervously pointed with their guns toward the place on the beach where the men were supposed to swim. With hundreds of others, Chaplain Taylor hurled himself off the port side of the ship into the warm shallows of Subic Bay. Taylor winced as the salt water bit into his fresh shell-fragment wounds. Guards positioned on the beach with tripod machine guns began to shoot at anyone who strayed too far one way or the other from the mainstream of swimmers.

When approximately half of the prisoners had vacated the listing ship, the men heard the growling approach of still more American planes. Three Navy dive-bombers, in tight formation, were streaking low and aiming straight for the *Oryoku Maru*. Americans on the decks began to wave desperately at the planes. At the last second one of the dive-bombers pulled out of the formation in sudden recognition. Finally, the pilots appeared to understand that these were American prisoners they'd been bombing and strafing with such tenacity. The planes banked over Subic Bay and disappeared in the late-morning haze.

Manny Lawton and one of his friends were among the last Americans to leave the sinking ship. When they climbed out of the hold and stepped on the carnage-strewn deck, they were startled to encounter the proud captain of the *Oryoku Maru*. "The captain looked sad but not as distressed as he might have been," Lawton wrote. "Short, stocky, and neat in his clean white uniform, he approached us. In broken English and in a not unfriendly tone, he urged us to go."

"You must hurry," he insisted. "Danger to explode."

Lawton and his buddy bowed politely. "The captain returned our bow with a half-smile," Lawton recalled, "then turned and walked toward where the bridge once was."

It took the better part of an hour for the last of the swimmers to reach the shore. They were assembled on the beach and then herded onto a nearby tennis court that had once been used by the U.S. Navy. There, under the blistering sun, loosely following the faded court lines, they were organized into long rows. Colonel Curtis Beecher clambered up to the old referee's platform and began to take roll. The head count was a laborious process. When it was finished, Beecher determined that their ranks had dwindled to just over 1,300—and many of those were seriously wounded, their flesh sliced and mangled by shrapnel.

Several hours went by, and then the Navy planes returned. Satisfied that the American prisoners had all vacated the smoldering ship, the pilots dealt the *Oryoku Maru* a deathblow. The prisoners stood on the baked slab of the tennis court and watched with glee as the hated ship went down. "The planes barreled down one right after the other," Chaplain Taylor recalled, "and dropped a string of bombs from bow to stern. That old ship went up in flames in just a few minutes. It didn't take long to sink."

The *Oryoku Maru* sagged and glurped in Subic Bay, belching black smoke. "Each of us harbored an intense hatred for the *Oryoku,* as if she were something beastly and alive," Lawton wrote. "After two hours, she settled a little deeper into the water as if nestling down to sleep, and there she rested."

On the tennis court, the men erupted in a malignant cheer.

The Americans were detained on the tennis court for six days. Exposed without protection to the roasting sun, the mostly naked prisoners became severely burned. The guards fed them a handful of raw rice each day and permitted access to a single trickling spigot. The several dozen prisoners who died on the court were buried outside the tennis court fence on the sandy beach, with Chaplain Taylor presiding over the funeral ceremonies.

The men had no inkling what the Japanese intended for

them now that the ship had been destroyed. Their health was deteriorating fast. Many of their shrapnel wounds had become gangrenous. The doctors, lacking surgical instruments, were forced to perform amputations by razor blade. In lieu of anesthetics, four or five men would pin the screaming patient to the concrete slab as the doctors methodically nicked the infected limb away.

As the general health situation worsened, the doctors pleaded with the guards to allow for the most severely injured prisoners to return to Cabanatuan or Manila for hospital treatment. Eventually, to the doctors' surprise, Mr. Wada agreed to the request. Fifteen of the worst American casualties were placed on a truck and taken east over the spine of the Zambales Mountains. Instead of transporting them to Cabanatuan, however, the guards drove to a remote spot in the jungle. The prisoners were told to crawl off the truck and assemble in a long line. The guards then drew their swords and, steadily working down the line, decapitated all fifteen Americans. The bodies were buried together in a shallow grave that would be discovered at the end of the war.

On December 20, the 1,300 denizens of the tennis court were trucked to the town of San Fernando and, after several more days of waiting, squeezed into narrow-gauge train cars—the same cars they'd ridden nearly three years earlier at the conclusion of the Death March. Hoping to discourage air raids, Mr. Wada ordered scores of bandaged prisoners to ride on the roofs of the boxcars so they might wave off attacking American planes. The tiny freight train rattled north through rice and cane country and finally creaked to a halt, fifteen hours later, at Lingayen Gulf.

The prisoners spent Christmas packed into an old

school building near the gulf shores. Then, on December 28, they were led to the docks and taken aboard a decrepit ship named the *Enoura Maru,* "an old scow," as Chaplain Taylor called it, "that was full of lice and looked as though it hadn't been cleaned in ten years." The day was cold and overcast, and the surging seas were the color of pewter. A freighter with a 10,000-ton displacement, the *Enoura Maru* rode high on the whitecapped water. Abovedecks, the ship was carrying several hundred badly injured Japanese troops. Wada told the prisoners to head for the ship's hatchways. When the men descended the rope ladder into the rusty hold, they were dismayed to discover that the *Enoura Maru* had formerly been used as a cavalry ship, transporting large numbers of horses belowdecks. The straw-lined floor was pungent with the ammonia of animal urine, and swarms of flies whined among the scattered heaps of manure.

The *Enoura Maru* slipped out of Lingayen Gulf in a small convoy, tacking sharply through the swells to elude American submarines. For four days the ship crept across the South China Sea, toward what was, for the prisoners, a mystery destination—Wada had never told them where they were going. On several occasions American submarines pursued the ship; the prisoners could hear the rumble of Japanese depth charges, followed by distant shudders in the water.

The hold was frigid and drafty, and the ship bobbed crazily in the turbulent seas. In one sense, though, the prisoners were grateful for the stormy weather—they could stand under the open hatches and collect rainwater in their mess tins and canteens, the only drinking water many would receive during the entire voyage. The Japanese occasionally lowered a wooden bucket of cooked rice, but by the time it reached the floor of the hold, the food was coated with black flies. Later the Japanese stopped feeding the prisoners altogether. "American submarines sink our supply ships—no food for you!" Wada reported with an edge of gleeful menace. Eventually, the ravenous men found themselves picking through the rancid hay for grains of oat feed on which to chew.

Prisoners died aboard the *Enoura Maru* at a rate of approximately four or five a day. They were, as Chaplain Taylor recalled, the "easiest deaths I have ever witnessed—the men went to sleep and awakened no more." Wada permitted the Americans to gather the day's dead and haul them up on deck. The naked corpses were wrapped in burlap sacks weighted down with stones. Chaplain Taylor would say a final benediction and then the bodies were eased into the sea.

On January 1, 1945, the *Enoura Maru* dropped anchor in the port of Takao, on the southwest coast of Formosa. The wounded Japanese troops above decks were loaded onto barges and taken ashore, but the American prisoners were kept in the hold for eight miserable days, as the boat rode at anchor in the harbor. Then, on the morning of January 9, the same morning that American forces were landing at Lingayen Gulf in the Philippines, the prisoners aboard the *Enoura Maru* heard the sound of dive-bombers in the skies over Takao. A plane swooped over the length of the ship and dropped a stick of bombs. Chaplain Taylor could hear the scream of the incoming explosives. Everyone in the hold leapt to the floor and buried themselves in the foul hay.

In one of his poems from Bataan, Henry Lee had

described an aerial attack from Bataan much like the one he was now experiencing:

> *I saw the bombs drop*
> *Tiny specks which grew as they fell*
> *Twinkling like silver coins*
> *Falling through clear water*
> *I felt neither fear nor hatred*
> *Only desire to have it over quickly*

The bombs found their targets. Hot shrapnel shot through the hold. As the *Enoura Maru* shuddered and rolled in the harbor, a black rain of splintered decking sifted down upon the men. An immense steel girder fell through the hold, pinning a hundred prisoners to the floor, instantly killing scores of men. After the dust settled, the sunlight shone brightly into the hold, and the scene was abominable. Manny Lawton recalled the "tangled, grotesque positions of violent death . . . limbs ripped from bodies and heads and torsos wrested apart." Those who were relatively uninjured tried to lift the massive girder, but finally they gave up, leaving their pinned comrades to slowly die.

The *Enoura Maru* was utterly disabled, but it didn't sink. It wallowed unsteadily in the sunny harbor, a bombed-out husk of a boat splattered with unimaginable gore. The prisoners had to wait three more days before the Japanese finally came aboard to offer assistance of any kind. The bodies were thrown several dozen at a time in a giant cargo net, hoisted by crane onto a barge, and taken four miles away to the beach, where they were buried in a mass grave.

The bombing of the *Enoura Maru* had claimed the lives

of 295 Americans. Of the 1,600 who had left Manila a month earlier aboard the *Oryoku Maru*, nearly 700 were dead. Chaplain Taylor was among the survivors. Lieutenant Henry Lee, the Cabanatuan poet, was not.

> *I could not know the meaning nor the way*
> *I was not one with all that time must end*
> *Until one hopeless, joyless, bitter day*
> *I looked on unmasked death and saw a friend*

It is believed that Lee died instantly in the blast. The letter his parents were to receive back in Pasadena would say only that he was "Killed in Action."

Incredibly, the guards were still determined to carry out their orders and transport these last remnants of Cabanatuan to Japan. Chaplain Taylor and some 930 other prisoners were off-loaded from the *Enoura Maru* and placed aboard a third ship, the *Brazil Maru*. On January 13, the vessel sailed out of Takao harbor, heading north for Japan.

Book Two

Harrow Hell

We are not pleasant people here, for the story of war is always the story of hate; it makes no difference with whom one fights.

The hate destroys you . . .

Agnes Newton Keith
Three Came Home

Chapter 8

The Pampanga River spills cold from the mountains of northern Luzon and courses south through the rice country before emptying into Manila Bay as a broad, mazy delta of brackish channels, aquaculture ponds, and mangrove swamps. One of the longest rivers in Luzon, the Rio Grande de la Pampanga, as it is sometimes called, is the island's central drainage, flowing thick with silt and volcanic ash. Much of the year the Pampanga runs swift and wide and deep, and even in the dry days of January it can be a treacherous stream in places, especially if pulsed by a surprise winter storm. For most of the dry season, however, the river braids quietly through the long reaches of the Central Plain, the turbid water swirling around sandbars, skimming low along the banks.

As the Rangers approached the Pampanga at a quarter past five on the afternoon of Tuesday, January 30, shortly after leaving Platero, they were pleased to confront the river in its more placid, winterized state. Spread out before them was a modest stream gently churning through a dry floodplain several hundred yards wide. Standing at the banks, Mucci realized that the raid on Cabanatuan, as it had been planned, would not have been possible in any other season. Hauling his men and equipment across the roil of a fully engorged Pampanga would have been logistically difficult, at best, while attempting to ferry 500 weak prisoners back across would have been unthinkably dangerous. Even now, the river was chin-high in places, the current formidable. Mucci anxiously scanned the skies to make sure no thunderclouds were mounting on the horizon. "I prayed that there wouldn't be any rain before we got back," he would later write, "because it was the kind of river that could rise a couple of feet in a very short time."

Fortunately, Pajota's guides were familiar with a spot in the Pampanga where the main stem forked into two shallower streams that coursed around a small island of silt. The current in these two subsidiary streams was weaker, and at their deepest points the waters rose only to the men's thighs. Marching single file with their rifles clutched over their heads, the Rangers easily forded the first stream, tramped over the soft sandbar, and then waded across the second channel to the far banks.

While the Rangers slipped across the river, Pajota's force split off to the left and Joson's men to the right, each group vanishing in the bamboo thickets along the banks. Mucci was more than a little concerned about the guerrillas. Never having worked with them before, he could only hope that they had the training, the wherewithal, and the inclination to hold the road for as long as it took. His skepticism wasn't merely grounded in U.S. Army chauvinism. Guerrilla warfare, with its reliance on small-scale sniping, lightning ambush, and subterfuge, was vastly different from the sort of fixed battle that the guerrillas were now preparing to wage along the highway. Mucci worried that in a direct confrontation with elite Japanese troops, the guerrillas might prematurely bolt, overwhelmed by the sustained potency of a well-trained, well-equipped regular army.

At one point, earlier in the day, he'd betrayed his suspicions by reiterating to Pajota the vital importance of holding the road at all costs. "We *will* hold, sir!" Pajota had reportedly answered. "If the enemy passes, it will be over our dead bodies." But now, as the guerrillas departed for their respective posts, the colonel still nursed his doubts.

It took fifteen minutes for the long file of Rangers to ford the warm brown waters of the Pampanga. Their pant legs soaked, they emerged from the muddy river into a cogon field. They were in high spirits. After holing up for nearly twenty-four hours in Platero, they found an almost giddy sense of release in forward movement, in the simple camaraderie of marching again. The delay had been a terrific boon, working wonders on their morale. Now the men were revitalized, with good local food in their bellies, a half-decent night's sleep, and a full day of catnapping in the shade.

As the men walked, Mucci strode up and down the column, slapping backs, rallying with his staccato pep talk. He was a bantam surging with resolve, the oldest man of the lot and yet stoked with twice the energy of the others—"a real pusher," as one Ranger called him. More than anything, Henry Mucci loved to march men. He took obvious pleasure in the élan, the sweaty effort, the sheer kinetics of it. For him, commanding achieved its highest form when it was on the hoof. Whether he was marching forward or backpedaling, his pace was always strenuous, his steps curiously large for a man so small. As one Ranger put it: "He consumed the ground with his strides." He had the drill sergeant's mysterious knack for being, or at least seeming to be, everywhere at once, seeing everything. He made himself heard, and he made sure the men believed what he believed. As he marched alongside the men, his coaching voice was clear and insistent without being shrill, and it had an irresistible quality that said *you can do anything*. "He didn't bellow or holler or swear," recalled Ranger Howard Baker. "He didn't need to. He had such a forceful voice that when he wanted something done, it got done in a hurry."

"Mucci was so charismatic you couldn't believe it," remembered Alvie Robbins. "He had this air of total confidence about him. If you ever had to go to war, that's the kind of man you wanted to go with." Vance Shears put it this way: "We all would have died for him. He was the very best."

Even the sober, circumspect Captain Prince, grimacing from the pain of his blistered feet, was inspired by Mucci's effervescence. "The man was just a born salesman," Prince recalled. "We knew he was selling us blue sky, but we would have followed him anywhere."

Not everyone was in good spirits, though. First Lieutenant John Lueddeke and the other combat photographers were dismayed to learn that the choice action of the raid would in all likelihood transpire in the dark. Mucci had brought them all this way to document history, and then he'd chosen, inconveniently, to schedule history after hours. It was the ultimate war photographer's tease—to be carried so titillatingly close to the action and then to be denied light. Flashbulbs or klieg lights were out of the question. Not only would artificial lamps be grossly insufficient to illuminate such a broad sweep of benighted terrain, but using them at all could be lethal, for any sort of flash would instantly give away the American position to the Japanese sentries.

The Signal Corps men had thus become a fifth wheel, or so they felt. Lueddeke and his men could shoot pictures of the marching to and from the camp (they'd already shot a good bit of material, in fact), but during the raid itself they'd be relegated to the role of "prisoner escorts." It was honorable duty, to be sure, but for proud combat photojournalists, a letdown. As one of the photographers would later put it: "It was as if I'd brought my favorite weapon into battle only to be told I couldn't fire it."

———————

Late afternoon was taking on the complexion of dusk. The sun's rays slanted low through the high grass and the temperature began to drop from the infernal to the merely intolerable. A gusty breeze made a constant play of swirls and ripples in the cogon, as though a distracted artist were beginning whimsical thoughts and ending them abruptly. As they snapped through the coarse grass, the men's collective mood was one of buoyant and almost carefree adolescence. They joked and gibed with one another. They boasted about how many Japs they would kill. They toted their weapons like toys. The gathering zeal of the march, it seemed, had momentarily suppressed their sense of the mission's gravity. As one Ranger described it, they could have been "bounding off to a rugby match."

After a half mile, the tall grass fields turned into rice paddies, a quilt of blond stalks and black mud stretching to the highway. The men adjusted their gazes. All conversation, all joking stopped. They squinted and shielded their eyes with cupped hands to break the glare. There it stood, a tattered city of thatch and razor wire swimming in the heat waves. The view was hazy but unobstructed, a straight shot south. The Rangers were startled and at the same time a little relieved to lay eyes, finally, on the target after three days of thinking about little else, to affix an image to the strange word they'd been uttering since Mucci first announced the mission. *Cabanatuan.*

The camp was imposing in size and appeared to be well guarded, but even from their safe remove the Rangers could see that it was no impregnable citadel. The enclosure enjoyed no height advantages, no defensive works, no intervening obstacles of water. Rising only slightly above the vegetational haze, the compound consisted merely of barbed wire stretched taut across a field, with wooden towers studding the corners. In an ordinary strategic sense, taking it should pose no insurmountable problems.

What made the target so intimidating was its emphatic isolation. Cabanatuan was a world unto itself, standing alone, a civilizational cyst. Nothing else broke the horizon for miles in any direction—nothing but the one nipa shack in which Nellist and Vaquilar had been crouched all afternoon.

Mucci and Prince surveyed the terrain with worried looks spreading over their faces. Trained to capitalize on the asset of surprise, Rangers instinctively shied away from open ground such as this. Considering how well armed his men were, Mucci might have been willing to risk forfeiting surprise in this case were he not also forced to consider the hair-trigger delicacy of the situation inside. One tiny mistake, he recognized, could provoke the very outcome they were trying to prevent—a slaughtering of prisoners.

Prince gave the signal and the men stepped forward, crouching in silence. They fanned out over the rice quadrants in broad waves of thirty men. Their boots crumped over the hard, cracked floors of the paddies, scattering flocks of field birds and reedy insects. Rice stalks rustled in a fickle breeze. The men were silent but for the random clicks and rattles of their weapons, the low friction of canvas rubbing canvas.

After a hundred yards of stooped marching, Prince gave another hand gesture, this one a signal to the men of F Company, releasing them on their separate errand. According to the plan, one platoon from F Company—thirty men in all—would break off from Prince's main group and, after describing a wide arc around the eastern perimeter, would assume attack positions in the rear of the camp. They had the longest way to go and would thus need more time to reach their destination than Prince's C Company would. The rear of the camp was more than eight hundred yards away from the main gate and impossible to see from the front of the enclosure, so Prince would have no way of knowing when F Company had arrived at its position. (The men had opted not to use walkie-talkies because they might create too much noise.) All of which explained why Prince had decided that F Company should initiate the raid by firing the first volley.

The men of F Company's 2nd Platoon were led by a young lieutenant from Springfield, Massachusetts, named

John Murphy. A sinewy man with a bony face and lugubrious, deep-set eyes, Murf, as nearly everyone called him, had graduated from Notre Dame and wanted to pursue a career in politics after the war. He was a cautious, understated leader in whom Mucci and Prince had implicit confidence. Prince figured Murphy's group would need about an hour to skulk around to the back of the camp. If all went according to plan, the next sign of F Company would be the deafening report of their weapons firing on the rear guard towers—the unmistakable fillip that would set everything in motion.

— — — — —

At approximately 5:45, Colonel Mucci, Captain Prince, and some ninety C Company Rangers and Alamo Scouts resumed their march to the south, aiming directly for the main gate. After traversing one more square of rice, however, Prince concluded that the danger of detection was growing unacceptable. They had drawn within less than a mile of the camp, with the guard towers not only visible but beginning to take on definition. Captain Prince lowered his hand in a sweeping gesture, and then all the Rangers fell to the ground. For the remaining three-quarters of a mile, they would have to chart a slow, steady advance on their bellies—an army of snakes.

Lying on the crusty floor of a paddy, the Rangers strapped their rifles to their backs or held them out in front, loosely cradled in their arms. Then they dug their knees and elbows into the dirt and began inching forward, pulling themselves through the long, straight rows of dried rice. The ground was strewn with old carabao dung, and the flat expanses were occasionally interrupted by shallow puddles faintly spluttering with tadpoles and schools of tiny fish. At one point, a group of Rangers disturbed an unseen nest, and armies of red ants skittered over them by the score, darting under their clothes, leaving trails of welts on their skin.

Even though the men were hugging the ground, Prince began to fear that the Japanese would spot them anyway. The dikes that delineated the paddies were as hard and thick as brick walls and more than two feet high in some places. Each time the Rangers came upon one of these earthen dividers, they had to climb up and over, exposing themselves even more conspicuously for a few terrifying seconds before dropping down into the next quadrant. This awkward hop, performed by so many Rangers in spasmodic intervals across the field, seemed like precisely the sort of unnatural movement that would snag a guard's attention.

Yet, for some reason, it didn't. Slowly, painstakingly, the Rangers advanced another five hundred yards with impunity—and another. They were smeared with mud and drenched in sweat. Their necks ached, their shoulders burned, their arms trembled from a hard hour's game of playing serpent. They were drawing tantalizingly close, close enough to see movement inside the compound and even make out the shapes of guards perched in the towers. When they passed by the lone nipa shack, Nellist and Vaquilar, the two Alamo Scouts who'd been patiently sitting inside, shinnied down the ladder and joined them.

The late-afternoon winds had gradually abated and a leaden silence fell over the plain. The sun grew fat and luxuriant as it lowered itself beside Mount Arayat, the vast dormant volcano to the southwest. In the sanguinary light, the jagged ridgelines of the Sierra Madre to the east broke through in sharper, richer blues, and the haze of the fields seemed to lift. Prostrate before enemy sentinels, enveloped by open earth and open sky, strung out over nearly a hundred yards, the men felt utterly exposed, as though the Shinto gods might be following their progress and waiting for the right moment to impale them. "I don't know why they didn't see us," recalled Ranger Alvie Robbins. "There was plenty of light. If they had been really looking with their glasses, they could have seen that there's something going on out there that's not right."

Then a strange noise pierced the silence—a signal of some kind, a loud bell coming from somewhere within the camp. It sounded and sounded and sounded again. Its tone was clangorous, businesslike, persistent, like an alarm.

Prince and Mucci traded glances of panic. By the dozens, the men reached for their rifles and unfastened the safety switches. The Rangers hissed at each other across the field:

"Hell is that?"

"Think they spotted us!"

The bell kept ringing. The men shoved clips into their rifles, trained their sights on specific targets. Mucci and Prince held steady, waiting for more definitive signs inside the camp.

If the Japanese opened fire, the Rangers' backup plan was crudely simple: Rise up from the rice paddies and charge the camp, John Wayne fashion. This had already been decided back in Platero. "There wasn't a whole lot else we *could* do," Prince recalled. "We were stuck out in the field. We'd come all this way. We tried to think about those guards. What would they be doing? Many of them would be off duty, we decided. They weren't likely to be near their weapons. They weren't going to be ready for combat. It seemed obvious to us. If they spotted us, we had to go for it."

On and on the bell pealed. Frantically, the men strained to see what was happening inside the camp. "We couldn't figure out what those chimes were," remembered Ranger Vance Shears. "We really thought we'd been spotted. We figured it was for the worst." Some Rangers found themselves bridling the impulse to stand and race toward the gate, to strike the first blow before the Japanese did. Others thought it was not Prince's group but rather the men in F Company who'd been spotted, over on the east side of the compound. Whatever the bell meant, it seemed inauspicious, and the men braced for a fusillade. Mucci and Prince still didn't budge.

The bell stopped tolling, and the camp was tranquil again. Prince lay as flat as he could, blood thrumming in his ears.

Then there was an explosion, coming from deeper within the camp. It sounded for all the world like a gunshot, or possibly a mortar. Panicked, one of the platoon leaders, Lieutenant William O'Connell, jumped up and motioned with his hands for everyone to run because he felt sure they'd all been spotted. It was a unilateral decision and completely impulsive. Somebody shrieked at O'Connell, sotto voce, to get back down, and the next instant he hit the dirt.

Captain Prince waited a few excruciating minutes to see whether a disturbance would develop inside the enclosure.

He could discern figures milling around inside the camp but nothing that indicated confusion or haste. To him, everything looked normal. A guard in one of the towers appeared to be enjoying a smoke. Prince lingered several more minutes before rendering his assessment: The Japanese hadn't seen them after all. The bell must have signified something else, he concluded. (In fact, it was the Navy watch bell, dutifully rung by one of the loyal prisoner timekeepers.) And the explosion must have been another backfire from one of those kerosene-fed Japanese vehicles.

The whole company gasped in relief and occupied a few long moments collecting their nerve, waiting for the adrenaline to settle. "I figured we had to be just about the luckiest people on earth," said Roy Peters. "I couldn't believe the guards hadn't seen O'Connell when he stood up. The Lord had just closed those Japanese eyes where they couldn't see—that's the only way I could figure it."

Prince glanced at his watch—6:40. Dusk was fast approaching, with a blood-orange sun half sunk in the Zambales Mountains. The Rangers were nearly within striking distance, less than a half mile from the gate. Captain Prince gave the signal, and warily the men resumed their measured, wriggling advance.

Chapter 9

One night in early January, as the men of Cabanatuan were clustered around their nipa barracks enjoying the stars and the cool, they turned their attention to the north-western sky, where a powerful and odd-looking storm was gathering strength. Somewhere over the South China Sea, the heavens seemed to be on fire, with an orange-red fluorescence rippling across the horizon. If they had been in the far north and not the Asian tropics, they might have been tempted to call it the aurora borealis. The strange light saturated broad reaches of the sky. It waxed and fizzed and waxed again, following an erratic pulse, growing feeble at times but never quite dying out. These slow red surges were punctuated by short bursts of yellow and white, scores of smaller flashes speckling the horizon like heat lightning. The storm must have been fifty or sixty miles distant, far enough so that the prisoners couldn't accurately gauge its force or location. It threw off a murky luminance, as though filtered through a thick lens of atmospheric moisture. Every so often, the ground shook beneath their feet with a faint, dislocated violence that could be felt but not heard.

That night Tommie Thomas was standing outside trying to remember where he'd left off on the imaginary house he'd been building in Grand Rapids. As he slapped mortar with his trowel, Thomas smoked a thin cigarette of coarse Filipino tobacco soaked in sugarcane juice. He was shirtless and barefoot, and he wore only his cloth G-string.

Then the skies lit up and pulled Thomas away from his construction reverie. The red glow startled him. The view was especially vivid because the Japanese had imposed a full blackout on the camp to discourage American air raids—no electric lights, oil lanterns, or open wood fires—and this rendered the evening sky impressively dark and untainted. He didn't quite know what to make of the spectacle in the skies, nor did his friends. They talked about it among themselves with great animation. If it was an electrical storm, they decided, it was the strangest one they'd ever seen.

Some of the prisoners who had acute night blindness or other ophthalmological maladies resulting from nutritional deficiency couldn't see the peculiar light—or if they did, they refused to trust their own eyes. Bert Bank, for one, was unable to detect anything on the horizon. But Thomas, confident of his vision and sure that something unusual was afoot, wanted a better explanation. He walked around camp soliciting opinions until he found someone who was a naval expert.

"That's Lingayen Gulf," the man said emphatically, his face tinctured by the rosy glow. "Those are star shells lighting up the place. The Yanks are preparing to land."

Thomas' spirits soared at the thought of it—*the reinva-*

sion of Luzon. This was a moment he'd been dreaming about for a thousand days. Not that it was any surprise that MacArthur's army was drawing close. The jury-rigged radio hidden in camp had kept the prisoners apprised of the Sixth Army's leapfrogging advance from New Guinea. They had heard accounts of the battle of Leyte Gulf, the largest naval engagement in history, in which the Japanese were decisively defeated by Admiral Nimitz's dreadnoughts. They'd heard that MacArthur had waded onto the Philippine island of Leyte, some four hundred miles to the southeast.

But more recently, the men of Cabanatuan didn't need a radio to grasp what was happening; they were getting firsthand evidence of America's return directly overhead. Increasingly, they'd seen dogfights between American and Japanese planes in the skies over Cabanatuan, and they'd heard American bombs crashing all about them. They'd watched in perverse delight as carrier-based planes destroyed the Cabanatuan landing strip—the same strip where their own prison details had spent so many months grading and leveling and digging out rocks by hand. "I don't think a single Japanese plane ever took off from that landing field," recalled Bob Body, who spent weeks slaving on the airstrip detail. "All of us were watching through the barbed wire when the planes came and turned it into a big hole. I can't tell you how ecstatic we were to see our own work go up in smoke."

The destruction of the airstrip came at a bitter cost for one POW, however: A .50 caliber machine gun on one of the Navy planes unjammed at precisely the wrong moment while its pilot was strafing the airfield. The wayward slug shot through the thatch roof of one of the Cabanatuan barracks and struck a prisoner high in the hip, severing a major nerve and, according to one prison diary, paralyzing him.

Of course, the men of Cabanatuan understood that misfortunes of this sort were inevitable in an aerial war, and they came to fear American air raids just as the Japanese guards did. At times they wondered whether Army and Navy intelligence knew that Cabanatuan was an American POW camp. And yet, as dangerous as flyovers obviously were, some of the men couldn't help themselves. Whenever planes streaked across the sky, the prisoners would scurry outside by the scores to wave at the pilots, sometimes leaving out crude SOS signs (with lettering scrawled in charcoal on white bedsheets) bearing semi-facetious messages like BRING MORE TOBACCO.

With so many tangible signs of America's comeback, Thomas knew that any day the Army would land on Luzon. Still, seeing the first flashes and feeling the first concussive throbs of the naval bombardment was an emotional turning point, and he brimmed with tears.

That night the prisoners began to talk about how they would be liberated—how the big day would unfold, the mode and style in which the rescue would happen. Knowing what they already knew about General MacArthur's taste for high theatrics, they imagined that the Army's arrival would be something grand. "Some of us thought MacArthur would personally enter the camp one day about noon with a large fleet of Harley-Davidson motorcycles and that he'd be sitting in a convertible staff car with a large entourage," said Bert Bank. "But I knew MacArthur wouldn't stop there—he'd be riding on a white stallion."

Like so many of the men, however, Thomas and Bank had ambivalent emotions about MacArthur's return. Their elation at the prospect of imminent freedom was soured by darker premonitions. The closer the American Army drew, the more fearful many of the POWs became that the Japanese would eliminate them. They felt that the Imperial Army, locked in its death grip, might resort to anything. Given what the men of Cabanatuan understood about the Japanese martial mentality, with its various echoes and borrowings from the stark codes of samurai days, the hope for Japanese mercy seemed naive. "The fear of a massacre was very prevalent," Thomas said. "Our hopes were high but we were also very, very scared. There were rumors running through the camp about how and when they were going to do it to us. We knew that was a distinct possibility. We figured the time was getting close. We didn't know how or when it would happen, but we figured anything might trigger it. We had to be on the alert all the time. Wherever we walked inside the camp, we kept an eye out for a pathway ditch we might suddenly need to jump in."

"We felt like pawns in an enormous game of chess," said Ralph Rodriguez, a medic from New Mexico who had fought on Bataan with the 200th Coast Artillery. "We wondered what they were going to do once the American Army advanced and the Japanese were stuck with their backs against Cabanatuan City. All we could see was that we were right in their way."

The prisoners seldom spoke of this scenario except in vague phrases like "at the end" or "when they get through with us." But most of the men doubted seriously whether the guards would be inclined to leave behind so many living prisoners. Although most of the men feared an outright liquidation, others conjured up even more elaborate nightmares. They imagined that the Japanese would try to slip them on a boat at night and ship them to Formosa, or take them into the mountains of northern Luzon and try to use them in some way for hostage bait, or even as a human screen in the face of American artillery barrages.

The Japanese master plan for the dispersal of prisoners had thus far made perfect sense. With their empire contracting and their leadership in Tokyo girding for the ultimate defense of the home islands, they'd removed all the reasonably fit Americans and put them on ships for Japan—including the unfortunates on the *Oryoku Maru*. They'd left the dregs in Cabanatuan, with just enough American doctors, medics, and engineers to keep the place feebly up and running. It was a hospital now, for all intents and purposes, full of crazies and dysentery cases and patients stuck in Dr. Hibbs's tuberculosis ward. The new American commanding officer of Cabanatuan was a doctor, a short, irascible fireplug of a fellow with white hair named James Duckworth, and Colonel Duckworth chose Dr. Hibbs to be his "adjutant," or personal assistant. The changes and reductions that had taken place since Duckworth assumed command had been astonishing. In just a few short months, the camp population had dwindled from 6,000 to the present 500 sickly souls. The musicals and movies and other offerings of the camp "morale program" had ceased. The fences were moved in, the work details canceled, the barracks consolidated. Little by little, the Japanese had closed up shop.

As far as the Japanese Army was concerned, this final batch of consumptives and cripples carried the same stigma ordinarily attached to prisoners of war, with several additional layers of undesirability. First, many had contagious diseases that could easily spread to Imperial Army troops. Second, because they couldn't work, these wasted men were deemed useless to the Nipponese war effort. They used up space and medicine and beds, and most significant, they consumed food needed by Japanese troops. Then, too, it was possible for the guards to see that if they spared these sick POWs, they could be sufficiently rehabilitated to become fighting soldiers again someday, perhaps even participating in the homeland invasion which the Japanese dreaded above all else. Why, as a matter of policy, would the Imperial Army permit today's POWs to become tomorrow's invaders? Finally, the prisoners surmised that the Japanese wouldn't want 500 or more American eyewitnesses to their cruelty lining up to testify in a war crimes trial, should the United States ultimately prevail. As Bob Body put it: "We figured they wouldn't want us around to tell the world what they'd done."

If this progression of reasoning failed to paint a dark enough picture, there was the undeniable example set by departing Japanese guards at other POW camps in the Philippines. The mass murder at the Puerto Princesa camp on the island of Palawan had occurred on December 14, only several weeks earlier, and vague stories about the atrocity were seeping into Cabanatuan via the Bamboo Telegraph. "The grim news filtered to us in bits and pieces," recalled Dr. Hibbs, "and by early January it was confirmed. That massacre only reinforced our fears that we would be liquidated."

On many different levels, the Palawan tragedy hit close to home. Puerto Princesa was a well-known satellite of

Cabanatuan. Many times over the past three years, work details composed of Cabanatuan men had left for Palawan, never to be heard from again. Everyone in camp had friends and acquaintances who were supposed to be there. Bert Bank, for example, was close friends with Dr. Carl Mango, one of the 141 Americans who were fatally burned or shot at Puerto Princesa.

And so that night, as the men watched the curious red glow radiating over Lingayen Gulf, they found it difficult not to think about the endgame and what had happened to their comrades at Palawan. "We figured that was going to happen to us," said Ralph Rodriguez. "We'd be the next Palawan. The Japs were retreating and the last thing they were going to do was turn us over to the Americans."

―――――――

Early the following morning, the naval bombardment of Lingayen Gulf began in earnest. The shell bursts were shuddering, deafening, relentless. All morning and through the day the countryside rattled with "smothered boomings and hissing screams," as Abie Abraham described them. The Japanese guards became increasingly alarmed as they watched thunderheads of smoke and debris swelling over the plain. "It filled us with joy," recalled Abraham, "to see the frightened Japanese as they exchanged hurried glances and hopped about uttering unintelligible phrases. You could see in their eyes they were panicked."

The day was dusty and cloudless and warm. Luzon was deep into the dry season. For weeks, the air had been powdered with a fine brown talc that made for labored breathing and gritted up the food. Recently the guards had shut down the Farm, the one sure precinct of greenery and life in the prison's vast circumference of beige. The Japanese had done this in part because the air raids had become so prevalent and in part because, after the *Oryoku Maru* draft of 1,600 men, there were so few Cabanatuan prisoners healthy enough to tend the crops. Now the fields lay in ruins. The tomato plants were stunted, the peppers and camotes ravaged by birds, the eggplants warped on the vines. Beyond the Farm, in all directions, the January landscape was one of similar desiccation—crackly cogon grass, dormant rice paddies, and guava trees whose every limb had been stripped bare of leaves by prison medics to concoct a homemade remedy for amebic dysentery. After three hard years, the camp looked as though it had already been abandoned.

Around noon that day, Colonel Duckworth asked Dr. Hibbs to accompany him to the Japanese headquarters. The commandant urgently wanted to meet with the American commanding officer. Something of major importance was about to happen. The tone of the summons, delivered by sentry, was even more brusque and impatient than usual.

The two doctors walked across to the Japanese side of the camp. They could still hear the typhoon of shells raging over Lingayen Gulf, and they wondered whether the purpose of the meeting was to discuss the turning tide of the war. Over the past few weeks, they'd observed that the Japanese had been behaving strangely. They were restless, distracted, preoccupied. They seemed to be falling into disarray. "Their command was breaking down," Dr. Hibbs recalled. "Their troop numbers were decreasing. The sentry towers were manned at all times but fewer guards filled the pillboxes on the corners. Even the commanding officers, unidentified by name, began to change frequently."

At the padlocked gate that opened to the Japanese side, Duckworth and Hibbs were met by a sentry, who led them to a small, bare room in the headquarters building. The camp commandant and his interpreter clomped across the creaky wooden floor and sat down in spartan upright chairs. Duckworth and Hibbs were not familiar with this commandant. He was unshaven and looked as though he hadn't been sleeping well. His eyes were bloodshot and nervous.

The commandant leaned across his desk and got straight to the point. "We leave in two days," he said. "No guards will remain here. However, you must stay in camp. If anybody tries to escape, *we kill everyone severely!*"

"What will we do for food?" Duckworth asked.

"We leave you one month's supply of rice," the commandant replied. Even as he said this, an American plane swooped impressively over the camp and banked east toward the Sierra Madre. The officer and his interpreter peered out the window and then darted nervous glances at each other.

Dr. Hibbs asked what might be considered an impertinent question. "The war," he said. "How does it look? What is the tactical situation?"

The commandant stood up awkwardly and seemed to be struggling with his emotions. It was impossible to ignore the roar of explosions coming from Lingayen Gulf. Hibbs recalled the strange look on the young officer's face, the look of a man who was "resigning himself to die in a foreign land."

After a long pause, the commandant said morosely, "Tactical situation is obscure. Very, very obscure."

He adjourned the meeting by reiterating his admonition to Duckworth and Hibbs that under no circumstances were the prisoners to vacate the compound. "If you do not obey," he said, "we kill all of you."

－－．－．－

Shortly before dusk two days later, just as the commandant had promised, the Japanese sentries stepped down from their towers, emerged from their pillboxes, and gathered on the little knoll in front of their headquarters. To everyone's astonishment, one of the guards hauled down the Rising Sun flag—"the flaming red asshole," which had been such a thorn in the men's morale all these years.

And then the unthinkable happened. The Japanese swung open the front gate and . . . left. The commandant departed in a small convoy of tanks and vehicles, with his personal prostitute and several officers riding along with him. The rest of the guards simply walked. Dr. Hibbs could barely stifle his glee as he watched the guards "marching down the road without song or cadence," heading toward Cabu. The prisoners didn't know where the guards were ultimately going, but undoubtedly they'd been ordered to rejoin the Imperial Army and take up defensive positions elsewhere on Luzon, as it was obvious that MacArthur's forces would be landing any day.

When the last Japanese sentry left, Colonel Duckworth summoned Tommie Thomas, who as the provost marshal was in charge of the American perimeter patrols that wore special white armbands and policed the fence line twenty-four hours a day to prevent a premature escape. "It looks like we're completely unguarded now," Duckworth said. "While there's still daylight left, get some men together and check it out."

So Thomas and a team of other American guards reconnoitered the entire fence line. Warily, they crossed over and explored the Japanese side of the camp, ducking into every building. Then they reported back to Duckworth. Sure enough, to the last man, the Japanese had quit the place. The prisoners were alone. Not only that, Thomas reported, the Japanese had left what looked to be a tremendous cache of food stored in their warehouse. Duckworth liked the sound of it. With the farm moribund, he had little idea where they would gather enough food to survive. "Marvelous," he said. "At daybreak, we'll raid the pantry."

The men of Cabanatuan didn't quite know what to make of their new freedom—if freedom was in fact what it was. This new predicament was baffling. Was it safe to leave, or would they all be mowed down the moment they tried to break from their apparently jailorless jail? Some prisoners thought the situation was a well-orchestrated trap to lure the men outside the compound so the Japanese would have provocation to shoot them all. Whatever the case, if the men harbored thoughts of a mass escape, they'd have to think again. Peering outside the fence, the prisoners could see much confusion along the highway. Japanese troops and vehicles hustled in both directions. Suddenly the prisoners realized that there had been a certain sense of safety in the guards' presence; now they were completely at the mercy of a large, hungry, chaotic army that was building all around them. "They say the devil you know is preferable to the devil you don't," said Bert Bank. "We began to realize we were in a precarious position. There were so many troops roaming around looking for food. If they were to come into our camp, there was no telling what they'd do, just for the sport of it."

In the meantime, Colonel Duckworth had to maintain order in the camp during this first night of quasi freedom. He was especially worried that some half-deranged POW would try to escape and that such an attempt would imperil the whole camp just as liberation was drawing nigh. He asked Tommie Thomas and his perimeter guard to tighten up their security. "I want everyone ordered to stay put—no escapes or shenanigans," Duckworth barked. "Now more than ever we've got to keep a low profile."

Duckworth's fears were well grounded, for in fact, the worm of conversation had already turned to escape. In the absence of guards for the first time in three years, the temptation to flee was overwhelming. The men even received encouragement from the outside: in one of the shacks, a prisoner found an arrow affixed with a goodwill message pledging help from the local barrios should the Americans decide to break out. "We talked about escape all night, and probably we would have except that so many of us were in such bad shape," said Bank. "Like me—I'm not sure I would have made it because my vision was so poor." Dr. Hibbs entertained the same thoughts of breaking out, but quickly realized the futility of it. "In my mind I strolled right across the cogon grass fields and the rice paddies and walked up into the foothills of the Nueva Ecija mountains," he wrote in his memoirs. "But then I said to myself, 'Patience. You must wait just a little longer.'"

"If we got out, where were we going to go?" Ralph

303

Rodriguez said. "There were tanks. There was traffic on the road, thousands of Japanese troops all around us. All we could hope for was a happy ending."

Duckworth was determined to put a firm lid on Thomas' enticing report about the Japanese food cache—at least until the morning when an organized search party could be dispatched. But, of course, an unguarded warehouse full of food was a white-hot secret at Cabanatuan, and inevitably the word got out.

Throughout the night various bands of men straggled over to the Japanese side to have a look, each group thinking it was the only one with the inside tip. In the warehouse, the plundering had become frenzied. The men hadn't seen this much food in four years. There were cases of Pet condensed milk, bottles of sake, stacks of canned goods, innumerable sacks of sugar and rice, as well as a small menagerie of fowl and a few pigs. There were also large stores of dry goods and supplies—medicines, mosquito nets, shoes, cigarettes, underwear, and blankets. The raiders couldn't believe their eyes.

"We grabbed up everything we could find that was light enough to carry," recalled Ralph Rodriguez's close friend John McCarty, a medic from Texas who had fought with the 200th Coast Artillery. McCarty snuck over to the warehouse with a couple of friends. "I saw someone carrying an empty cigarette ashtray. Someone else got some saltshakers, the first salt for food seasoning they'd had in three and half years."

All the men knew this was an unauthorized raid, and they skulked about in the dark, bumping into one another, whispering and laughing under their breath like adolescent pranksters. At least one of the looters was a high-ranking officer—none other than Dr. Hibbs. "I couldn't very well discipline the others," Hibbs wrote, "since my hand was stuck in the same cookie jar." Hibbs broke open a can of condensed milk and took a sip. "The richness nauseated me," he said. "My stomach was so accustomed to bland food that I had to swallow three times to keep it down once."

John McCarty was poking around in the warehouse when a live duck practically flew into his arms. A friend of his found a butcher knife and cut the duck's throat to save it for a stew they planned to prepare later.

Shortly thereafter a couple of perturbed-looking POWs came running in. "Did you see a duck come in here?" they demanded.

"A *live* duck?" McCarty inquired.

"Why the hell you think we'd be chasing him if he wasn't alive?"

"Couldn't have been this one, then," McCarty said. *"Our duck is dead."*

The duck's original "owners" were livid until they opened up an oven in the kitchen to find an entire baked pig. Evidently the Japanese had left in such a hurry that they'd forgotten about it. McCarty watched as the two lucky POWs "began grabbing and tearing the meat off with their dirty hands and cramming it into their mouths. We tried to trade our duck for half of the pig, and you can imagine where they told us to stick that duck."

––––––

The following morning, immediately after roll call, the "official" ransacking began. Duckworth wanted everyone who was reasonably able-bodied to participate in raiding the Japanese bodegas and transferring the goods to the American side of the camp. It was one work detail at which nobody balked. Quickly the Japanese compound took on the jumbled chaos of a Moroccan souk. Men were running crazily down the pathways and corridors chasing geese and chickens and squealing pigs. Merely at the sight of so much food, the men were noticeably invigorated. "To our hollow eyes, it was manna from heaven, cream on the lugao," one of the prisoners recalled. "We felt like colts in clover," Bert Bank said. "There was sack after sack of rice, thousands of cans of American milk, and enough wood to feed our ovens for weeks."

While a couple of MPs kept a close eye on the front gate for Japanese, the prisoners spent the entire day hauling food in buckets, in crates, in wheelbarrows. They placed the heaviest stuff on an oxcart and pulled it across to the American side. Instead of storing all the goods in an obvious public place (like the mess-hall kitchens), they decided to conceal it throughout the camp so it would be harder for Japanese soldiers to steal it back should they wander into Cabanatuan on a foraging mission. By nightfall, the happy pillagers had picked the Japanese storehouse clean. "Everyone had worked hard and without a complaint," said Tommie Thomas. "Not even the Japanese could have made us work that hard."

Among the more popular items confiscated from the Japanese storage room were several piles of old futons. The men excitedly brought them over to their barracks and looked forward to their first comfortable night's rest in years. As the evening wore on, however, they found the cotton mattresses to be intolerably soft. "This was the first bed I had lain down in since December 1941," John McCarty would later recall in his co-authored memoirs, "but I couldn't get to sleep, I couldn't get comfortable." Finally McCarty hurled his mattress outside and then fell fast asleep on his ordinary bamboo mat. The next morning, he discovered that he wasn't the only one. Outside his barracks, the ground was strewn with futons.

Later that morning, a smaller group of men, including McCarty, decided to push their luck and go back over to the Japanese side to see if the previous night's raiding party had missed anything. In an hour or so they emerged from the Japanese compound bearing several litters piled high with more food and supplies. They rounded a corner and were angling toward the American gate when they suddenly confronted two Japanese soldiers standing beside a tank. Soon a larger group of infantrymen appeared, clutching rifles with fixed bayonets. "So this was the trap," McCarty thought in horror, bracing himself for the end.

Yet the soldiers only stared in bewilderment and sucked air through their teeth in the Japanese fashion, as if this were an entirely unfamiliar situation for which they were hopelessly ill prepared. McCarty thought these newly arrived troops were "stunned" to see them. "I guess we looked like ghosts, all skin and bones and tangled hair. They obviously had not expected to find anyone in the camp."

Not knowing what else to do, McCarty and his buddies bowed politely and continued walking with their sumptuous litters of food, past the tank and the gauntlet of soldiers, toward the American gate. They tried to affect an air of nonchalance as they shuffled by, as though of course they were *supposed* to be pilfering food from the Japanese side of the camp. McCarty and his buddies found themselves saying, in an exaggeratedly chipper tone, "Okay, okay, okay."

The prisoners noticed a tall Japanese lieutenant standing alongside the gate, and they held their breath as they brushed past him. "I looked toward the lieutenant," recalled McCarty, "and damned if he didn't 'okay' us back."

Once they'd made it safely inside the American compound, McCarty and his friends were greeted by a clutch of relieved prisoners who'd been watching every moment of this harrowing encounter. The men of Cabanatuan needed no more close calls for them to realize they'd best get out of the kitchen-raiding business. Several dozen Japanese troops had trickled into camp, and it looked as though they were staying for a while. Nevertheless, they were a different breed from the guards who left two days earlier. They had recently returned from fighting at the front. Shell-shocked and bedraggled, many of them bandaged, they wore tattered uniforms stained with blood. One prisoner described them as "the walking wounded." In his prison diary, veterinarian Herbert Ott said, "They came straggling in—they sure look all fagged out and can hardly walk." Their forlorn expressions and postures spoke volumes about the changing fortunes of the war. "They looked plenty worried," said John McCarty, "but they still had the guns."

These new neighbors treated the prisoners with a strange deference. They kept to themselves and didn't seem to mind, or even notice, that the Americans had plenty of food. At one point they even gave the prisoners some of their rice. "They weren't anything like our regular guards," recalled Thomas. "They were running scared, I think. They kind of let us run the camp." These Japanese troops didn't make the men go on work details. Beatings were a thing of the past. On several occasions a soldier would come over to consult with an American doctor or to ask the Cabanatuan cobbler to repair his shoes, proffering a few cigarettes as payment. Medic Ralph Rodriguez treated one Japanese soldier who had an advanced case of gangrene on his arm. "Nobody would treat him, so I say, okay, I'll do it," said Rodriguez. "That young soldier was so appreciative when he left." Through the fence, John McCarty befriended another Japanese soldier who had studied a little English and "wanted me to tell him about cities in the U.S.A." Other than a handful of relatively pleasant workaday encounters like this, however, it was as though a wall had been erected between the two camps. "As far as we were concerned," one POW said, "they didn't exist."

—————

For a brief period in early January, the men of Cabanatuan camp ate quite well, principally as a result of their having robbed the Japanese stores. And eating well, they found, could work miracles. The sap of life was returning. Astonishing things began to happen to their bodies. For some, the sharp throbbing aches of beriberi diminished. Their night blindness improved. With stronger immune systems, the men recovered from all sorts of miscellaneous low-grade infections that had persistently tormented them. Tropical ulcers shrank, rheumy eyes cleared up. Odd sounds—whistling, humming, laughter—were heard around camp. Here and there, one could see small instances of wasted motion, the superfluous dips and gesticulations of a spirit that abides in vitamins and calories. Atrophied interests revived. The men began to think about sex, and in the mornings they noticed with some curiosity that they were occasionally waking up with erections again.

Mainly, though, they put on weight, as much as a pound a day. It seemed impossible that a body could accrue mass and girth so quickly, but nursed on a steady diet of canned fish and syrupy Pet milk, everyone in camp experienced almost miraculous gains. Ralph Rodriguez, who ordinarily weighed 150 pounds but had plummeted to 90, was back to 120 in the two short weeks following the storehouse raids.

With new stamina, the prisoners grew bolder. One day a few of the men spotted a Brahma cow grazing in the fields outside the fence. Its Filipino owner was nowhere in evidence, and the Japanese, cloistered in their barracks, didn't seem to be paying attention. All the guard towers were empty. The large-humped cow quietly cropped what little grass it could find in the dry field, its hide spasmodically twitching to shoo off the flies. With the peculiar malice of the protein-starved, the men strode out the gate, slipped a rope around the animal's neck, and pulled it into camp. This first step seemed like a move of Promethean audacity: No one had set foot outside the Cabanatuan fence on his own before and lived to tell of it.

Straightaway, Dr. Ott was summoned. The veterinarian looked the animal over to make sure it wasn't obviously diseased. The cow was stunned with a large hammer and then Ott slit its throat. A bucket was placed under the dying animal to collect every ounce of blood. A large group of prisoners looked on as the Brahma cow was cut open, and some of the men wept with joy as they joined in the butchering. Dr. Ott inspected the condition of the organs to look for infections or other abnormalities. When he sliced open the liver, trematode worms boiled out by the hundreds. These writhing parasites were better known as liver flukes, common in the Philippines and harmless when ingested as long as the meat was thoroughly cooked.

Dr. Ott gave the cow his seal of approval and a feast was planned on the spot. Standing in a circle around the fire, the men cooked and ate the flesh within a few hours. They prepared an immense vat of beef stew. They fried up the clotted blood or simmered it to make a consommé. They sucked the marrow from the bones, and boiled the hooves to make a broth. By the day's end, every part had been eaten. "We couldn't imagine it, a whole animal for five hundred people," Dr. Hibbs wrote. "The soup even had fat floating on top of it."

Savoring the foreign sensation of full bellies, some of the men spontaneously threw a party. They sang songs and passed around bottles of confiscated sake. Conversation turned appreciatively to women, their shapes and smells and other attributes. Someone brought out a radio that had been swiped from the Japanese side of the camp and they listened to KGEI out of San Francisco. In the glow of good food and drink, the men of Cabanatuan caught glimpses of a life with grace notes. They were surrounded by Japanese who seemed to wish them no harm. The war was radically tilting in their favor. Even as they listened to a radio signal from home, the vast American armies were coming, after long delay, to fetch them. They were drinking a wine made from a grain they hated, the distillate of a culture they hated even more, and yet somehow they found pleasure in it.

Then a news bulletin on the radio confirmed a rumor they'd been hearing for two days—that General Krueger's Sixth Army had landed on Luzon and was driving south toward Manila. Liberation could be any day. "There were prayers and tears of rejoicing," recalled Abie Abraham. "Many people danced, or at least they tried to. It was quite a startling sight to see those skeletons stand up and make brave attempts at clogging and Highland flings as the Japanese radio blared through the night."

The morning after the party, life at Cabanatuan continued more or less as usual. As welcome as it was, the new dispensation left the prisoners acutely suspicious. They sensed that the favorable situation in camp, the seeming beneficence or at least indifference of the several dozen Japanese in residence, was but a temporary aberration to be enjoyed while it lasted.

And they were right: In mid-January, the picture began to change abruptly. The population on the Japanese side dramatically swelled. As many as three hundred more soldiers marched in from the front to set up temporary living quarters. Tanks rolled through the main gate and parked ominously in the center of camp. Armed sentries returned to the guard towers and sandbagged pillboxes to resume a twenty-four-hour watch. The Japanese eyed everything more closely and began to issue new orders and warnings. The prisoners bristled at the realization that they were prisoners again.

Chapter 10

As the Rangers of C Company crept ever closer to the gates of Cabanatuan, Captain Prince's fear of being detected immeasurably deepened. Then, from the northwest, a godsend. They heard a low and indistinct rumble that seemed to emanate from deep within the ground, but in a few seconds it clarified into a more familiar sound—the clean, metallic hum of prop engines. A fighter was hurtling across the sky toward them at low altitude, coming from the direction of Lingayen Gulf. Soon the aircraft was on top of them—a strange-looking plane, black as anthracite. It had a long capped snout, a swollen abdomen set with cannons, and sweeping black tails—*two* of them. There was a hooked needle stuck in its nose that looked vaguely like a stinger. Stair-stepping back from the cockpit was a confusing array of nacelles and bulbous Lucite housings. On the side of the nose was painted a zaftig nude, in the style of Vargas, with the hand-sketched moniker *Hard to Get.*

Mucci smiled as the plane shot past the camp. This

menacing, insectile-looking thing was, he realized, the answer to his prayers. He'd asked for a plane and the Sixth Army had provided one. In truth, Mucci had half assumed that his request had been bungled, stuck somewhere in the vast mire of inexplicable snafus for which the Army was infamous. Instead, headquarters had come through with the most impressive new fighter in the U.S. air force. *Hard to Get* was a P-61, better known as a Black Widow. The Rangers had seen these strange twin-fuselage war birds back in New Guinea, where they'd been introduced in 1944. Aside from its wicked appearance, what was most remarkable about the Black Widow was what it harbored inside its domed fiberglass proboscis: The P-61, newly sprung from the factories of Northrop, was the first American plane to be equipped with radar—in this case, a large, cumbersome internal dish contraption known as the Radiation Laboratory SCR-720. The air force chose to paint the aluminum-alloy skin a matte black because the plane was expressly designed to be a night fighter, employing radar to chase down targets from dusk to dawn.

The P-61 had proven to be an immediate success in Europe and the Pacific alike. With its arachnid name and appearance, the Black Widow perhaps inevitably acquired a noirish reputation (which its pilots, of course, did nothing to dispel). The plane was invariably talked about and portrayed in archly sinister terms. Nose artists for the Black Widow had obvious good fun coming up with images that conveyed a peculiar combination of vampy salaciousness, love of the night, and a predilection for just plain evil. The various nicknames of the Black Widows clearly captured the spirit: *Sleepy Time Gal, Shady Lady, Moonhappy, Midnight Madonna, Blind Date, Impatient Widow, Satan 13.*

Earlier that afternoon, Mucci's radio request for air cover had been forwarded by Sixth Army headquarters to an outfit called the 547th Night Fighter Squadron, the air force group that flew Black Widows from new airstrips set up along Lingayen Gulf. There were thirty-eight pilots in the squadron, but the assignment to fly over Cabanatuan camp went, more or less by luck, to a twenty-six-year-old pilot from Rainier, Oregon, named Kenneth Schrieber. Accompanied by a radar specialist, Bonnie Rucks, Schrieber took off just before six o'clock from a prefabricated airstrip fashioned out of pierced-steel planking—a new material of connectable galvanized-metal sheeting that enabled the air force to build in a matter of hours runways that once took weeks to construct. Climbing high above the blue scallop of Lingayen Gulf, Schrieber veered southeast, barreling straight over the Central Plain for Cabanatuan.

For the Rangers, pinned down on the rice paddies, *Hard to Get*'s grand entrance inspired awe. The arrival couldn't have been more perfectly timed. The plane banked low over the camp and roared across the Pampanga River, circling back for another pass. Few of the Rangers had been briefed on the possibility that a plane would make an appearance that night, and for a split second they feared that a Japanese plane was pursuing them—or that an American pilot had mistaken them for enemy soldiers. But soon the Black Widow's intent became clear to the Rangers. With their eyes fastened on the gloaming sky, they grinned at each other and shook their heads in delighted admiration.

The Japanese were terrified. Sixth Army headquarters couldn't have dreamed up a more malevolent-looking aircraft to instill fear or attract attention. At first the guards and transient troops thought they were being attacked, and naturally they scrambled for cover. For a short while the scene inside the camp was one of utter confusion. Once the shock wore off and the Japanese realized this probably wasn't an air raid after all, they simply stared up at the Black Widow, stared in wonder, consternation, and disbelief. They were transfixed. They'd never seen such a plane.

For good reason, the Japanese couldn't figure out what the P-61 was doing. Pilot Schrieber did his best to make *Hard to Get* behave as oddly as possible. Without firing a single shot, he performed a series of taunts and feints, wheeling and stalling and reversing directions. At one point, he killed an engine and let the plane falter, as though it was crippled. Feathering the "malfunctioning" engine to make it sound as though it were fatally wheezing, he aimed the plane for a ridge of foothills miles in the distance, trying to convey the impression he was about to crash. For a few moments, he vanished behind the hills. Then at the last possible second he pulled out of it and turned back for another tease.

On and on it went for twenty minutes, this coquettish dance in the twilit sky. Schrieber and Rucks could see the Rangers creeping in the fields and clusters of spindly-legged POWs waving up at them from within the compound. If an emergency developed, the two airmen were prepared to strafe the Japanese with the 20mm cannons that were part of the Black Widow's onboard arsenal. Such an action would have brought its own dangers, however, and thankfully it wasn't necessary. The ruse appeared to be working precisely the way Captain Pajota hoped it would: The guards were looking skyward instead of groundward, and the Rangers were inching forward.

"The idea of an aerial decoy was a little unusual," said Prince, "and honestly, I didn't think it would work, not in a million years. But the pilot's maneuvers were so skillful and deceptive that the diversion was complete. I don't know where we would have been without it."

———————

Captain Juan Pajota and his force of 200 guerrillas had already taken their positions along the highway to the northeast of the camp, spread out on either side of the road in a great "V." Crouched low in the field stubble, holding Springfields and BARs and manning large water-cooled .30 caliber machine guns set on tripods, they could see the Japanese camps clustered in the miasmal bottomlands of the Cabu, just a few hundred yards to the east. Large numbers of enemy tanks and armored vehicles were visible across the river, parked in the feathered thickets of bamboo. At times, in the shifting breeze, the Filipinos could hear muffled fragments of Japanese conversations. As they'd done for the past several nights, the enemy soldiers were cooking their dinners while there was still light; fearing that bright flames might too clearly give away their position after dark, they would stamp out their fires by dusk to forestall an American air attack.

Pajota's men were both frightened and excited to have the chance, finally, to confront the Japanese straight on. This was their first great battle. For the past three years, they'd been a phantom army—farmers by day, soldiers by night. They were skilled at picking off the enemy a few at a time, blowing out their truck tires, swiping their food, stealing their weapons—subverting the Japanese in a thousand little ways before disappearing into the jungle. They were talented and courageous sneaks, but the question remained whether they were talented and courageous soldiers. At the Cabu River, they now had an opportunity to prove their valor and battle savvy in something other than a hit-and-run conflict. They were well armed for the most part, carrying both prewar Springfields and weapons of a more recent vintage that had been smuggled into the occupied Philippines by submarine. Yet some of Pajota's "men" were merely teenaged boys armed with nothing more than bolo knives.

Pajota was heartened to find that the Japanese had neglected to station guards on the Cabu River bridge. This oversight allowed Pajota's men to lodge some twenty land mines in the road. An explosives expert also succeeded in strapping a time bomb to the understructure of the bridge. The bomb was timed to detonate at 7:45. This calibration was a matter of supreme delicacy. If the bomb went off any earlier, the loud blast might prematurely set the Ranger raid in motion. If it exploded any later, substantial numbers of Japanese troops and vehicles might cross over the span, overwhelm the Filipinos, and join the battle at Cabanatuan camp. Ideally, the bomb would go off precisely when Japanese armored vehicles were trundling across the planked floor of the bridge, thus taking down a few unsuspecting members of the onrushing enemy along with the structure.

That, at least, was Pajota's firm hope, but in the tropical humidity of the Philippines, explosives quickly became corroded and were thus often unreliable. The odds were good, Captain Pajota realized, that the bomb would fail to detonate. This would leave his modest force of a few hundred men in an extremely precarious position. In a fire-fight with an entire mechanized battalion of Japanese troops, Pajota's men would then enjoy but one slim advantage, that of surprise.

Approximately one mile away from Pajota's location, straight down the highway toward Cabanatuan City, Captain Eduardo Joson's forces had assumed their positions without incident. They were crouched in the irrigation ditches lining either side of the road, poised to annihilate anything that blundered down the road. Joson scanned the empty highway and realized that, most likely, his was an all-or-nothing situation: Either he would see no action whatsoever or he'd encounter an overwhelming force. Cabanatuan City was four miles away, close enough so that a convoy of Japanese vehicles could arrive within minutes should the garrison receive a distress call. Once the assault began, Joson could only hope that the Japanese inside the camp would never get a chance to telephone their comrades in Cabanatuan City for help. Joson knew that Captain Pajota had dispatched a few of his scouts to snip all telephone lines leading to the prison compound. Eventually the guards would probably figure out that something was amiss and send a team of electricians to learn where the breaks in the line were. But for the moment, Cabanatuan camp lay incommunicado, marooned in the waning twilight.

— — — —

While Joson and Pajota held their corresponding road-blocks on the main highway, Lieutenant John Murphy and the thirty Rangers from F Company crossed *under* the

319

highway, one by one. They crept through a culvert and emerged on the other side in a dry wash that coursed along the east edge of the camp. This ravine trended to the south and was deep and weedy enough to conceal the men from the Japanese guards for the first hundred yards. But then it grew progressively shallower until it played out altogether, emptying into a flat field where the grass was clipped short. Lieutenant Murphy could see that reaching the rear of the camp would require a slow, laborious crawl within frighteningly close range of one Japanese guard tower and two fortified pillboxes. An extremely wary platoon leader—one F Company man called him "kind of a skittish, nervous little feller"—Murphy had a bad feeling as he contemplated this extremely risky traverse.

His hunch was borne out almost from the start. When the long line of thirty Rangers inched beneath the guard tower on the northeast side of the camp—the first in a gauntlet of manned installations they'd have to sneak past—one of the Imperial Army sentries suddenly blurted out a warning in Japanese and drew his rifle. The F Company men pressed themselves even closer against the bank of the arroyo. They felt sure they'd been spotted and prepared to leap up and charge the fence at the next unmistakable sign. Stealing peeks over the rim of the ditch, they could tell that the guard knew something was afoot. He was a mere forty yards away, close enough so that the men could see that he was wearing eyeglasses. The sentry clutched his rifle and trained it nervously from side to side, aiming it straight at the ravine.

The Rangers carried on a tense debate of whispers. "Shit, he's looking at us."

"Right at us!"

"Should we blast him?"

"No, Murf wants *him* to make the first move."

The Rangers kept stone-still in the ravine. The Japanese erupted in shrill discussion, but gradually the voices trailed off. After a few long minutes, the guard rested his rifle and appeared to relax, as though he'd decided the trouble either had passed or had merely been a vision of some kind, a figment of his bored ruminations. No aspect of Army work was more tedious or stultifying than standing sentinel. It was easy to fall asleep up in the guard towers—or to hallucinate, especially in the famously blue twilight of the Philippines, where, as in all tropical lands close to the equator, the setting sun seemed to hurl itself at the western horizon.

Murphy's F Company moved on. The men noticed that the Japanese guards had ceased looking down at the fields, that they seemed to be entirely focused on the sky. To Murphy's delight, the Black Widow was streaking impressively over the camp, and it proved to be a lifesaver for his platoon just as it had been for Prince and his C Company.

As the column of men writhed through the ditch, smaller groups fell out and took positions beneath each of the major Japanese fortifications along the eastern fence. There were two pillboxes and two guard towers, each of which appeared to be manned by two or three Japanese guards. The F Company plan was one of simple and decisive violence: Upon hearing the signal shot fired by Lieutenant Murphy in the rear, the men intended to annihilate these various nests simultaneously and with such concentrated force that the Japanese would have no opportunity to return fire. Although the Rangers called them pillboxes, these low-lying fortifications were actually a much cruder construction consisting of a large tripod machine gun set in a shallow dugout that was bermed all around and further reinforced with sandbags. Certainly they were far from impregnable. In addition to covering them with tremendous fire, the F Company men planned to lob fragmentation grenades onto the unsuspecting machine-gun crews within.

At approximately 7:30 the vanguard of F Company emerged from the ravine and crawled a final two hundred yards on hard, open, well-mown turf. This was the part of the perimeter crawl that Murphy dreaded most. All that enabled them to pass through it was a bit of incredible good fortune: With the sun now completely set, the camp environs were plunged in darkness and would remain so for only twenty-five minutes before a full moon would launch itself over the Sierra Madre, washing everything in bright silver light. The timing was extraordinary, as if a magical black veil had been thrown over them just when they needed it most. Though they were no more than twenty yards away, the guards couldn't see them. "If there had been even an ounce of light, we couldn't have made it that last stretch, no way," said William Proudfit of F Company. "But when we came out of that ravine, it was like ink." Sergeant Joe Youngblood, who was crawling alongside Proudfit, said he'd never seen a night so black in his life. "In the Philippines, when it got dark, it really got dark quick," said Youngblood. "We couldn't see our own rifles. We didn't have flashlights. It was a mystery how we saw enough to do anything."

To reach their firing positions, the last remaining F Company men had to crawl, without realizing it, over the shallow, unmarked graves of untold numbers of

Cabanatuan prisoners—coffinless crypts that had long since been plundered and disturbed by burrowing rodents and dogs. This was not the main Cabanatuan burial ground, but a smaller one, where, according to diagrams later found hidden inside the camp, the Japanese had interred the bodies of executed Americans. Sprawled among the moldered remains of their countrymen, they squirmed across a field of pungent grass that smelled to some of the Rangers like wild sage.

In the rear of the camp were several large nipa barracks where approximately one hundred transient Japanese troops were quartered. If all went according to plan, every single one of these troops would be cut to pieces in what was supposed to be the raid's most ruthless point of attack. The barracks were situated off to themselves, in the extreme southern end of the camp, several hundred yards from the American section. The Rangers planned to rake these Japanese billets with such intense fire that not a single occupant would have a chance to flee. Murphy knew that the last thing Captain Prince wanted was a surprise coming from the rear while the C Company men escorted the prisoners out the front gate.

Among the F Company Rangers assigned to fire on these rear quarters were Francis Schilli and Corporal Roy Sweezy. They were close friends, both big, unassuming farm boys from the American Midwest. Sweezy was from Allegan, Michigan, a tiny, cold town on the Kalamazoo River less than twenty miles from Lake Michigan. Schilli had grown up in Farmington, Missouri, a rural community south of St. Louis and not far from the Mississippi River. They were boon companions, having trained and bunked with one another in New Guinea. Together Sweezy and

Schilli crept up on the dimly lit Japanese barracks and peered inside the large windows, which were swung wide open for ventilation. They could hear laughing, singing, and yawning. The Japanese had stripped out of their uniforms and were enjoying each other's company for a relaxing hour before bed. They smoked, told stories, played games, passed around bottles of sake. Some of them appeared to be wounded. "We watched them right through the fence," recalled Schilli. "They were maybe twenty, thirty yards away. They were sitting around in their underwear, getting ready for bed."

Lieutenant Murphy was crouched in a shallow ditch not far away from Schilli and Sweezy. Murf was supposed to fire the inaugural shot, and the gravity of that assignment was beginning to weigh on him. He glanced at his watch and saw that it was 7:40, ten minutes past the scheduled starting time. It had taken a little longer than expected for him and his men to sneak all the way back to the rear. Along the full length of the fence, all the way around to the front where Prince and his men were waiting in what must have been agonizing anticipation, Murf knew that every Ranger ear was tuned to receive and instantaneously react to a single sound. He braced himself for the thunderous ferocity of a hundred American weapons replying at once to his cue. It was a dazzling, unnerving feeling to hold such latent power in the tip of a digit. He brought his M-1 rifle to his shoulder and switched off the safety. He drew a deep breath and settled his sights on a Japanese soldier inside the barracks, resting his index finger on the cool crescent of metal.

By 7:30, Prince's C Company Rangers had slithered the last quarter mile to the highway and were resting in a shallow, brushy ditch directly across the road from the padlocked gate. They'd been in attack position for more than a half hour. Now they only had to remain silent and wait for Murphy's men to ignite the fireworks. The fence was close enough so that the Rangers could see the individual barbs on the individual strands of wire and, rising beyond, the shaggy forlorn rooftops of the prisoner barracks.

The men grasped their weapons with the barrels resting in the weeds just inches below the level of the road. The highway still held the day's heat, a narrow strip of cooked asphalt half ruined by neglect and by war, the surface rubbled with potholes and forced open by thistles. Realizing that Japanese convoys had jammed this same stretch of highway just twelve hours earlier, Captain Prince was heartened to see that it now appeared empty in both directions. He trusted that it would stay that way, that the two guerrilla groups had safely reached their destinations and were ready to destroy whatever trouble should come.

The Black Widow receded into the night, and in its void the men could hear the Japanese guards talking excitedly among themselves. The plane had clearly riled them, and judging by their desperate, scattershot speech, they seemed worried and confused. At one point a sentry stationed in the front tower got a strong whiff of something suspicious. He leaned out the window and restlessly scoured the field. "He was squinting and sniffing and looking down at us," recalled Vance Shears. "I think he near about ruptured his eyeballs trying to see us. Luckily, it was too dark. He knew there was something wrong, but he didn't know exactly what."

Captain Prince eyed his glow-in-the-dark watch—7:40. Where was F Company? he wondered. They should be in position by now. At any moment, he expected Murf's gunfire to erupt.

The minutes dripped by. The men kept still as mannequins, pressed low against the ditch wall, facing the gates of Cabanatuan. Their nerves flitted and raced. They imagined that every noise was trebled, that the Japanese could hear the sound of their dripping sweat, their chattering teeth, the train of their own thoughts. Fingers hooked around triggers, muzzles fell on shadowy forms within. "We felt like they could hear us breathing," Roy Peters said. "They were just thirty feet away. We sat in the dark listening to them talk and talk, wondering which of them would be the first to die."

Chapter 11

During the last weeks of January 1945, Cabanatuan continued to expand as a Japanese way station. On some nights there were more Japanese soldiers staying inside the prison stockade than American prisoners. With so many more people sleeping and eating and defecating in the camp, sanitation soon became of paramount concern again. In particular, the men had to grapple anew with the problem of blowflies. For several months they'd been under control, but now the pests swarmed everywhere, ubiquitous clouds at the latrines, buzzing over mess kits, crawling in the refuse heaps. The doctors had been down this black road before, of course, and they sought immediate intervention. As Colonel Duckworth's adjutant, Dr. Hibbs sent out a memo to the various American barracks:

MEMORANDUM
TO: All Concerned

A fly-killing campaign is now very much
in need. Everyone is requested to obtain

some form of swatter and kill flies
whenever possible. All prisoners not
employed at regular duties must kill at
least 20 flies a day.

For the Commanding Officer: RALPH
E. HIBBS

Not only were many more Japanese sleeping in the camp; they were incessantly entering and exiting through the main gate, by day and by night. Cabanatuan had become part billet, part matériel depot. The constant racket of grinding tanks and backfiring truck engines set the Americans increasingly on edge. Having become creatures of routine, like most inmates in most prisons, they found this around-the-clock chaos especially nerve-racking. They couldn't sleep for the noise. They dwelled in a state of perpetual alertness. Every changing circumstance, every stray sound, had to be investigated.

An even more worrisome development was taking place outside the fence. Only a mile to the northeast, several hundred Imperial soldiers had established a new encampment. The prisoners could see their cooking fires curling over the Cabu River in the morning and the late afternoon. The troops were nestled in the bamboo groves along the banks, drawing their water from the river and hoping to derive at least some cover from the riparian brush. Every now and then, the prisoners would see some of these soldiers snooping around the surrounding barrios, sometimes even walking up to the perimeter of the camp. Obviously they were hunting for food. Hibbs grew concerned that one of these freelance foraging expeditions might easily devolve into an incident that could trigger a mass execution. "We were surrounded and entirely defenseless," Hibbs said. "Our options were zilch. Any wild, undisciplined Japanese outfit could wipe us out just for kicks—or for the Emperor."

Worried that these roving Japanese troops might catch wind of the Americans' relative prosperity—in particular, their enormous cache of condensed milk—Colonel Duckworth had Dr. Hibbs fire off another memo to all members of the camp.

MEMORANDUM

TO: All Concerned

It is urgently requested that you do not
expose milk cans, empty or filled, to the
view of the Japanese. It is felt that if they
know we have milk they may demand
that we turn it over to them. Attention is
called to the fact that there are Japanese
camping on the east side of the camp,
and there are roving guards all around
this area. Please consider the safety of
others if not of yourself.

In addition to the new Japanese encampment along the Cabu River, the word (gleaned from discreet conversations with Filipinos through the fence) was that as many as 8,000 troops were stationed at the garrison in Cabanatuan City. With so many troops massing around them, the prisoners began to entertain a fresh new fear: that a major battle might occur in their midst. It seemed to them that the

Japanese were preparing to make a stand against the American Army right there in the rice paddies of Cabanatuan. "We didn't know what to do, because we didn't have foxholes dug at the camp," said Ralph Rodriguez. "We worried that if the Americans started firing artillery in our direction, we'd be sitting ducks. We had nowhere to go, and those nipa shacks were thin as paper."

However, this fear gradually receded as the month of January dragged on. By radio, by rumor, and simply by following the trend of the visible explosions to the west of camp, the prisoners realized with much disappointment that the Sixth Army's primary thrust was toward Manila. "It looked like the American lines were getting away from us," said Bob Body. "They were going right past the camp, as if we weren't there." Even more terrifying than the prospect of getting caught in the heat of battle, they realized, was the prospect of being missed altogether. "We followed the progress of the American troops down the length of Luzon and knew that they had taken Clark Field and Tarlac," said Bert Bank. "But the thing we couldn't understand was why they didn't come farther east to rescue us. It looked like they were going to drive all the way to Manila before coming back to get us. And we were afraid that by then the Japanese would certainly have moved us out of the camp—or killed us all."

If the American ground forces appeared to be heading in the wrong direction, at least the American planes were everywhere in evidence. Each day the skies overhead brought more surprises. Usually the planes would career past the camp on their way to other assignments. But on Friday, January 19, as one prisoner wrote in an unsigned diary, "we had some fine visitors." Soon after lunch two

Piper Cub observational planes appeared in the skies. "They crossed and recrossed the camp, just clearing the rooftops," the prisoner recorded. "We all stood outside and grinned and waved to the pilots, who grinned and waved back at us. They seemed astonishingly unwarlike to be venturing out by themselves." The men could see that the pilots were taking surveillance photographs of the camp. "They were so low," recalled Bob Body, "you could see the wristwatch on the pilot's arm." So slowly did the planes drone overhead that a prisoner made the rather specious-sounding claim that he sprinted beneath one of them from fence line to fence line—and outraced it. As Herbert Ott put it in his diary: "They practically stopped in the air."

One of the Piper Cubs crossed back over the camp and dropped a small object with a long streamer attached to it, but it landed in the most inconvenient place, right beside the Japanese guardhouse. A dozen Americans ran over to retrieve it, but the terrified Japanese, who refused to emerge from under the eaves of the low-roofed guardhouse, "commenced shouting and motioning for the Americans to stay away from the object." The Piper Cub pilot, meanwhile, circled around and around waiting for someone to pick the item up. "No doubt he was completely baffled as to why we didn't," the diary continued. "Finally he flew off, I suppose in disgust, and the Nips came out and carried off the object."

The prisoners never learned what the plane had dropped, though they imagined it was a note of encouragement or perhaps a package of cigarettes. Of greater importance was the fact that the plane had come expressly to them, and that it had lingered. The pilot quite evidently understood that Cabanatuan was an American prison. Twenty minutes after the Piper Cubs vanished, six very impressive-looking fighter planes—P-38s—shot past the camp in what seemed to the prisoners like a resounding encore. "They roared over our heads in a flash," the diarist wrote appreciatively, "leaving the grass roofs of the buildings rustling and shaking." After this flyover the Japanese guards became "more and more indignant," according to the author of the diary. Finally they told the prisoners that "such air shows were not to be tolerated, and that in the future when airplanes came over we would all stay out of sight. Such flights of planes over the camp, they said, were highly improper, and they could have 'killed all the planes and shot all the prisoners' but refrained from doing so because they 'had pity.'"

The next day, Dr. Hibbs was at his typewriter again, pecking out another order to the camp population:

MEMORANDUM

TO: All Concerned

The Japanese at the present time guarding this camp have expressed concern regarding the large groups of men outside of their barracks watching and waving to planes. The following orders were laid down by the Japanese for the future:

Whenever planes are flying over the camp, particularly when low, everyone must go inside their barracks, not under the eaves. There must be no waving or signaling of any type. The only exceptions allowed by them are guards on post and men working on outside details who are to continue working and must not in any way signal. The Japanese stated there would be severe punishment if this order is not obeyed. It is suggested that now, so near the end, let's not jeopardize our liberation by unnecessary acts.

———————

By late January, the Japanese in camp were becoming progressively more anxious and mercurial. Not only did the American planes continue to harry them each day, but the guerrillas of Nueva Ecija stepped up their campaign of harassment and ambush. Across the countryside, the chatter of distant gunfire and small explosions was heard with such frequency that it became a kind of white noise. The Japanese lodged within and around Cabanatuan knew that the knot was tightening fast. Although the Imperial Army high command was notorious for concealing discouraging developments from its own troops, now even the lowliest young conscripts could see that their effort in the Philippines was doomed. They were staring at a long, grim, Bataan-like delaying action whose sole purpose was sacrificial, to buy time for the defense of the home islands. Steadily, the desperation of the whole situation was sinking in for them, and it became more and more evident in their behavior.

One day four Japanese burst into the American side of the camp thrusting rifles with fixed bayonets. They were furious about something. "They looked like an execution squad to me," recalled Dr. Hibbs. With much shouting and gesticulating, they raced down the footpaths, peering under the American shacks, overturning crates and supplies. They were frantically looking for something or someone. Eventually, after a long, intense exercise of charades, the prisoners ascertained that the Japanese were hunting for a Filipino guerrilla. "The affair was a complete mystery to us," said Hibbs. "A guerrilla would be crazy to venture inside our camp."

The exchanges between the Americans and the Japanese grew increasingly strained and at times a bit cryptic. One day a Japanese officer who appeared to be in charge walked over to the American side with an odd and potentially disturbing inquiry: He wanted to know how many of the Americans could walk and how many would need to be carried. "It was apparent to us that they intended to move us," said Bert Bank. "Well, as you can imagine, that threw us all into a fit."

On another occasion a Japanese second lieutenant stormed into the medical quarters loudly demanding the services of an American doctor. An unconscious Japanese soldier with a serious head wound was brought in and placed on a bare wooden table. Dr. Hibbs and a colleague named Dr. Merle Musselman examined the patient. He was an eighteen-year-old kid who had apparently fallen from a tank while napping. Dr. Musselman inserted a needle into the patient's spine and gross red blood squirted out under considerable pressure. This confirmed the diagnosis: The boy had a severe hemorrhage from a skull fracture and was not likely to live.

"No good-o," Dr. Hibbs said to the Japanese officer, shaking his head and gesturing awkwardly, but the officer "gave me the impression that we'd better save the boy—or else."

Hibbs and Musselman stayed up all night watching the patient. "We didn't need to resurrect the Hippocratic oath," said Hibbs. "Although he was the enemy, the thought never entered our mind to do anything but to try to save the young soldier's life." The following morning the Japanese officer returned in a huff. Hibbs and Musselman made it clear that the situation was grave, that the boy must not be moved under any circumstances. Ignoring their advice, the officer peremptorily ordered several Japanese soldiers to haul the unconscious boy out of the medical ward. They placed him on a tank, tied him loosely to the turret, and took off, grumbling down a fatally bumpy road. "We both felt sorry for the lad," Hibbs wrote. "Our best estimate was that he wouldn't last half a kilometer."

Troubled by the strange, callous mistreatment of the soldier, Hibbs viewed the episode as typical of the irrational behavior the Americans were increasingly encountering among the Japanese in camp. It seemed to the prisoners that the soldiers across the way were slowly descending into madness. They were alternately wrathful and defeatist, arrogant and self-destructive. The POWs could never anticipate what they'd do next. Clearly the Japanese felt spooked and threatened and were beginning to lash out in erratic ways. As one prisoner said: "We were more alert than ever to the old saying that every animal is most vicious when he's backed into a corner."

In this taut environment, new warnings began to flourish about a coming massacre. The rumors assumed greater, and more lurid, specificity. According to one version, the Japanese were preparing to dig a large burial trench several hundred yards back from the road. They would order the Americans to march out to the lip of the ditch (which explained, to some, why the Japanese had recently inquired about the mobility of the prisoners), whereupon machine-gun executioners would drop wave after wave of their victims into the mass grave. Filipinos in Cabanatuan City had heard permutations of this plan discussed among Japanese troops stationed at the garrison. During a meeting held at the Japanese headquarters in camp, Dr. Hibbs believed he caught a glimpse of the signed execution order, complete with a diagram showing how and where it was to take place.

The most prevalent rumor, however, had it that a couple of Japanese tank crews were going to rampage through the camp, mowing everyone down. "We heard that *very* strongly," recalled Bob Body. "We were positive they were going to kill us. There were three or four tanks right there inside the camp, and we got the word from the grapevine that they were just going to run those tanks right through us—roll over us, machine-gun us, blast our barracks. My experience with the Filipino grapevine was that it usually didn't miss by much."

When Body first heard this rumor sometime during the last week of January, he immediately hatched a plan to escape. "I said, well they're not going to run them tanks through me, because I'm not going to be here. I figured, I've made it this far, I'm not going to be killed like that." Body convinced two other prisoners to join him, and on the morning of Monday, January 29, they discreetly finalized their plans: They would leave at nightfall, climbing through the fence when the tower guard went to urinate. They would cross the road, cross the Pampanga, and head north, following what they thought would be the most direct route to the American lines. They knew that pulling off the plan would be tricky, as they'd have not one but two sets of guards to sneak past: Duckworth had urged Tommie Thomas and the American night watchmen along the perimeter to be especially vigilant for escapees. Body conceded, "We hadn't thought it through very well. We were just going to *go.* Just as we were. We figured it was time to move on."

However, their escape plans were emphatically thwarted. To Body's dismay, a northeastward exodus of enemy soldiers and commandeered local vehicles began shortly after dark and lasted until dawn. A prison diary vividly described the tumult that swept past camp. "The Japs seem to be moving to the mountains to the east. Perhaps a hundred trucks and more carabao carts and calesas rattled and honked and creaked thru the darkness. The animal drivers added to the din by their shouts to their animals and to the unlighted trucks bearing down on them."

Body and his two confederates shook their heads in befuddlement at their colossally bad timing—and vowed to try again the next sundown.

—— —— ——

At six-thirty the following night, Tuesday, January 30, most of the men of Cabanatuan were squatting outside their barracks in their G-strings and burlap rags, sucking the runts of old cigarettes, enjoying the stillness of the gathering twilight. Evening chow was over, and the mess-hall details were busy rinsing out the cauldrons, scraping the charred rice from the bottoms of pots. Everyone knew it was six-thirty because one of the Navy timekeepers was sounding the six-thirty watch on the "camp clock." The loud, sharp peals reverberated in all directions. Taking the alarm as his cue for the changing of the guard, Tommie Thomas donned his provost marshal armband and set out from his barracks to march the perimeter of the fence. In the medical wards, several hundred men lay on the hard tatami mats, coughing sclerotic coughs, brushing away flies with languid sweeps of their hands.

The Japanese could be heard across the way, frantically moving vehicles about, hoisting burlap sacks, and stacking crates of supplies. In the late afternoon, three light tanks along with two new platoons of Japanese soldiers had been seen slipping into the camp. The smells of salty fish and simmering miso tendriled through the barbed-wire fence. To the northeast, a loose constellation of campfires speckled the scrubby margins of the Cabu River.

Shortly after the six-thirty chimes went off, one of the perimeter guards anxiously reported to Tommie Thomas that he thought he'd detected a suspicious movement in the grass several hundred feet beyond the fence. Something, or someone, appeared to be crawling out there.

"What'd it look like?" Thomas asked.

"Don't really know," the American watchman said. "Only saw it a couple seconds."

Thomas scoured the field carefully and didn't spot anything. "Bet you it was a dog," he said. "There was a couple of 'em out there last week. Did the Jap in the tower see anything?"

338

"Don't think so," the guard replied. "That guy's napping all the time."

A few minutes later an airplane shot across the sky. It seemed to have appeared out of nowhere, as though a trapdoor had opened in the firmament. As the aircraft streaked low over the camp, Thomas caught a momentary glimpse of the twin-tailed contraption. It was black, futuristic, sleeker than any plane Thomas had seen before. He observed that the guards up in the tower were apoplectic, hurling themselves upon the floorboards.

The plane flew exceedingly low, low enough so that Abie Abraham thought he could "easily hit it with a rock." All about the camp, the prisoners stared up in awe, wondering what the strange ship had in mind for them. John Cook thought the aircraft looked like "Buck Rogers come to life." The plane looked so different from anything else they'd seen that at first they thought it was German, or possibly Russian. Other prisoners described it as "a black barn swallow," "a *War of the Worlds* rocket," and an "angel of death." To the men of Cabanatuan, the plane, whatever it was, seemed a powerful, almost eerie emblem of how far American technology had evolved in the three years of their captivity. Mechanically, logistically, *conceptually,* this was a different Army. On Bataan, they'd starved in their shallow metal helmets fighting old-fashioned pitched battles with dud shells and rusty artillery. Thirty-odd months later, they had only to gaze upon this sci-fi lozenge streaking through the clouds at 300 miles per hour to understand that everything, the whole social and industrial universe back home, had changed. It was as though they were looking at a new country, a new era.

As night fell upon Nueva Ecija, the airplane vanished

and the camp seemed preternaturally quiet and dark. Except for a few flickering coconut-oil lamps lighting up the interiors of the medical wards, the grounds were thoroughly blacked out, in accordance with a standing Japanese policy to prevent air raids.

At approximately 7:45, Dr. Hibbs was sitting on the steps of the American headquarters, enjoying a postprandial seminar on the stars with Dr. Musselman and two other close friends. Tommie Thomas was smoking a cigarette and conversing with the camp tailor outside the last building on the south end of the compound, only thirty feet from the Japanese fence. One of the British prisoners, a deaf elderly man named Edwin Rose, was sitting on one of the thrones at the latrine, struggling with a chronic case of amebic dysentery. Bob Body and his two fellow conspirators, pleased to note that no Japanese traffic had been spotted on the highway, were preparing to slip through the barbed wire within the hour. "That night was do or die," Body said. "I'd gone as far as I could go. One way or the other, I was going to get through that fence. I said to the others, 'Okay, we go tonight at eight-thirty.' "

Ralph Rodriguez was working at his typewriter in the medical office and playing records on a rickety phonograph that had arrived two years earlier in a Red Cross package. "We only had a couple of records, so we just played them over and over again," Rodriguez said. He put on an extremely groove-worn version of the old Tin Pan Alley song "Wait 'Til the Sun Shines, Nellie," and stared out the window at the flashing lights of the American bombardment in the distance. The vapid tune seeped through the camp:

Then she heard him softly say . . .
Wait 'til the sun shines, Nellie, and the clouds go drifting by
We will be happy, Nellie, don't you cry . . .

A few seconds later the scratchy melody was overwhelmed by a fusillade of gunfire erupting from the rear of the camp. Rodriguez could hear the screams of men, could see the traceries against the night sky. Bullets chewed through the nipa thatching and drilled into the far wall. The song wouldn't shut up—*Through the window pane, she looked at the rain*. A squall of mortars, machine-gun staccato. On instinct, prisoners everywhere hurled themselves into latrines, crawled under their shacks, burrowed into anything that felt like a hole. Dr. Hibbs and Dr. Musselman dove into an irrigation ditch, and listened to the sound, as Hibbs put it, of "whistling slugs, Roman candles, and flaming meteors sailing over our heads." Bob Body and his two would-be fellow escapees were pulling together a few belongings when the firing began. "We were sitting just outside the barracks where we slept, waiting for the right time to leave," Body said. "When the shooting started, I said, 'Guys, hit the dirt, it sounds like they're starting to kill us.'"

Abie Abraham heard his buddies desperately conferring in their barracks—*Mother oh mother . . . What a way to die . . . They've fattened us up just to murder us all*. Abraham's first instinct was to defend himself. "They won't get me," he thought, "not without a fight." Abraham crept under his barracks and retrieved a long, knotted club that he'd buried beneath the floorboards weeks earlier. He returned to his bunk wielding the club, vowing to bludgeon the first Japanese executioner who ventured through the door.

341

In the kitchen, where John Cook had just finished up the dishes, the hanging stockpots rattled and clinked in the relentless spatter of lead. A few seconds later, he heard the rupture of a grenade, then another. Rodriguez hurled himself on the floor of his office. "Ralph, shut that fucking thing off!" *Must we stay home, Joe? she cried.* At the latrine, deaf Edwin Rose was still shitting, oblivious to the firestorm all around him. "I said shut it off, goddamnit!" John McCarty jumped off a chair outside his barracks and hit the dirt. "The bullets were thick as swarms of bees," he said, "and flying so close I could feel their heat on my bare skin." On the south end of camp, Tommie Thomas rolled into a drainage ditch, his heart thudding in his chest. "I heard screaming and moaning all around us," he said, "and I thought the Japs were finally massacring us."

Crouched on the floor, Rodriguez reached over and shook the leg of the table, but the phonograph wouldn't stop. *Maybe we better not wander, maybe we better not roam.*

Chapter 12

If the slaughter could have been viewed without sound, one might have been disposed to call it beautiful. In an instant, the entire fence line lit up in a corona of frenetic glitters soon numbering in the thousands, each burst crisp and discrete against the black night. The orange flashes came in pleasingly random and inscrutable patterns like the semaphore of fireflies in a dense forest. Occasionally gold stars streaked across the field and ended abruptly in warm blooms of yellow and vermilion, leaving the sky crisscrossed with trails of smoke.

Yet the sounds, shrill and fulminant, were at odds with the majestic visuals—splintering bamboo, the whine of stray slugs, glass fracturing into shards, sputters of pulverized dirt. The blunt sound bullets make when they enter flesh, sending up aerosol clouds of blood. Polyrhythmic jackhammerings and ricochets of BARs, of carbines, of M-1s and tommy guns. The bilious rip of fragmentation grenades, of antitank missiles piercing metal, of walls riven apart.

Once the crack of Murphy's rifle rang out, the vast fusillade was unleashed from one end of the compound to the other. Within fifteen seconds, all the towers and pillboxes had been neutralized, or obliterated altogether. The Japanese were unable to reply. The surprise was so complete, the firepower so massive and omnidirectional that the enemy was left paralyzed.

Hunkered along the front road, Prince's C Company opened fire with a barrage that was so immense it was plainly overkill. As one Ranger described it, "We mowed them down like hay." Since there were only a few visible human targets at which the waiting Rangers could aim their rifles, they lavished those targets with absurd amounts of fire. The sentry in the front pillbox was riddled with so many bullets that his head and upper body "atomized," as one Ranger put it. A guard in the northeast tower was ripped completely in half at the waist. The torso dropped over the ledge of the guardhouse window and landed with a sodden bounce, smoke rising off the flesh.

In the midst of this lashing gunfire, a C Company Ranger named Teddy Richardson leapt up from the ditch, bounded across the road, and tried to bash open the padlock on the gate with the butt of his tommy gun. This proved impractical, so he fished out a .45 automatic pistol from his side holster with the intention of blasting the lock open. Just as he drew this weapon, however, a Japanese guard from within the compound managed to raise his rifle and fire at Richardson. Judging by the muzzle flame, the assailant appeared to be only thirty feet from the gate. Incredibly, the bullet missed Richardson but glanced his pistol with sufficient force to jar it from his hand. He responded impulsively, squeezing off a few rounds from his tommy gun in the general direction of the guard, who was never heard from again. Then Richardson retrieved his pistol from the ground and resumed what he'd been doing before this unpleasant distraction. With a single shot, the padlock clicked open.

Richardson flung the lock to the side, pulled back the hasp, and threw open the ponderous gates of Cabanatuan. Now all the Rangers jumped up from the ditch and poured through the breached gate, scurrying to their assigned positions inside. The next Ranger who entered Cabanatuan after Richardson was a BAR man from Minnesota named Leland Provencher. As Richardson and Provencher dashed past the guardhouse area they encountered a dim form standing in the pathway. "What's going on here?" the man yelled in an odd accent. Richardson and Provencher assumed this person must be an American prisoner, so they lowered their weapons. Then the figure wheeled about and took off toward the enemy quarters yelling frantically in Japanese. Realizing it was a ruse (Americans fighting in New Guinea and Guadalcanal had often encountered Japanese soldiers speaking snippets of convincing English to confuse GIs and thus buy a few precious seconds in tight situations), the two Rangers opened fire and dropped the imposter in his tracks.

Following the camp's central thoroughfare, Provencher and several others raced back to the Japanese officer quarters and raked the buildings for several uninterrupted minutes. Provencher's heavy rifle was set to automatic, so that he only had to depress once—*Brrrrrrrrrrrrphtttttttt*—and the flimsy nipa barracks were chewed to pieces at rate of 550 rounds per minute. He heard screams and groans inside, but didn't see the enemy. Encountering no resistance whatsoever, Provencher moved on to what appeared to be a utility shed. He raised his rifle and started to fire when he heard a voice cry out: "Don't shoot! Please, I'm an American." Given what had happened at the front gate Provencher was skeptical, but for some reason he held his fire. The man turned out to be an American after all, a Navy engineer whom the Japanese had impressed into doing maintenance work on the generator that powered the camp lights. Provencher came within a beat of killing him. "I don't know what the hell saved him, because it was only by pure instinct that I didn't shoot," Provencher said. "I had my gun on him, it was just a matter of pulling the trigger."

Provencher ordered him to come out very slowly so the Rangers could examine him carefully. With mincing steps, the man emerged from the maintenance shed holding up an old *Life* magazine he'd just been reading that was now lanced with a fresh bullet hole.

"Get to the main gate!" Provencher cried, as gently as he could under the circumstances. The prisoner, still blanched with fright, stumbled nervously in serpentine fashion toward the front of the compound.

While the riflemen maintained a constant wall of fire, a bazooka team led by a staff sergeant from Texas named Manton Stewart sprinted farther down the same central road and came to a halt directly across from the corrugated sheds that Bill Nellist had spotted earlier in the day. They were so far back in the compound that they could clearly see the muzzle flashes of F Company as they riddled the rear barracks. Stewart crouched in the gravel and hoisted the ungainly steel pipe to his shoulder. Another Ranger inserted a finned three-and-a-half-pound rocket into the rear of the smooth-bore tube and rapped Stewart on the arm when it was loaded.

Stewart swiveled the launcher in the direction of the sheds and was about to mash the trigger when he detected a movement in his peripheral vision. A long-bed truck, packed with Imperial Army soldiers, was chuffing beside the shed. The driver had just switched on the ignition and was desperately pulling out, evidently with the intention of fleeing the camp while there was still a chance. Stewart squeezed the trigger, which ignited the electric fuse, and in a bright steady arc the self-propelled rocket fizzed across the compound, striking the body of the truck and piercing its engine block. Within seconds the vehicle had been reduced to a pyre of exploding fuel, shattered glass, and melted rubber. Several dozen injured men, some of whom had been set aflame, crawled half alive from the carcass of the truck only to be finished off by Ranger gunfire. They were pitifully easy targets, clearly silhouetted in the flames.

Then Stewart turned back to his original target, the galvanized-metal sheds that were believed to house Japanese tanks. It was imperative that he attack the garages before the Japanese had a chance to start up their tanks and put them to deadly use. With several bursts, Stewart's bazooka was able to puncture and destroy the thin-skinned buildings—and whatever vehicles were stowed inside. The structures warped and yawed in the billowing flames before collapsing into mangled heaps. Better able to see in the waxing light of the fires, several of the Rangers thought they glimpsed the outline of two tanks. Stewart fired in that direction and, by most accounts, scored a direct hit.

No longer having to concern themselves with the specter of tanks raging through camp, C Company could now turn to the most satisfying aspect of the evening's work—storming the bastille. A group of Rangers ran toward the American section of the compound, brandishing wire cutters. A Ranger named Lester Malone ran up to the main American gate and inspected the lock. He took two steps back and fired his M-1. Then Malone yanked off the lock and opened up the gates to the American prison. "We're Yanks!" he yelled. "This is a prison break! Head for the main gate!"

At first, the prisoners failed to understand. They were too mentally brittle to process the chaos. Fearing the worst, they took refuge in the barest and most pitiful of hiding places. To one Ranger, who had sliced his way through the fence with wire cutters, the inmates of Cabanatuan looked like "scared vermin scattering for cover after you switch on the kitchen lights." They huddled in corners, cowered in black-water ditches, lurked behind frail bamboo posts, praying for a slimness that even they could not affect. Some were literally scurrying from their deliverers. At least one prisoner wet himself. Still others "were praying and running around in circles," as Abie Abraham recalled, "because they didn't know where to run *to.*" Ranger Alvie Robbins almost bayoneted one of the terrified prisoners who sprinted around the corner of a nipa building and surprised him. "I didn't recognize him as being American," said Robbins. "I thought he could have been Japanese. The adrenaline was flowing, the battle was raging, it was dark outside. I raised my rifle and came within an instant of running that bayonet right through him."

To the prisoners, the scene didn't make sense. There were troops running from barracks to barracks, dim forms crouched along the camp's dirt pathways. They were gesturing wildly, shouting orders. "Buddy, you're free," a voice said. "Up quick and get over to the gate! You're a soldier again!"

Like many others, Bert Bank was convinced it was a trick. He felt sure the Japanese were using English to lure the Americans outside so the executioners could more conveniently gun down their victims. "We whispered to each other not to move, that it was a trap to get us to run and then the Japanese would open up on us." Bank was lying on the ground, trying to persuade his buddies not to acquiesce in this enemy scheme, when a Ranger walked right up to him and tugged him on the arm.

"C'mon, we're here to save you," he said. "Run for the gate."

Bank still wouldn't budge. The Ranger looked into his eyes and saw they were vacant, registering nothing.

"What's wrong with you?" he asked. "Don't you want to be free?"

A smile formed on Bank's lips. Something in the Ranger's accent had reached him. "Where you from, boy?" he asked.

"Oklahoma," replied the Ranger.

Bank tendered his hand. "Oklahoma's good enough for me. Say, give me a lift here—I can't see a thing."

For prisoners who could see, the Rangers looked exceedingly strange. They wore unfamiliar uniforms, carried unfamiliar guns. To starved men, the strapping soldiers looked impossibly huge, even menacing. Ralph Rodriguez was thoroughly frightened by the first Ranger he encountered.

"This guy looked like a giant. I thought, what kind of a man is this? He had guns everywhere. Big hands. He could have been a man from Mars. He yelled out, 'Any more Americans?' I was trembling when I raised my hand—'*Here!*'"

Even when the fear of a massacre had passed, even when most of the prisoners understood that the Rangers were Americans come to liberate them, many were still curiously reluctant to go. They seemed suspicious of their good fortune. They couldn't shed the dour pessimism of captivity long enough to understand that captivity was over. Or perhaps on some half-conscious level, they still found it hard to transgress the order of the Japanese, the only authority they'd known for three years.

Some of the POWs appeared almost ungrateful at first. John Cook, wearing only a G-string and high-top leather shoes, practically interrogated his liberator. "I said, 'Hey, who in the hell are you?' The guy had the funniest uniform on, with a funny-looking cap, and he was carrying something that looked like a grease gun, like he was going to grease up a car. He said, 'We're Yanks. Get your ass out the main gate.' This guy is trying to save my life, and I'm sitting there carrying on an argument with him. I said, 'No Yank ever wore a uniform like that.' He said, 'The hell we don't!'"

Bob Body was similarly combative with the first Ranger he met. "I was lying on the ground, and all of a sudden I looked up and there was this huge guy looming over me. I said, 'Who the hell you think you are?' 'Never mind. We're U.S. Army Rangers. Get out of here.' I said, 'What's a Ranger?' He said, 'Never mind, get the fuck outta here. We've come to get you outta here. Don't ask any more questions—get out, get out!'"

Body finally got the picture—his planned escape had been trumped by a full-scale rescue. The American Army had beaten him to the draw by no more than a half hour. Yet like many of the other prisoners, Body wasn't sure where he was supposed to go. Some Rangers were yelling, "Head for the cut fence!" while others were saying, "Head for the main gate!" Not only that, the prisoners were thoroughly confused about what the Rangers meant by the "main gate." It was a basic orientation problem. For the past three years, the main gate had always meant the gate to the American compound, not the central exit of the entire prison. This ultimate portal to the outside world was generally viewed as a forbidden concept, something one didn't talk about because it was depressing and futile and could all too easily lead to subversive thoughts that might get a prisoner shot. The area around the main gate was strictly out of bounds, a dangerous piece of real estate, a dangerous *idea*.

So, like many of his fellow prisoners, Body scurried about the compound in utter confusion. "Too much was happening too quick and I wanted out of there," Body said. Finally, not knowing what else to do, mad with fear and glee and adrenaline, he charged right into the fence, badly scraping up his face as he nosed impatiently through the razor ribbon in the dark. "What in the hell did you do that for?" a perplexed Ranger asked him when he emerged on the front road, blood streaming down his face. "I didn't know what to tell him," Body said. "I didn't care, not a bit. I was free!"

As the precious minutes ticked by, the Rangers became more and more irritated by the strange stubbornness of the POWs. They didn't seem to understand the urgency of the situation. "I was getting annoyed," recalled Alvie Robbins. "I'd say to them, 'Listen, I've got a job to do here. I can't spend a lot of time arguing with you. There's thousands of Japanese just up the road. We gotta get out of here in a hurry.' " In some cases, the Rangers actually had to use physical force. "We just turned them around and booted 'em," said Lester Malone. "We couldn't fool around and explain nothing. They just didn't want to believe we were Americans." One of the prisoners Malone "booted" was Herbert Ott, the camp veterinarian. "I told him, get the hell out of here. I just turned him toward the gate and kicked him on out."

Dr. Ralph Hibbs was another prisoner who needed a little physical convincing. "What the hell is going on?" Hibbs shouted at three Rangers who came bounding down the path toward him "with their tommy guns blazing" from their hips. "Where'd you come from? Are you guerrillas?"

"We're Rangers—General Krueger's boys."

"What are Rangers?" Hibbs demanded. He was taxing their patience. Finally, one of them picked up the doctor, muscled him around, and gave him "a ten-foot kick squarely in the ass."

The most recalcitrant prisoner of all was Hibbs's immediate superior, Colonel Duckworth, the American commander of Cabanatuan. Duckworth was digging in his heels, refusing to go, even refusing to let the Rangers escort others out. The colonel, who'd been suddenly awakened by the shooting and still seemed perplexed by the whole fracas, was strutting through the compound buttonholing Rangers and shouting in their faces. He seemed unwilling to surrender authority to people whose identities and motives had been inadequately explained to him. Alvie

Robbins was almost shocked by Duckworth's belligerence. "He says, 'I'm Colonel Duckworth, and I'm in charge here! Who the hell are you!' I said, 'We're Americans. We've come for you.' He said, 'You can't do this! You're going to get us killed. The Japanese told us no escapes! No one leaves here until *I* say they do.' I said, 'You go see Captain Prince,' and I went on about my business." Duckworth continued storming about the camp, demanding explanations, imploring the raiders to cease and desist. Finally, another Ranger grabbed him by the arm and said, "With all due respect, you are not in charge here, General MacArthur is. Now I suggest you head to the main gate before we kick your ass there. I'll apologize in the morning.' " Still grousing about the situation, Duckworth shambled out the American gate. Plagued by night blindness like so many others, he promptly fell into a ditch and fractured his right arm.

Slowly, the awareness that this was a jailbreak was beginning to sink in among the rest of the prisoners. They were reacting with a kind of catatonic ecstasy, numb and inarticulate. One prisoner wrapped his arms around the neck of the first Ranger he saw and kissed him on the forehead. All he could say was, "Oh boy! Oh boy! Oh boy!" Alvie Robbins found one prisoner muttering in a darkened corner of one of the barracks, tears coursing down his face. "I thought we'd been forgotten," the prisoner said.

"No, you're not forgotten," Robbins said. "We've come for you."

Abie Abraham, still clutching his bludgeon, spotted a

Ranger with a tommy gun sprinting for his barracks. The Ranger poked his head through the open doorway and, discerning Abraham's dim outline inside, asked, "Can you walk, Mac?"

"Yeah, I can walk," Abraham replied. "I walked out of Bataan, and by God I can walk out of here."

Now several Rangers leapt into the barracks to assist anyone who needed a hand. Abraham spied a friend of his, a civilian from Norway named Aksel Svendsen, lying in a heap on the floor of the shack. Under his breath, Svendsen pleaded, "Please don't hurt me. I'm Norwegian. Please help me, God!"

The Ranger was taken aback at the thought that he'd caused such trepidation. "I'm not God," he said. "Now c'mon, buddy, let's go."

"Please don't kill me!" Svendsen still didn't understand.

Abraham intervened, gently taking Svendsen by the arm. "Aksel, it's okay," he said. "It's Abie, your friend. It's okay."

The Rangers had forgotten, or never knew in the first place, that Cabanatuan camp held men from other nationalities—Norwegians, Canadians, Dutch, and, the largest non-American contingent of all, British. A Ranger cried out, "You're free—all Americans assemble at the main gate!" To which one of the proper English prisoners yelled gleefully, "I'm not American, but shall I come too?"

Outside Abraham's barracks, the exodus was proceeding in a more orderly fashion. Every prisoner who could walk was emerging from his crawl space or cubbyhole and moving toward the front. Tommie Thomas and his friend the camp tailor pulled themselves up from the ditch where they'd been hiding since the shooting started. The tailor couldn't walk very well, so he jumped on Thomas' back and they bounced awkwardly down Broadway as fast as Thomas' huge, shambling frame could go. "We moved and we moved fast," said Thomas. "We kept our heads down and headed for the main gate." Finally they encountered one of the Rangers leading prisoners out by the arm. "Are you a Yank?" Thomas asked, and when the Ranger said he was, Thomas extended his hand and said, "Put 'er there."

"I was glad it was dark so he couldn't see my tears," Thomas recalled. "I said, 'Are we ever happy to see you!' "

"Here," said the Ranger. "Let *us* carry your buddy."

All of this time, the shooting had continued, first in a merciless storm, now in sporadic coughs and splutters. As the prisoners made their way to the gate, they had to pick their way through several Japanese corpses, with stray bullets pinging this way and that. On his way out, John McCarty saw a couple of Japanese guards cut down by the Ranger fire. "What a sight it was watching those soldiers fall," he said. "Some of them were so near to me that I could see the puffs on the front of their uniforms."

Many of the POWs had belongings they wanted to fetch— documents, medals, souvenirs, clean uniforms they had planned to wear out of camp when and if the glorious day came. They yearned to walk out of there with dignity. All about the camp, hidden in floorboards and thatched roofs, the men had stashed their little mementos and sentimental valuables for safekeeping, hoping to drag them out on liberation day. Dr. Hibbs had a beautiful polished cigarette holder he'd made from the brass jacket of a spent .30–.06 shell fitted into a mouthpiece whittled from carabao horn—"an enormous enhancement to your smoking pleasure," as he later remembered it ruefully.

Tommie Thomas had a musette bag filled with various "goodies I was saving for a time like this." Herbert Ott prided himself on a beloved chess set that he'd carved out of narra wood. Others kept Bibles, photographs of sweethearts, sketchbooks, letters, and prison diaries. But now that the hour of freedom was upon them, they had no time to retrieve their valuables. Every time a prisoner ran back to the barracks to rescue some cherished item, a Ranger would have to block his path and show him the way out.

A Ranger named Marvin Kinder led a prisoner by the arm and hustled him outside. Suddenly the man resisted, as though he'd forgotten something. "I have to go back in and get some documents I hid," he said anxiously.

"No, sir," Kinder insisted, "we have to keep moving."

"But I need my documents! When I get back to the States, I'm going to court-martial a man who ate my cat. A beautiful cat, it was! The man ate my cat, I'm telling you!"

Then the prisoner burst into tears and collapsed on the ground. Kinder tried not to consider for even a second the world of despair suggested by this man's predicament; there wasn't time for it now. Kinder lifted him in his arms. Through his sobs the POW said, "Thank you! Thank you! Thank God you've come!"

Even though they had prepared themselves for the worst, the Rangers were truly appalled at the grotesque condition of many of the prisoners. A nearly full moon had just risen over the Sierra Madre, flooding the countryside and making it possible for the Rangers to get a vivid look at the men they were liberating. It was a ghastly parade—amputees, consumptives, men with peg legs, men without hair or teeth, men with the elephantine appendages and scrotums indicative of wet beriberi. One Ranger described them as "sickly old birds that had just been plucked." The half-naked prisoners were dull-eyed and louse-infested, and they seemed old beyond their years. Most were barefoot, or they hobbled around on homemade sandals fashioned from string and slats of cardboard. Their hair was greasy and raggedly shorn close to the scalp with blunt knives. Lesions and battle scars marred their skin, and many had tropical ulcers as big as dinner plates. Out of the psychiatric ward emerged a florid and oddly grandiose fellow everyone called "Napoleon" because in his delusions that's who he had convinced himself he was. Another Ranger escorted a prisoner who was crudely festooned with what he good-naturedly called his "vest-pocket asshole"—a colostomy bag. Some of the Rangers welled with tears at the hideous procession and tried to offer comfort. "They tucked our men under their arms like babies," said Ralph Hibbs. "They shook their heads in disbelief and cried at the sight of these emaciated countrymen so far down the starvation trail."

Standing next to the young, strapping Rangers, the prisoners realized anew how sorry they must look, and some were overcome with self-pity and shame. "The pallor of death shone on our faces," Abie Abraham later wrote. "Our hip bones protruded sharply through our thin underwear. We stared vacantly, unable to believe we were no longer prisoners of the Japanese."

As soon as the captives began pouring out the front, Dr. Jimmy Fisher and his medics sprang up from their trench along the highway and positioned themselves at the gate to assist the sickest ones. Scores of the prisoners, particularly those quartered in the medical wards, were completely immobile. The Rangers had to pick them up in their arms and carry them out the gate. "They were skin and bones," said Robert Anderson. "You could reach around their calves with your thumb and forefinger." The POWs were light enough so that some Rangers were able to carry two prisoners on their back at once. "With some of them," said Lester Malone, "it was just like you were carrying a ten-year-old kid." Malone encountered several who clearly couldn't move but were too proud to acknowledge it. "I can walk!" one prisoner insisted as he reclined on his mat in his barracks. "For God's sake I'm an American soldier!" He staggered to his feet, took two defiant steps, and tumbled in agony in the doorway. Malone called a Ranger to come carry him out.

A Ranger named August Stern found himself carrying a chaplain named Hugh Kennedy, pickaback style. At one point they stumbled into an irrigation ditch that was flowing with raw sewage. Stern began to curse a blue streak, then caught himself, embarrassed for taking the Lord's name in vain. "Son, you're forgiven," Kennedy said into Stern's ear. "There's a time and place for everything, and this is the time and the place."

Dr. Hibbs raced toward his TB ward to check on his patients and make sure the Rangers did not overlook them. Many of his patients were especially fragile, and he knew they would need to be ferried out with great care. He popped his head in the doorway and cried, "We're all free! The Americans are here. We've got to get ready to go!" No one answered. He ascended the steps to look in on his prisoners, but found to his consternation that the ward was completely empty. The Rangers had already removed them all. "It gave me an odd feeling," Hibbs said. "I thought, 'My God, how did they do it?'"

In a different medical ward, Corporal Jim Herrick found another of the sick POWs curled up on a bamboo mat. He pleaded with the man to try to stand up.

"No, no," the prisoner replied. "I'm a goner. Go save the others."

According to historian Forrest Johnson, Herrick gathered this faintly breathing husk into his arms. Even though the two young men were about the same age, Herrick felt he was carrying a frail old wizard in his eighties, bony and light, a man aged on some strangely accelerated scale of time.

A few moments later, the prisoner lost consciousness. Herrick checked his pulse—nothing. He was apparently the raid's first American casualty. It was too much excitement for him. He died of a heart attack (or so it would later be declared) in Herrick's arms, twenty feet from the gate.

———————

While the prisoners hobbled manically out of Cabanatuan and made their way across the moonlit fields toward the river, a Japanese soldier scrambled from his barracks in the rear of the camp and hid himself in a shallow ditch. Quickly, deftly, he set up a small weapon known as a knee mortar. He kicked out the prop legs and ran his fingers over the cool metal tube with the rote dexterity of one experienced in battle. He tipped the weapon toward the front of the camp, where he must have logically assumed that the greatest numbers of Americans would be found, pouring out the bottleneck of the main gate. Squinting in the subdued silver light, he hurriedly estimated the distance—approximately six hundred yards—and roughed out his ballistics calculations accordingly. He dropped a round into the muzzle and braced for the cough, *ssss-thunk*. With a faint sibilance, the projectile arced high over the camp and homed toward the gate, meeting ground in a loose, ragged explosion. The soldier revised his calculation slightly and dropped in another shell—*ssss-thunk*—and a third. It is not unreasonable to imagine that the last feeling surging in his breast was one of pride and soldierly accomplishment, for in poor visibility, under trying circumstances, he had struck his distant target with precision.

Francis Schilli, Roy Sweezy, and several others from F Company were the first men to detect the mortar. The bright muzzle flame and low pneumatic burst of the weapon unmistakably gave the soldier's position away. Schilli and the others turned to spray him with heavy automatic fire, and abruptly the mortar attack ceased.

Around the front gate, at the point of impact, the mortar shells had thrown up clouds of dirt and left a triad of large divots in the road. All the Rangers and prisoners in the vicinity had hurled themselves on the ground; now they lay shaking off the shock and fingering their wounds in the hope that they'd been hit only by rocks or soil debris and not by the lethal shards of a mortar round. The Rangers began to suspect that the rounds had incompletely fragmented, because many men standing close to the explosions (such as Captain Prince) had been left unscathed while a few others caught large hunks of hot shrapnel.

One of the unfortunates was an Alamo Scout named Alfred Alfonso. He had received a significant fragment in his lower abdomen, and he was losing much blood. A medic ran over to give Alfonso a syringe of morphine and quickly patch him up so he could be ferried across the river. Quickly scanning the area around the front gate, Prince could see that there were a half dozen others down, and he remembered thinking how oddly random the casualties appeared. "It could have been me, it could have been anybody," Prince recalled. "There was no rhyme or reason to it." One Ranger, PFC Jack Peters, was struck almost directly in the groin. "A half inch higher," said Prince, "and he would been emasculated."

A few yards away, another Alamo Scout, Tom Rounsaville, had also caught a large chunk of metal—in his rear end. Bill Nellist had been standing close by and saw Rounsaville collapse from the wound. In a second, Nellist hastened to his friend's aid. Dr. Fisher was apparently busy somewhere else, so Nellist decided to take charge. Although he had no medic's training to speak of, he removed his field knife and commanded Rounsaville to roll over.

"What are you doing, Bill?" Rounsaville asked suspiciously.

"Gonna operate on you."

Before Rounsaville could form a protest, Nellist had slit open the bottom of Rounsaville's fatigues and trenched the wound so that the dark metal fragment could clearly be seen, firmly lodged in glistening flesh. Rounsaville grimaced and swore at his friend, "Damn you, Bill!" Without pausing a beat, Nellist produced a pair of wire cutters and yanked out the offending gobbet of shrapnel like a nail from plywood, quipping to Rounsaville that "when you get your Purple Heart they'll pin it on your ass."

Now Captain Prince ordered a couple of Rangers to

scour the area and learn the total number of casualties. The report came back better than he had feared. Although dozens were cut or scraped, only five men needed attention. Miraculously, none of them was a prisoner, and no one seemed to be critically injured.

But then a sixth casualty was found. He had been hard to spot because he was lying down in the roadside ditch and capable of only feeble speech.

"Where you hit?" asked John Nelson, one of the medics.

"Stomach."

The wound was bleeding profusely, warm rivulets spilling through his fingers. Nelson couldn't see his face in the darkness, but with the alacrity and calm haste of a seasoned medic, he began to dress the wound. "Go find Captain Fisher!" Nelson said. "This man is badly hurt."

The injured man lifted his arm. *"I'm* Captain Fisher," he said.

"What?" Nelson said distractedly.

"It's me—*Jimmy.*"

Nelson squinted in disbelief. Fisher and he were the best of friends. Nelson was the "number one boy," as he called himself, Captain Fisher's first sergeant. Ever since New Guinea, they'd spent endless hours bullshitting with each other. They'd dreamed about taking a long sailing trip around America after the war was over. Now Fisher couldn't move. He lay awkwardly on his back, breathing thinly, the color flushing from his face. The blast from one of the mortar shells had hurled him into the ditch. Fisher knew it was extremely serious. He grimaced and bit his lip. His pulse was thready. The wound was large and jagged, the blood hemorrhaging with his heartbeat. Embedded in his viscera, the shrapnel was hot and serrated, a sharp pressure against the wall of his abdomen. It pained him to draw breath, as though the shard were biting a little deeper into him each time he inhaled. He wasn't positive, but he thought the fragment had struck his liver. As he faded in and out of consciousness, a team of medics moved in fast with a litter to carry their fallen doctor across the Pampanga River toward Platero.

─ ─ ─ ─ ─

When the long straggle of inmates left their blazing prison behind and tore out, many of them barefoot, across the stubbled fields, their spirits soared with an optimism they hadn't known in years. The stunned disbelief they had initially felt had given way to a guarded giddiness that seeped down to their feet and kept them moving at a spry clip. To watch Cabanatuan consumed by fire was unimaginably cathartic for them. "I turned back toward camp once more to see flames leaping skyward," Dr. Hibbs wrote. "The fire from our captors' headquarters building illuminated the Cabanatuan water tower on the knoll. We would no longer have to listen to 'Kimigayo' anymore. For the first time I was finally convinced that we were honest-to-God going to make it."

A hundred yards out, the escaping prisoners were met by the radiant countenance of Henry Mucci. The colonel had spent the opening moments of the raid crouched in the rice fields carefully watching the fireworks go off. Now he rose up and made his considerable presence felt. Mucci projected just the sort of steady confidence and air of authority that the skittish prisoners needed as they emerged into the world. He came across as his usual stentorian self, offering bright words of praise and encouragement, taking the more tentative prisoners by the hand, doubling back again and again to greet each fresh wave of the newly freed inmates. Unaware that Captain Fisher had been hit by a mortar-shell fragment, Mucci was unequivocally ecstatic about the raid. "Everything went off exactly as we'd planned," he said, "by luck and by the grace of God."

Mucci would lead the vanguard toward Platero, a Pied Piper figure. "We would have followed him to hell that night," said Ranger Thomas Grace. "And when we got there, he would've opened up the goddamn gates." The prisoners instantly responded to his command. "In that crazy situation out there in the field, we desperately needed a leader, and that was Mucci," recalled Bob Body. "We could see that what he said counted. We respected him. He was tough and colorful and somehow reassuring. He led the way, and we followed."

Mucci was thrilled by the generosity and game spirit that he saw in his Rangers. "Some of them gave their shoes and most of their clothes to the prisoners who needed them," the colonel later fondly recalled. "They gave the prisoners cigarettes and held them up when they needed it. I cannot say say too much for them."

Yet as they made their way over the rice fields, the faltering chatter of gunfire in and around the compound was soon engulfed by another, even more terrifying ruckus. Less than a mile to the northeast, at the Cabu River bridge, an enormous firefight had erupted between Captain Pajota's men and the Japanese troops camped along the Cabu. As they hopped and limped due north toward Platero, the prisoners could hear the deafening roar and see the riverbed coruscating with gunfire and explosions. Stray Japanese slugs streaked across the field and riddled the dirt around them. As one Ranger recalled: "Those bullets were singing a pretty tune over our heads." The prisoners and Rangers zigzagged their way across the paddies to avoid getting hit.

It was impossible to see how Pajota's guerrillas were faring, but the prisoners understood that the Japanese were trying to pursue them, and the fear acted as a new stimulus, prodding them to walk even faster. As Abie Abraham put it: "Some who were too weak to walk were possessed of sudden strength." For the past several days, the prisoners had known enemy troops were camping beside the Cabu River. The POWs had fretted over their presence and suspected that if there was to be a massacre, these troops would have a hand in it. Now it seemed that their dread scenario was materializing.

Fearing that their white cloth G-strings and underwear shone too conspicuously in the moonlight, many of them elected to shed this marginal attire of the tropics and march buck naked. Yet for many, the Japanese cross fire proved to be only a temporary goad. Even some of the stronger prisoners discovered that they couldn't walk very fast, or very far. Their true condition was manifesting itself. By the dozens and scores, they would have to be carried, or at the very least escorted arm in arm. Bert Bank, too blind to see his own feet, was one of many who were led across the field by hand.

John McCarty, who had lost first one sandal and then the other on his way out of camp, hobbled gingerly over the crackly paddies, his naked feet fast collecting scrapes and bruises. McCarty was so anxious about the bullets "whistling all around us" that one of the Rangers handed him a .45 side arm and a bowie knife, which gave him at least a semblance of self-defense, real or imagined. "I was a walking skeleton," said McCarty, "but I was ready to fight the enemy."

Other prisoners pushed themselves as far as they could go and then squatted in the field, eagerly awaiting a rescuer to come fetch them. The Rangers ran back and forth, balancing these bony apparitions on their backs for the long mile to the Pampanga, where oxcarts were supposed to be waiting. Several pairs of Rangers formed makeshift litters by tying fatigue shirts between their two rifles and grasping the four ends like stretcher poles, with a prisoner borne like an ailing rajah inside.

For a half hour this ungainly procession of the halt and the blind worked its way north. As they plodded along, Mucci kept darting nervous glances off to the right, where the fighting at the Cabu bridge continued to rage with undiminished ferocity. The Imperial Army soldiers were still obviously trying to break through and come after them. Mucci couldn't quite make out what was happening over there; Pajota appeared to be putting up a good fight but it remained to be seen whether he could hold long enough for all the prisoners to cross over to the other side of the river.

Finally, Mucci led the men down to the banks of the Pampanga, where he rejoiced to learn that Pajota's lieutenants had made good on their promise: In the bright moonlight, Mucci could clearly see a dozen carabao carts parked down in the riverbed, the great yoked beasts stamping along the muddy margins. They were unlikely Charons, encrusted in slop, reeking of various wet musky odors, their massive horns bobbing in the darkness. Their presence was a testament of local loyalty to Pajota as well as to the Americans. A peasant of Nueva Ecija didn't lightly offer up his carabao—the bulwark of his livelihood—to anyone. Pajota's men had to fan out in all directions locating animals and wagons from faraway villages. Yet as remarkable as this fleet of beasts of burden was to behold, the colonel could already see that a dozen carts weren't enough. The condition of the prisoners was much worse than he had expected. Before the night was through, Pajota's minions would have to return to the countryside and scare up a few dozen more of these quixotic conveyances.

With the gunfire roaring as loud as ever at the Cabu bridge, Mucci didn't waste any time getting the prisoners moving. They were to ford at the same sandbar where the Rangers had crossed over late in the afternoon. Those who thought they could get across on their own power went ahead, some of them stumbling in the warm, turbid waters. Some prisoners who didn't know about the sandbar tried to cross at other places in the river and soon found themselves in over their heads. It was a baptism no one seemed to mind—although John Cook was mildly distressed to see that the immaculate white boxer shorts he'd proudly donned as his "liberation uniform" before leaving camp were now "stained an ugly muddy brown." Cook, who didn't know how to swim, was heartened to find that the river, at his place of crossing, only came up to his waist.

At one point the column was chased by a group of Japanese who had presumably broken away from the camp. "Suddenly a hail of bullets peppered the water," recalled Hibbs. "But it was soon quieted by the rearguard Rangers." Athough memories differ on this question, several prisoners insist they were pursued to the water's edge by Japanese vehicles. Tommie Thomas recalled that a Japanese light tank was spotted following them as his group crossed the Pampanga. "The Rangers waited while one of them held a rocket launcher on his shoulder," Thomas said. "When that vehicle reached the water's edge—*pow!*—it was a pile of smoldering metal."

To some, the Pampanga was both a literal and a metaphorical line of demarcation; crossing it was to cross over into freedom, for many prisoners doubted that the Japanese would elect to give further chase beyond the river. One POW thought the train of prisoners approaching the banks of the Pampanga looked like the Hebrews of Exodus "waiting for the Red Sea to part before Pharaoh's warriors arrived in hot pursuit."

The most incapacitated prisoners were brought over to the oxcarts and placed inside the straw-lined beds, five to a wagon. Using pliable cane poles, the drivers, who in most cases were the actual owners, prodded their animals across the river. One of the oxcarts tipped over into the water and a group of men had struggle to right it. Although it was swift, the river was shallow enough so that the water came up only to the axles of the wagon wheels. With maddening slowness but without a hint of physical strain, the carabao tugged their cargo across the channel, the creaky wagons heaving behind them.

Chapter 13

While the prisoners of Cabanatuan haltingly made their way to safety, Juan Pajota was engaged in the fight of his life near the Cabu River bridge. As the American guerrilla leader Robert Lapham would write: "It was Pajota's finest hour."

The shooting had commenced only a few seconds after Murphy fired the initial volley at the rear of the compound. The Filipinos caught the Imperial troops at the precise moment of the day when they had most injudiciously let down their guard. Having eaten their suppers, they'd been lounging around their doused campfires enjoying the afterglow of sunset. As Pajota's men began to take aim, they could hear the Japanese laughter, the lilt of their conversation. The beads of one hundred rifles leveled on individual Japanese soldiers. Once the Filipinos heard the stutter of Murphy's F Company, more than a mile distant, they let loose. They fired with a hatred and a vengeance that had steeped in three years of mostly unexpressed resentments. For the Rangers, the killing was a necessary and perhaps momentarily enjoyable but not especially gratifying aspect of the mission; for the Filipinos it was personal, tribal, national; they considered it a blessing of fate, long overdue, to strike back at the invaders with all they could bring to bear.

At first, the Japanese withered. They were utterly taken by surprise. It was several minutes before they could muster even a tepid response. Just as they were trying to launch their first sortie over the Cabu bridge, the ponderous log structure was torn asunder by a terrific explosion. The time bomb secreted beneath the span had detonated on schedule. The Cabu bridge had been rebuilt several months earlier by the camp wood detail at Cabanatuan, but now the hard-wrought handiwork of the prisoners was going up in smoke. When the dust cleared, however, Pajota's scouts discovered with some alarm that although the overpass was now pitted with a gaping bomb crater, the blast had destroyed only a portion of the bridge. As Pajota later told historian Forrest Johnson, the damage appeared sufficient enough to stymie any tanks or other armored vehicles that might attempt to pass over, but the Japanese foot soldiers could still step around the ragged fissure and race across the bridge.

This is precisely what they tried to do. Approximately fifty Imperial Army soldiers gathered on the bridge and mounted a charge, "chanting weird incantations," as the official Ranger report would describe their deafening "Banzai!" cries. But Pajota's men, spread out in a great "V" athwart the highway, were ideally positioned for the ambush. They had set a snare of wicked simplicity. By concentrating their fire directly on the bridge, they were sure to catch the onrushing enemy.

370

The first barrage lasted no more than thirty seconds. To the last man, the Japanese were cut down by the enfilading fire. The Japanese commander, Tomeo Oyabu, responded with bold obtuseness by sending another wave of men over the bridge. When they too were sawed down, he dispatched a third, and a fourth, each squad sending up spirited battle cries before meeting certain death. As Colonel Mucci would tell the *New York Times,* "Those Jáps kept coming and the guerrillas kept mowing them down until their bodies were three deep." Their shrieking became an open invitation for the Filipinos to shoot; Pajota's men would hold their fire until they heard the banzais, then prepare themselves for the next predictable sally of Imperial troops.

A truck filled with Japanese soldiers rushed toward the bridge, the driver apparently not aware that it was impassable. From across the river, a Filipino guerrilla took aim with a bazooka. Having been trained by Rangers in how to use the rocket launcher only that morning, he fired on the vehicle and scored a solid hit. The maimed truck erupted in flames, and several dozen troops were hurled out the sides. Those who weren't killed by the blast feebly attempted to charge, but Pajota's marksmen made quick work of them. Startled by the power of this strange new weapon, the Filipino bazooka man then fired on several tanks that were hidden in a clump of mango trees. Within a few short minutes, he had succeeded in crippling or destroying all of them.

At the bridge, the Japanese continued to expend themselves. On and on it went for a half hour, a scene of revolting carnage, with bodies piling up by the hundreds. "They will keep coming," Captain Pajota predicted to one of his lieutenants. "They know no other way." Many of the corpses fell through the bomb crater and plunged into the river, while others ended up draped in queer postures over the supporting timbers beneath. As they raced across the bridge, the Japanese had to climb over the bodies of their comrades. The Filipinos didn't comprehend the Japanese battle zeal, which seemed to be composed, in equal parts, of superhuman courage and an obedience of extraordinary self-abasement. At one point a small group of Japanese soldiers attempted a flank attack but the guerrillas quickly detected it and obliterated them. The Japanese failure to find an alternate route across the river was inexplicable. Their kamikaze charge was a chilling spectacle to watch, but Pajota's face, lit by the flames of the siege, creased with a barely perceptible smile.

— — — —

At five minutes past eight o'clock, Cabanatuan camp lay still in the pearl moonlight. Twists of smoke rose from some of the rear quarters and sheds, and the tang of singed thatch hung in the air. The Japanese officer barracks were eaten with bullet holes, and figures lay crumpled in pathways and irrigation ditches. One of the guard towers was consumed in a crackling fire. The Ranger shooting had dwindled to occasional stitches that sounded like uninspired afterthoughts.

Captain Prince stood at the front of the compound, clutching his Garand rifle, studying the embers of the raid. The stream of inmates emerging from the main gate had thinned to a trickle and then stopped altogether. Those Rangers responsible for escorting the prisoners reported to Prince that they believed the camp was now empty. They hadn't had time to perform an exact head count, but they felt certain that all Americans had been removed and were well on their way to Platero.

Prince removed his Colt .45 pistol from his side holster and set it at half-cock. Stepping around several bodies that had dropped just inside the entrance, he ran down the camp's central road and bore a sharp left into the American compound. Briskly, he walked from barracks to barracks, ducking into each structure to make sure that no prisoner had been left behind. He gripped his pistol tight and kept it poised at his right ear as he clambered up the buckled wooden stairs and peered into the shadowy dwellings.

"Anybody home?" he said. "Anyone still here?"

He heard nothing but crickets and the far-off sputter of Pajota's guns.

"Hello. Anyone? We're leaving—the Americans are leaving."

But not a single soul was in evidence. The shacks were vacant except for the long rows of sleeping mats and the odd scatterings of personal effects that had been left behind—a hand-carved backgammon set, a stethoscope, mosquito nets, an Underwood typewriter, a pith helmet, stacks of playing cards, a King James Bible, a phonograph, small troves of Japanese occupation money, a flyswatter. The barracks smelled of sweat and coconut oil and human grime. The large swinging shutters were propped open, and a steady cross breeze rattled through. One of the quarters had a little hearth set in a sandbox in the middle of the floor where the evening fire was still faintly burning, casting a molten radiance over the bare room. "That was an eerie feeling going into those big barracks," recalled Prince. "It was nearly pitch black in there except for the faint glow of the ashes. If a Japanese soldier had come around he could have cut me to ribbons. I kept yelling, 'Is there anybody here? Anybody left?' But I got no response."

Captain Prince was spooked by the moonlit desolation of the American compound. He wanted to get out of there in a hurry. He felt certain that although many Japanese soldiers had been killed in the raid, a good number were probably still lurking on the far side of the camp. The report from the Alamo Scouts had suggested that well over 200 soldiers had been quartering there. They couldn't *all* be dead. The Japanese were holding their fire, Prince felt, waiting quietly for the last rattles of the firestorm to pass before emerging from their barracks.

Prince didn't plan to hang around and test his theory. Besides, he'd accomplished his mission. He felt satisfied that his men were correct: As far as he could tell, the premises had been completely evacuated. Now it was time to make a fast exit. He produced his flare pistol and dropped in a cartridge that resembled a small Roman candle. Pointing it heavenward, he fired a single shot. The skies high over Cabanatuan fizzed in a brilliant red glow, with dazzling contrails descending like confetti from the central burst and then tapering into smoke. Visible for miles in all directions, Prince's crimson flare was the definitive signal every Ranger, Scout, and guerrilla was supposed to recognize. The assault was officially concluded. Any Rangers who might still be lingering inside or around the compound were now expected to return with haste to the Pampanga River and assist with the mass exodus of prisoners.

At approximately 8:15, thirty minutes after the raid had begun, Captain Prince returned his flare gun and his .45 to their holsters, strode out the main gate of Cabanatuan, and took off across the rice paddies, searching in vain for a gait that wouldn't aggravate the blisters seething inside his combat boots. Aside from any Japanese survivors, Prince was, he felt sure, the last one out.

But there was one more: Edwin Rose, the deaf Englishman. During the raid, Rose had been at the latrine, laboring mightily. He was not exactly sure what happened, but he believed that he dozed off while he was perched there. Somehow he missed all the shooting and the explosions and the salutations of the Rangers. Nor could he hear Prince's last call. Prince had inspected only the barracks and other large buildings; he didn't think of checking the latrines. So all this time Rose had been sitting there, unaware of the maelstrom swirling around him. Rose was an elderly civilian who had lived in Toronto and was believed to have served as a postal worker in Shanghai before the war. He'd been a purser on a British ship plying between Hong Kong and Singapore, and early in the war he'd suffered a shrapnel wound which had never completely healed. He was a sweet but slightly skittish gentleman of sixty-five years with downy white hair. His vision was depleted from vitamin deficiencies, and his mind was generally addled by his years in prison. "He was a slow thinker," recalled Tommie Thomas, who shared a barracks with Rose. "He was a pleasant enough fellow but he didn't seem to want to associate with anybody. In the mess hall, he was always the last one in line." As another POW who knew Rose put it: "Edwin wasn't all there—his elevator didn't go to the top floor."

Sometime that night after Captain Prince ignited his

flare and departed, Edwin Rose's eyes blinked open. Smelling smoke, he staggered out of the closed latrine and onto the dirt pathway. He was confused. Something didn't seem right to him. The moon shone brightly, but he still couldn't see. On sore feet racked with dry beriberi, Rose fumbled his way back to his barracks. He failed to notice that the room was empty. All of his fellow Englishmen had vanished. He surmised that he had been at the latrine for a long time, that the inmates had turned in for the night. He had no idea that the camp was in ruins, the gate breached, the paths littered with corpses. As the haze of battle cleared, the last prisoner of Cabanatuan lay down on his straw mat and drifted off to sleep.

––––––––

Several hundred yards away, out in the fields beyond the eastern fence, a group of men from F Company were making their way toward the Pampanga. They had seen Prince's flare and thus knew it was time to leave, but since they had to come all the way from the back of the stockade, they were the last stragglers, the rear guard. In their group were Francis Schilli, Roy Sweezy, and Charles Brown, an F Company sergeant. They were moving at a brisk pace, wide-eyed with the adrenaline of combat but relieved that the raid was over, when a lone Japanese soldier opened up on the group from behind. The gunman was too far away to attain accuracy in the darkness, perhaps three hundred yards away. The enemy bullets zinged by without hitting anyone. Francis Schilli, who was ahead of most of the group, had spotted a drainage ditch in the middle distance. The men raced for it and jumped in.

From the safety of the ditch, Schilli turned and watched as the other Rangers streamed across the field. "Where's Roy?" another F Company man asked.

"Right behind us," replied Schilli. Sweezy was standing only a few feet away. He'd turned to look back at the compound. The shooting had stopped; the Japanese rifleman had apparently given up. Just then, the Rangers were startled to see two muzzle flashes leap from a gun no more than five feet away. Schilli watched in horror as Roy Sweezy was hurled across the field, landing with a dull thud on his back. He had two gaping bullet wounds in his chest. From the shadows emerged Charles Brown, holding his rifle, his face white with shock.

The men gathered around Sweezy. The light was going out of his eyes. The bullets passed all the way through his body. A peculiar rasp came from his chest, with a sibilant urgency, and a froth of blood faintly sprayed from the two bullet holes. He had a "sucking chest wound," as the medics would have called it, the failing lungs desperately trying to take in air through the newly created passageway. Sweezy was a dead man.

"God, God, God," he said, writhing. He looked blankly into Schilli's eyes. "Killed by my own men."

His comrades tried to convince him otherwise. "No, no," they said. "Japs." They didn't want him to go with such a sour thought. But Sweezy knew, and he was dying with adamance on his lips. "My own."

The others cut a sharp look at Brown. He didn't say a word. He was incredulous. Everyone had seen what had happened. "I was standing right there," said Schilli. "It could have been me. Roy was two feet away from me." Brown had evidently panicked. For a split second, he'd thought Sweezy was Japanese. There was something about the way he moved, his body language. It happened in a flash. The darkness, people darting about in the moon shadows. On an ill-starred impulse, Brown had apparently fired twice, at point-blank range.

There were a few long awkward moments during which no one knew what to do. Sweezy was still faintly breathing, but they knew he only had minutes. The men decided they would leave him here where he'd fallen and ask the Filipino guerrillas to come retrieve his body in the morning. They hated to leave him behind, but if they didn't go now, Murphy and Prince would wonder what had happened to them. As it was, they would have to hurry to catch up with the main column, where they were needed to assist with the prisoners.

"We're going to baptize him," said Schilli. As a devout Catholic, he thought it was the right thing to do, and everyone seemed to agree. Schilli took his friend in his arms and poured a dribble of canteen water onto his forehead. Solemnly, he mumbled, "The Father, the Son, and the Holy Ghost," and everyone, even the unbelievers, said, "Amen."

———

At 8:40 Captain Prince and the last of the prisoners had reached the cattailed banks of the Pampanga River. The bedraggled caravan of men and beasts stretched to Platero, two miles away. To the east, Pajota's gunfight was still in progress but had diminished in intensity. The threat of a Japanese pursuit lingered, but with Pajota's men holding the road admirably and with the hindmost section of the column now fording the river, the Rangers had good cause to be sanguine. After everyone had crossed over, Prince shot a second signal flare into the skies. This beacon was intended for Pajota and Joson. It was a signal for them to withdraw from their positions and slowly fall back to Platero, where they would be needed as scouts and armed escorts for the twenty-five-mile exodus to the American lines.

Captain Joson, fortunately, had not engaged the enemy forces—in fact, he hadn't seen a hint of them. Since 7:30, when he and his men had set up the roadblock, his stretch of the highway had been a lonely strip of tarmac. With the phone lines cut, the commanders of the 7,000-man Japanese garrison in Cabanatuan City had apparently remained unaware of the raid. Not having to worry about defending himself, Joson could thus heed Prince's flare and easily remove his forces to Platero posthaste. Captain Pajota would not have that luxury. His withdrawal would necessarily be a much more complicated and delicate procedure, one that would require several hours to complete.

On his way into Platero, Dr. Hibbs ran into "a slouched hulk" leaning against the dike of a rice paddy. It was a very tired-looking Colonel Duckworth, taking a brief rest. Hibbs wasn't aware that the colonel had broken his arm while fleeing the camp, and in greeting his commanding officer, he gave the bad arm a vigorous, friendly tug. Duckworth yowled in pain and screeched, "Don't pull on that arm!" Profusely apologetic, Hibbs helped him get back on his feet and they walked on into Platero. "The bones grated as he moved," Hibbs recalled, "but he refused anything for the pain. I managed to make him a sling with handkerchiefs and my precious socks."

By this time, Platero was a crowded way station bustling with gleeful shouts and laughter. Several hundred prisoners and Rangers were already ensconced there, and Captain Joson's forces formed a tight ring around the town to guard against a Japanese incursion. Mucci announced that the column would take a half-hour break so that the men and carabao could get water and a brief rest. The Rangers offered chocolates and American cigarettes to the POWs—or, one should say, to the ex-POWs—while local Filipinos circulated fruits and coconut cakes, crying, *"Mabuhay!"*

Both the liberators and the liberated were trying to seize a sense of military order from the pandemonium of the raid and the headlong flight across the river. It was here in Platero that the prisoners had their first opportunity to conduct a proper roll call. Tommie Thomas, who in addition to being the provost marshal was one of the barracks leaders, performed a quick head count and made a frightening discovery: One of the English prisoners from his barracks was missing. The Brits did a little investigating among themselves and determined who it was—Edwin Rose. "There was a great deal of concern," recalled Thomas. "We checked around. No one had seen him since the afternoon." Everybody was genuinely worried for the poor fellow. Cabanatuan camp and its environs were still inhabited by Japanese soldiers who, it could now be assumed, were in a decidedly vengeful frame of mind. If they found this innocent old fool stumbling about the camp, there was no telling what they'd do to him.

Abie Abraham promptly reported the disturbing development to Mucci. "We've got a man missing, Colonel," said Abraham. "We have to do something." Though troubled by the news, Colonel Mucci decided that it was far too late—and too risky—to double back for Rose. "I can't send any of my men," Mucci told Abraham. As it was, he explained, they had a long, hard march ahead of them, one that would tax the sleep-deprived Rangers and push the very limits of the prisoners' endurance. Instead, Mucci would ask Pajota to dispatch a squad of guerrillas to return and search for Rose at first light.

At the Platero schoolhouse, Dr. Jimmy Fisher was lying on one of the operating tables that had been fashioned by pushing several desks together and layering them with clean bedding and sheets. He'd been brought in a few minutes earlier by oxcart. The irony wasn't lost on anyone: Fisher was the only seriously wounded patient lying in the field hospital that he himself had set up earlier in the day to treat the numerous casualties he expected the raid to produce. His condition was grave. He was losing enormous amounts of blood. He'd been given morphine to blunt the acute pain in his gut, but the field hospital had no proper anesthetic. Dr. Carlos Layug was standing over Fisher, shaking his head darkly. He'd seen abdominal shrapnel wounds of this sort before and recognized immediately that Fisher's prognosis was desperately serious. Layug's wife, Julita, was at his side, her eyes filled with worry as she took Fisher's pulse. From the start, Fisher had made a deep impression on the Layugs, and even though they'd known him for only twenty-four hours, they were visibly shocked to see him languishing before them, in extremis. "We felt he was an old friend," Julita Layug later wrote, "and almost regretted coming to know and love him, for if he had been a stranger we would not have felt as miserable as we did."

The Layugs understood that Fisher desperately needed to be moved to a better-equipped hospital, but moving him at all would kill him. They would have to operate immediately. The Layugs were joined by Merle Musselman, the POW doctor who had just arrived from the prison camp, and James Duckworth, who could only play an advisory role since his fractured right arm was now bound up in a sling.

With the patient fluttering in and out of consciousness, Layug made a long incision across the belly. When he pulled back the outer tissues and began to inspect Fisher's organs, he realized that the damage was even worse than he'd feared. The liver was hemorrhaging massively and bits of shrapnel were lodged in his colon and small intestines. The doctors exchanged sober looks. They all felt the situation was virtually hopeless, but they had to give it a try. "There was a job to do, and we did the best we could," Dr. Musselman later wrote. "One doesn't count the odds until it is all over and one has time to think. I didn't want to be haunted by the thought that I had overlooked a hope."

Methodically they worked through the liver, removing the little specks and shards as they went. Periodically local women would come in with fresh sheets and pots of boiling water. Dr. Musselman, having been liberated but an hour before, felt an especially intense feeling of responsibility toward the patient lying before him. "As we worked on Dr. Fisher that night," Musselman recalled, "I kept feeling the debt I owed to this man and to his family, and the impossibility of ever fulfilling it by word, by thought or by action. I knew that I would never forget him and the others who made possible any good that I might do or any success that I might enjoy."

One of the Rangers, Eugene Kocsis, had to enter the schoolhouse to deliver another patient wounded in the same mortar-shell attack that had felled Dr. Fisher. He was shocked by the scene inside. "I couldn't believe my eyes," said Kocsis. "There was Captain Jimmy, lying on the table. The Filipino doctor had cut him open from one side all the way over to the other. He was holding up his intestines in one hand, and picking out shrapnel with the other." The men were distressed beyond words to see their beloved battalion surgeon so gravely wounded. Several Rangers who entered the schoolhouse left in tears. "He was in loving hands," Julita Layug wrote. "It was touching to see the Rangers crying, and wishing they could take his place."

At one point during the operation, Fisher came to and for a few moments seemed to pierce the fog of the morphine. His eyes trolled the room for a familiar face. "Did we get them?" he asked. "The prisoners—did we get them all?"

"You bet we did, Captain," said one of the Rangers who happened to be standing nearby. "Every last one of 'em."

Fisher smiled weakly and drifted off again while Dr. Layug began to suture his abdomen.

The train of men pulled out of Platero around 9:30 that night on what Abie Abraham called "the last of many marches." More Filipino farmers had arrived to donate the services of their carabao; now the caravan had expanded to more than thirty carts. The column would need to trudge all night and well into the next day to cover the twenty-five miles to Guimba, and that was assuming there were no unforeseen holdups or encounters with the Japanese. An oxcart trek of such length would be far too grueling for Dr. Fisher. The wounded surgeon would have to stay behind in Platero, lying in a state of semiconsciousness on a teacher's desk in the dimly lit schoolhouse. A group of men volunteered to look after him, including Dr. Musselman, veterinarian Herbert Ott, and Chaplain Hugh Kennedy. The Alamo Scouts and a handful of Rangers would serve as bodyguards, and Pajota's men, who were just now beginning to disengage from the Cabu Bridge battle, would provide a rearguard force.

Within a half hour, the last of the POWs had left Platero. In the rear of the column, Captain Prince walked with a hobbling gait that made him seem as bad off as many of the prisoners he was "delivering." By asking around, Prince was disappointed to learn that the two friends he'd trained with back in the United States, Bataan veterans Reed Shurtleff and Van Geldern, whom he'd hoped to find among the Cabanatuan prisoners, had both died in prison camp years earlier.

For the veterans of Bataan, the prospect of a wearisome trudge with fellow stick figures across rural Luzon sounded nauseatingly familiar, a cruel déjà vu. As they found their stride, more than a few of the prisoners observed that the long hike to safety felt like the direct opposite of their trek out of Bataan, a kind of reverse image in which all the emotional valences had been flipped. "It was a long, slow, steady march," said John McCarty, "but this was a life march, a march of freedom."

The prisoners felt as though they were traveling in a protective envelope. The marching prisoners could look off to the sides, to the front or rear, and see the silhouettes of a hundred armed men, Rangers and guerrillas, insulating them from the uncertainties of the countryside. Other Rangers were walking right with the prisoners, offering a hand, a canteen, or a morsel of food to whoever was in need. As the night grew colder, the Rangers shed their clothes and offered them to the scantily clad prisoners. John Cook was hiking in nothing more than boxer shorts and high-top leather shoes when a Ranger insisted that the shivering Texan take his fatigue jacket. "He said, 'Have this—you need this worse than I do.' It was a blessing." Another Ranger removed his T-shirt and ripped it into rags so John McCarty, who was walking without shoes, could bind his scratched and bleeding feet.

Soldierly pride prevented many of the prisoners from accepting the assistance they genuinely needed. "Some of the men told the Rangers to stop holding them up," recalled Abraham. "They were stubborn about it. They'd say, 'We want to walk by ourselves, like free men!'"

The carabao teams tramped onward, kicking up thick shrouds of dust as they went, puncturing the ground with their odd, two-toed hooves. They seemed confused and irritable in their heavy yokes; they weren't used to working after sunset and their night vision was poor. Sometimes one of the buffaloes would veer off on a subsidiary trail, and the train would have to halt while the animal's owner took off to fetch it. Ponderous and ungraceful, the carabao ambled at a pace that was almost comical, even though their drivers relentlessly fussed at them. "They couldn't be made to move faster," complained Abraham. "They just took their good old time. But if they spotted water, they moved toward it at a brisk run."

The men had ideal weather for a march—cool and clear and dry, with a sugaring of stars and a nearly full moon, occasionally scarved in high cumulus clouds, that gave the prisoners a convenient night-light by which to walk. "The good Lord knew what He was doing," Tommie Thomas mused. There was rain somewhere off in the Cordillera Central. The northern horizon flickered with heat lightning. Overhead, the prisoners could hear the steady hum of American night fighters, which were supposed to be clearing the main roads throughout Nueva Ecija of any Japanese convoys that might harry the Rangers' return to Guimba.

On timeworn trails and roads of rutted dirt, the glacial hike went on and on, crossing the Morcan and Casili rivers, passing through the barrios of Balincarin and Mataas Na Kahoy, where even more oxcarts and buffaloes were added to the growing cavalcade. The villagers streamed out of their huts. Ralph Hibbs was given an entire meal to eat. A small, gray-haired Filipina emerged from the darkness holding in her outstretched hands a cooked chicken wrapped in banana leaves. "I could see tears glistening in her wrinkled face. 'You eat,' she said. 'I pray for you many years.' She crossed herself and moved away."

———

All night long Colonel Mucci had to play the role of pacesetter and morale czar. He was good at it, pushing the prisoners just as far and as fast they could go without collapsing. He didn't want to rest too long in any one place, not only because the Japanese might find them but also because it seemed to him that momentum itself was keeping the march alive. The longer the break, the harder it was to get everyone moving again. He practiced the classic prevarication of the drill sergeant—distance deflation. "Just a few miles to go," he'd say, "just a few more," knowing perfectly well that they still had another fifteen or twenty ahead of them.

"Mucci's miles stretched into more miles," said Abie Abraham, who appreciated the psychology behind the colonel's white deceit. "But I didn't care, because I was happy for the first time in years, sucking in the fresh air." In fact, the prisoners, even many of the sickest ones, grew more buoyant as the march progressed. With each mile, a visible euphoria grew on their faces. Abraham observed one gaunt man with tuberculosis who had "a permanent smile on his face. He said, 'Oh, my folks will be so happy.' He gazed up at the stars and said, 'Mother, I love you!'"

Many prisoners who started out the march in poor condition were astounded at how far they could walk. Part of their new vitality sprang from all the protein-rich beef and condensed milk they'd consumed during their last few weeks in the camp. Their raiding of the Japanese storehouse now seemed providential; it had afforded them the sustenance they needed to break from their shackles. They were running on stolen fuel, without which, they now understood, this long trek would not have been possible.

But there was more to it than that, for the prisoners seemed to gather strength as they went. The foretaste of freedom was like a blood transfusion. They responded powerfully to a carrot-and-stick motivation, the lure of home ahead and the threat of Japanese avengers at their backs. "Sometimes I wonder how we did it," said Ralph

Rodriguez. "You have to remember, those Japs were behind us, we could hear them shooting, they were trying to break through." Rodriguez came to feel as though his legs moved by their own volition. "I could walk but I couldn't stop," he said. "If I stopped, even for a few seconds, my legs wouldn't hold me up and I collapsed. The muscles went rigid." Bob Body, who had been in the hospital with a variety of maladies and weighed only 100 pounds, figured he'd make it only a few miles and then find a seat on a crowded carabao cart. "When I started out from that camp," said Body, "I would have bet a thousand bucks I couldn't walk twenty-five miles. But you'd be amazed at what you can take if you have to. We were sure the Japanese were going to come track us down and annihilate us."

The other stimulus that kept the captives moving was the good cheer of the Rangers and the spirited conversation that filled the long hours. "The Rangers seemed as happy as we were," remembered Bert Bank. "All during the night they ran up and down the columns inquiring if anyone was from their hometowns." They talked about the exotic and fearsome new weapons the Americans were wielding throughout the world—bazookas and flamethrowers, napalm and radar-equipped planes. They talked about the two wars, the war that was lost three years ago and the war that was now being won. "We wanted to know where they had been and what they had seen," wrote Tommie Thomas. "And they were anxious to know how it had been with us, and whether it was as rough as they had heard. We regarded them as heroes. They regarded us as heroes. It was a mutual admiration society."

The Rangers wouldn't accept congratulations from the internees—they kept responding with demurrals like "It was just a job" or "You're the brave ones, not us." They didn't understand the extent to which the men of Cabanatuan had instantly come to venerate them. "They were a breed of men like none we'd ever seen before," is how John Cook described the Rangers. Bob Body was more emphatic: "As far as we were concerned, they were gods."

Yet even gods eventually get tired. As the night progressed, the Rangers grew noticeably sloppy and zombie-eyed from lack of sleep. Some began to doze or mildly hallucinate as they marched. The Rangers had slept only five or six hours over the past seventy-two, and, in truth, they'd been so anxious during the previous night's rest in Platero that few had gotten any real slumber. "Just to keep us awake and give us that last needed bit of energy," as Mucci put it, one of the medics distributed a vial of little white tablets that were described as "pep pills." It was the new pharmaceutical offering of the U.S. Army, the new sleep fighter: Benzedrine.

Although it was first synthesized back in 1887, amphetamine wasn't employed for medical purposes until thirty years later, when pharmaceutical companies marketed it as an inhaler for asthmatics. During World War II, amphetamines became all the rage as a stimulant, with some 72 million tablets handed out to both Allied and Axis soldiers by the end of the war. It was said that Adolf Hitler underwent a daily regimen of amphetamine injections. Certainly, this was the first time any of the Rangers had taken speed. They found the drug both startling and wonderful. It increased the heart rate and breathing rate, dilated the pupils, pumped fresh adrenaline into the system. "We were having the devil of a time staying awake that night," recalled

Ranger Homer Britzius. "But those bennies did the trick. That was a new thing in the Army. It felt like your eyes were popped open. You couldn't have closed them if you wanted to. One pill was all I ever took—it was all I ever needed."

A few of the Rangers, like Roy Peters, failed to receive a dose and the comparative results were remarkable. "Somehow I missed out on those pills," Peters said, "and boy I sure could have used them, because a couple of times I fell asleep right there on the trail." The Benzedrine worked so well that some of the men began to wish for a veterinary equivalent. "If only we could have given some of that stuff to those buffaloes," one Ranger said, "then we really would have gotten somewhere."

––––––––

Their nerves were fairly thrumming by the time the Rangers reached the Rizal Road, the major north-south thoroughfare which they'd crossed over with several close calls two nights previously. It was now 2:30 on Wednesday morning, January 31. Mucci was deeply concerned about the Rizal Road. Not only was the highway controlled by the enemy, but the Japanese convoys had been most active at precisely this time of the morning. If enemy traffic appeared while they were crossing, the "life march" would be in jeopardy. They were pitifully vulnerable. The present caravan of shambling prisoners and water buffaloes was not nearly so agile as his light-traveling Rangers had been two nights earlier. The column now stretched back for more than a mile behind Mucci, with more than 600 people and fifty oxcarts in the train. Even under the best of circumstances, it would take them a half hour to get everyone across.

Mucci was unaware that earlier in the evening—at about eight o'clock, as the Cabanatuan raid was being carried out—a Black Widow night fighter had destroyed five troop-carrying trucks and a Japanese tank on this same road, approximately six miles to the south. Ten other Black Widows were fanning out over the roads and arteries of Nueva Ecija just now, seeking prey. Even though they were friendly aircraft, the night fighters made an unnerving chorus of Furies in the night sky. The Rangers found it vaguely nerve-racking to have this unseen menace droning above them.

As Mucci approached the Rizal Road, his scouts informed him that the embankment on the far side of the highway was too steep for the carabao carts to negotiate. Instead of crossing right over, the cavalcade would have to backtrack, proceeding due south on the highway for over a mile before they could find a suitable place to pass over.

Mucci assigned two parties to set up barricades. Armed with bazookas and antitank grenades, the two teams assumed corresponding positions to the north and south of the main column. Beyond the roadblocks, Mucci sent scouts on calesa ponies to serve as advance warners. Then, in ones and twos, the men and beasts climbed up from the rice paddies onto the road and began to inch southward. Mucci understood that it was a tremendously precarious endeavor. If an enemy motorcade were to come along, neither of the two roadblocks would be able to hold for more than a few minutes. The long file of prisoners would then lay hopelessly exposed. "It was a pretty bad stretch," Mucci conceded, "but we couldn't avoid it."

Silently, the exodus crept down the road, the men enjoying the feel of the smooth asphalt under their feet even while they dreaded the circumstances of this risky pass. The two barricade crews scoured the highway and prayed that no one would come. "It was a tense hour or so," remembered Roy Peters. "We couldn't have done much with those roadblocks if there had actually been Japs coming. But as with the rest of the raid, we had good luck every step of the way."

Finally, "after what seemed an age," as Mucci put it, the long queue reached a spot where the carabao could safely vacate the road and slip back down into the relative safety of the countryside. At about 4:30 A.M. the maneuver was complete, with the blistered Captain Prince, now hitching a ride in an oxcart, bringing up the rear. As Mucci later wrote: "It was the longest hour I've ever sweated out in all my life."

—·——·—

A few hours earlier, at one in the morning, Bill Nellist and the other Alamo Scouts who had stayed back in Platero to guard Dr. Fisher, decided they must evacuate the barrio. Their safety was in jeopardy. Reports from the guerrillas indicated that the Japanese were active again along the highway. It was only a matter of time before the garrison in Cabanatuan City would discover that the phone lines to the camp had been severed and that something was amiss. Pajota's forces had completed their withdrawal to the Pampanga River. By their admittedly vague estimates drawn from the dim visibility of the night, they had eliminated over half of the Japanese battalion camped along the river.

Pajota had secured a remarkable victory, but now he fully expected that the Japanese would regroup and attempt to retaliate.

Bill Nellist's immediate fear was that the enemy might dispatch patrols to comb the surrounding countryside and hunt down prisoners or any other American stragglers. Nellist asked Dr. Musselman whether he thought Fisher could be moved to Balincarin, the next barrio to the north. Musselman's reply was fatalistic. "Fisher's prognosis is very poor," he said. "I doubt it will matter one way or the other."

Still, they had to devise a suitable way to convey him. An ordinary stretcher wouldn't suffice. In his present state his body couldn't withstand the violent torquing and swaying of a crude litter. So the Scouts improvised a solution. From one of the fancier dwellings in Platero, they removed a thick Spanish door from its hinges and hauled it over to the school. Gingerly, they slid Dr. Fisher onto the ponderous slab. It required six strong men to carry the semiconscious captain on his stretcher of wood. Glancing nervously over their shoulders for enemy sorties, the bearers disappeared down the carabao path toward Balincarin, some three miles away. "I don't think anybody thought he was going to make it," said Ranger Thomas Grace, who was one of Fisher's six litter carriers. "You could look at him and tell. But we couldn't just leave him behind to die." Dr. Musselman, Herbert Ott, Chaplain Kennedy, Bill Nellist, and the remaining Alamo Scouts soon followed.

Since his operation earlier in the evening, Dr. Fisher's condition had steadily worsened. The Layugs had succeeded in addressing the numerous perforations in Fisher's bowel, but the liver was still hemorrhaging. His life was steadily pouring from him. He punctuated every shallow breath with a sharp grunt of discomfort. The medics gave him another dose of morphine to dull the pain. Even when he was awake he was seldom lucid. At one point he rose through the narcotic haze just long enough to ask what was happening and how everyone was getting along. "He actually apologized for being any trouble instead of being able to direct and help in the care of his own men," Dr. Musselman later recalled in a note to Fisher's mother. "He spoke of you and of his wife and hoped that the news of his wound would not worry you."

Lying on the door with his sallow face turned toward the stars, Fisher survived the hour-long journey to Balincarin—but just barely. Fisher was placed on a cot in one of the stilted nipa huts. Dr. Musselman and Herbert Ott continued to monitor his vital signs. Musselman suspected that the move from Platero, although necessary, had considerably harmed Dr. Fisher.

If Fisher was to be saved, Musselman concluded, he absolutely required the facilities and expertise of a fully equipped Army hospital. By radio, a request for a small airplane was called in to Army headquarters in Guimba. The request was granted. A plane would fly to Balincarin in the morning to evacuate Fisher. There was a glaring problem, however: Balincarin had no airstrip. With the audacity peculiar to his outfit, Bill Nellist ordered his Alamo Scouts to go build one—overnight. Quickly they went canvassing from door to door and assembled a crew of local people. By torchlight, they selected a suitable swath of land on the barrio outskirts. For five hours, as darkness segued into dawn, the workmen stooped in the rice fields with hoes, rakes, even wooden spoons. They graded and leveled, tore down the paddy dikes, and pulled away vegetation. "I'd never seen anything like it," recalled Alamo Scout Gilbert Cox. "Not once did they stop to take a rest. Every man, woman, and child was out there all night clawing in the dirt. Some of them were using their bare hands."

By dawn the airstrip was complete. It was crude, bumpy, and short, but the tiny Piper Cubs didn't require much distance on which to land and take off. The Scouts marked the parameters with bedsheets so the pilot could plainly spot it from the air. Utterly exhausted, Bill Nellist fell asleep in his clothes with ears tuned to the skies.

Unbeknownst to the Scouts, Dr. Fisher's already grave condition began to plummet around dawn. Accustomed to improvisational medicine like all POW physicians, Dr. Musselman undertook a desperate and seldom-performed procedure: a vein-to-vein blood transfusion, with an IV line directly attached to the arm of a Scout who shared Fisher's blood type. "We used two needles and the rubber tubing left from a long-since-expended plasma set," Musselman recalled. "Jim was semicomatose during this time and did no talking. He suffered none and showed no apprehension of his condition."

The unorthodox transfusion failed to arrest Fisher's downward spiral. "It was futile," medic John Nelson later wrote in a letter to Fisher's mother. "Everything possible had been done to save the captain's life, and even under the most favorable conditions the outcome would have been extremely doubtful."

The airplane never came. In the forenoon, Captain Fisher roused for a brief moment. With glazed, uncomprehending eyes, he glanced over at his friend and first sergeant, John Nelson, who was at his side. Fisher's expression was opaque, his voice thin and whispery. "G'luck," he said, struggling to muster a smile.

"What, Jimmy?"

"G'luck on the way out," he said, and then his eyes closed.

An hour later, he died. The body was carefully wrapped in canvas. With several hundred Filipinos in attendance, Chaplain Hugh Kennedy performed the solemnities. Then the Alamo Scouts buried James Canfield Fisher at the base of a fruit tree at the edge of Balincarin.

———————

All through the morning, Henry Mucci steadily marched the prisoners toward the northwest. The colonel was on the brink of exhaustion, his eyes bloodshot, his face stubbled with a three-day beard, his nerves frayed. Yet somehow he still gave the impression of being indefatigable, coaxing the others in a voice that conveyed optimism and strength. Around six in the morning, the skies over the Sierra Madre assumed a pinkish tint. The sun's first suggestion lifted the men's morale impressively. "At last, I saw the horizon," Abie Abraham later wrote. "I gazed back at the sunrise, then at the skeletons plodding along in the column behind me, their sunken eyes emitting joy."

Around 6:30 the column came to an abrupt stop. Something was awry. One of Pajota's lieutenants hurried over to inform Colonel Mucci that the barrio ahead was controlled by the Hukbalahap, a rebel outfit that had for years been a staunch and sometimes bloody rival of the pro-American guerrillas. The village, which was guarded by more than 150 armed men, was strictly off-limits. The column of POWs would not be allowed to pass through.

Mucci asked the obvious question. "Is there a road around this barrio?" The answer came back, negative. They'd have to retrace their steps for miles and then take an alternate route, a laborious backtrack that Mucci was not prepared even to consider.

The colonel reacted to this unforeseen wrinkle with an incredulity that quickly sharpened into outrage. He squared his shoulders and fixed a gimlet stare on the little village gleaming before him in the morning light. Unable to assess the rebel faction's true strength, Mucci couldn't tell where the bluff ended and the legitimate threat began. The Huks, as the Hukbalahap were more commonly known, were a shadowy and thoroughly unpredictable force in the life of rural Luzon. They were an indigenous organization of agrarian reformers and insurgents heavily influenced by Marxist ideas. Rabidly anti-Japanese, but also anti-American, they enjoyed considerable popularity in the rice-dominant plains of Nueva Ecija, where a handful of wealthy landowners had long held the tenant-farming majority in a state of virtual serfdom. The Huk leaders disagreed over some of their ultimate goals, but in general they wanted to incite a peasant revolt that would sweep the Philippines and lead to the installation of a Communist, or at least socialistic, regime once the Americans rid the country of the Japanese and set it on the promised course toward total independence. The well-armed Huks could be ruthless if provoked. Robert Lapham, the American guerrilla leader, considered them "treacherous." Throughout the occupation, they had persistently tangled with American-led Filipino guerrillas. Province by province, barrio by barrio, the two organizations bitterly vied against one another for local loyalty and support. There had constantly been ambushes and reprisals—and, inevitably, reprisals to the reprisals. At times the internecine fighting had grown bloodier than the common effort against the Japanese occupiers.

Generally, the two groups tried to respect each other's turf, which explained why Pajota's lieutenant was now loath to trespass on the tiny village ahead. The Huks were doubtless annoyed that their rival had been selected to guide the American force on a mission of such importance, and they now jealously sought to exert, through sabotage, what little influence they had left over the situation.

It was an absurd impasse that called for a bit of diplomatic finesse, but Mucci was tired and ornery and growing more impatient by the second. Finally he decided to bull his way through, a style of problem solving more in keeping with his temperament. He turned to his Filipino scouts. "Go explain to them," he said. "We're coming through. Don't ask—*tell* them."

The mile-long cortege of oxcarts and bleary-eyed prisoners halted at the edge of town while overtures were made with the village elders. After a few long minutes, Pajota's people returned with the verdict. "They will let Americans through," the lieutenant reported. "But we guerrillas are forbidden to enter."

Mucci had had enough. He didn't want to stick his nose in a local squabble, but they'd left him no choice. He thought it highly imprudent to lead his vulnerable caravan through a potentially hostile village without the protection of the guerrilla escorts. "Tell them we're *all* coming through," Mucci barked. "If they have any objections, tell them I'll get on the radio and call in the American artillery. This village will be *leveled*."

It was a bluff, of course. Mucci's radio wasn't even working. The radioman had been trying to reach headquarters since dawn, but was getting only static. But the bluff worked—one of the guerrilla captains came back with official approval to enter the barrio. At this point Mucci had understandably grown a bit paranoid and was no longer sure whom to trust. He entertained the possibility that somehow this captain might be in collusion with the Huks. "Are you absolutely sure the road will be all clear?"

"Yes."

Mucci removed his .45 from his side holster and cranked a shell into it. "It's like this," he told the captain. "It *better* be all clear. Because you're going to head the column. I'll be right behind you. If there's even a hint of trouble, I'll shoot you first." He glowered at the young Filipino.

Bob Body was standing ten feet away from Mucci, watching this terse exchange. "I thought, Jesus Christ, this Colonel Mucci is one tough little guy," Body said. "I sure wouldn't want to be that captain, walking through that town with a forty-five in my back."

Mucci gave the signal, and the column resumed its march, threading through the center of the barrio. The Huk warriors lined the shoulders of the road and stared. They stood proudly, clutching their weapons, with their families arrayed behind them. The prisoners could feel the tension as they slipped through this curious gauntlet. The Huks and the guerrillas traded spiteful looks at each other, the glares of men who would surely revisit the morning's sentiments at another time and place.

Yet the entire column passed through without incident. Mucci apologized profusely to the guerrilla captain whose loyalty he had questioned, and the column carried on toward Guimba.

—————

At eight o'clock, Colonel Mucci's radio man finally got through to Sixth Army headquarters. The news was felicitous: During the three days of the raid, the Americans had advanced more than fifteen miles toward Cabanatuan, which meant the "life march" had fifteen fewer miles to go than Mucci thought. They wouldn't have to go all the way to Guimba. The day before, the Sixth Army had captured the town of Talavera, which was about ten miles away from Mucci's present position. The radioman told the colonel to head for Talavera; American forces would be waiting to intercept them there.

The pace was as slow as ever, but nearly everyone who needed a ride could find one now, for the caravan had swelled to a magnificent seventy-one carts. The men in the carts kept their eyes fixed on the west, for the first sign of American presence. Some of the men passed the time singing songs—"Amazing Grace," "Home on the Range." By ten o'clock, the hot sun bit at the prisoners' bare backs and warmed the dirt beneath their bare feet. Suddenly the morning calm was punctured by the sound of planes in the distance. The Rangers turned and saw four silver specks growing on the eastern horizon. They were fighter planes, diving in low. The Rangers became suspicious. The aircraft seemed to be perfectly aligned for a strafing attack, as though they would pass right over the full length of the column. "They're Japanese!" one Ranger yelled. "Take cover!" The prisoners jumped from their oxcarts and sought protection in the surrounding rice paddies. "Oh God, not now, not after all this," Abie Abraham heard one POW lying next to him moan. Mucci's men hoisted their rifles and set their sights on the incoming planes. The Rangers were just about to shoot when the planes pulled out of their dives, revealing bright stars on the undersides of their wings.

They were P-51 fighters and they'd simply come to pay aerial tribute to the men of Bataan and Corregidor. They circled back and passed over the column again and again, waggling their wings in greeting. "They roared over us with earsplitting screams from their powerful engines," recalled Abraham. "They were waving their wings as if to say, 'Welcome back!' " Finally, the fighters turned north and assumed a tight formation as they streaked away. It was a moving spectacle, yet for some prisoners possessed of bitter memories, the air show was three years overdue. As Dr. Hibbs put it: "Hundreds of planes had arrived just like they promised in 1942—but oh my God, they were so late!"

Up ahead, the prisoners riding high in their carts could spot a flurry of activity in the distance. Soon ambulances and trucks began to appear on the road, then a Red Cross van. An American tank approached, swiveling its turret and bobbing its guns in salutation. The border had been an invisible one, but somehow they'd crossed it: They were now inside American lines.

While everyone else cheered and screamed in exultation, Dr. Hibbs suddenly became preoccupied with one of his TB patients, a man named Johnson, who was in critical condition. Hibbs had spent much of the evening tending to Johnson, but he was going down fast. The all-night ride had been too much for his frail constitution. "I hurried over to the straw-filled cart where Johnson was breathing his last," Hibbs later wrote. "I climbed in and cuddled his head on my lap. I could see medics running toward us with IVs, but it was too late. He was in the twilight of consciousness." Johnson died in his cart outside Talavera, only minutes after crossing out of Japanese-held territory.

A convoy of large troop-carrying trucks motored down the road and halted alongside the column. The prisoners were told to vacate their oxcarts and climb aboard. For the last ten miles into Guimba, they stood up and clung to the side boards. They rode as champions at the end of a long campaign, inspecting the new world from a high perch. The roads were lined with thousands of GIs who waved at them and threw candy and cigarettes. They were speeding to a place that had medicines and hot food, clean quarters with soft cots and cool fans and cold beer. They were seven thousand miles from home, but they'd passed again into America.

Along the way they saw an American flag set in the turret of a tank. It wasn't much of a flag, writhing in a weak breeze, but for the men of Cabanatuan, the sight was galvanizing. Ralph Hibbs said his heart stopped, for he realized that it was the first Stars and Stripes he'd seen since the surrender. All the men in all the trucks stood at attention and saluted. Then came the tears. "We wept openly," said Abie Abraham, "and we wept without shame."

We are all ghosts now

But once we were men.

from an unsigned diary
recovered from Cabanatuan camp

Epilogue

The transport ship churned without escort across the blue bulge of the Pacific, making a long, circuitous loop close to the equator to avoid the major shipping lanes. The boat left from Leyte in mid-February, stopping briefly in New Guinea before cutting across the open ocean, tacking with metronomic regularity to evade Japanese subs. The usual seven thousand miles to San Francisco would thus become closer to twelve thousand, with the hammocks belowdecks swaying in unison as the ship heaved and groaned with every sharp turn.

The SS *General Anderson* was a 20,000-ton troop transport painted battle gray and kept in constant blackout to forestall air attacks. The ship was filled with a few thousand sailors on rotation furlough as well as 272 former residents of Cabanatuan camp. Ralph Hibbs was on board, as were Tommie Thomas, Bert Bank, John Cook, Herbert Ott, Ralph Rodriguez, John McCarty, and Robert Body. The transport held most of the American prisoners rescued by the Rangers except for a few of the highest-ranking officers and the gravely ill, who were hospitalized in the Philippines or sent home by airplane. Also on the boat were several survivors of the massacre on Palawan, including Eugene Nielsen, the private from Utah who had swum across Puerto Princesa Bay to escape the atrocity. The *Anderson*'s evasive maneuvers were not an idle precaution. The captain of the ship had been informed that the Japanese Navy knew not only the name, description, and destination of the transport but also the precise nature of the cargo. Shortly before the *Anderson* left Leyte, Tokyo Rose, the queen of the Japanese Department of Propaganda, had been heard on the radio talking explicitly about the ship. Possessed of eerily accurate intelligence, she'd placed a kind of curse on the *Anderson*. "This is Tokyo Rose," she was reported to have said in the odd, tremulous English for which she was famous. "At this moment the murderers and criminals who took advantage of our Japanese guards at Cabanatuan are boarding the American ship *General Anderson* in Leyte Harbor. They have been spreading malicious lies about the Japanese people. Japanese warships, submarines, and planes in the Pacific have been alerted to destroy this ship at all costs."

The Ranger raid on Cabanatuan had evidently caused the Imperial Army to lose considerable face in the international propaganda wars. If Tokyo Rose was to be believed, the Japanese were determined to obliterate the homeward-bound POWs before they could tell their stories to the world. The relentlessness of the Japanese hex against them was chilling: The prisoners of Cabanatuan, weeks after their rescue, still appeared to be marked men. Stunned by the accuracy of Tokyo Rose's information, the prisoners had boarded the *Anderson* with the quiet despair of hounded fugitives. "You guys are powder kegs," one Navy man said to John McCarty as the prisoners boarded the ship. "Loading you is like loading dynamite."

The *Anderson* was virtually defenseless, armed only with a single six-inch gun mounted on its fantail that was operated by an inexperienced gunnery crew. If a Japanese submarine made good on Tokyo Rose's promise and put a torpedo in the hull, the *Anderson* would surely sink to the bottom of the Pacific in one of the great maritime disasters of the war. When the ship reached Hollandia, New Guinea, Tokyo Rose again conveyed Nippon's peculiar wrath toward the *Anderson*. Uncannily, Japanese intelligence had already pinpointed the ship's new location. "The *Anderson* has reached Hollandia, New Guinea," she announced. "Japanese submarines have been ordered to destroy the ship." Trying to respond to the situation with humor, John McCarty said, "Somebody call up the bitch and ask her what we're having for breakfast."

The skipper of the *Anderson* came down from the bridge and tried to reassure the prisoners. "We're confident they won't get us, but we want to be cautious," he said. He instructed them to wear life preservers at all times—in case of a sudden sub attack. The captain was charting an unusual course, bearing south, then east toward Mexico, keeping the ship as close as possible to friendly islands or the known locations of American vessels. "You're precious cargo," the captain assured them. "The people in the States want you more than those Japs do." At one point a life raft was spotted off the bow of the ship, but the skipper did not slow down to investigate. He later explained to the prisoners that enemy submarines had been known to rig up open-water decoys in the hope of getting American ships to stop long enough for the Japanese to blast them out of the water. "We stop for no one," the skipper said, "not even the President."

Assuming that they did not become entangled with the Japanese along the way, their zigzagging voyage to San Francisco would take a full month, perhaps longer. One unforeseen advantage of such a long journey was that it gave the men more time to fatten up. Gorging themselves was their only responsibility. They were under direct orders from the U.S. Army to eat as much as they could possibly fit into their starved frames. America didn't want its war heroes to look like skeletons. The Cabanatuan passengers were expected to avail themselves of a twenty-four-hour buffet, six meals a day, groaning boards of meat and mashed potatoes with gravy, milk and doughnuts on demand. "A dietary orgy," Dr. Hibbs called it. Most gained a pound every day, their gaunt cheeks popping out like the pouches of chipmunks. For many, the food was too rich and plentiful for their shrunken stomachs and debilitated livers, but the men stuffed themselves anyway.

"Every day we ate and ate until we got sick," said Bert Bank. "It was our job."

— — — —

The prisoners had been treated like royalty ever since they reached the safety of the American lines on the morning of January 31. They were brought to an evacuation hospital at Guimba, where they were deloused, treated to hot showers, and issued fresh clothes. Their filthy G-strings and patchwork shirts were heaped into a pile and promptly incinerated. Then the men were given hot meals and cots outfitted with a radical luxury—blankets and sheets. They half dozed through the afternoon heat, contemplating the happy nuances of freedom and comparing notes on their spectacular rescue.

At their bivouac site not far away, the Rangers were doing much the same thing—reliving the events of the previous seventy-two hours. The Benzedrine had worn off, but the high of their "audacious enterprise," as the official Ranger narrative would call it, kept many of them buzzing far into the day. Said Prince, "We all felt a glow of satisfaction that in the midst of the fighting we had participated in a life-saving operation." Theirs was a delicious victory, a jailbreak on an epic scale, the largest and most triumphant mission of its kind ever undertaken by the U.S. Army. It was estimated that the raid had resulted in the deaths of approximately 1,000 enemy troops, if one included all the Japanese soldiers who had fallen at the hands of Juan Pajota's guerrillas at the Cabu River bridge. In stark contrast, only four Americans died during the night—two Rangers in the firefight and two prisoners who perished for reasons of poor health. Although Pajota's guerrillas had sustained some twenty casualties, none of his men had been killed. In official "after-action reports," the death of Corporal Roy Sweezy was attributed to a stray Japanese bullet.

By the following day, February 1, every prisoner, Ranger, and Scout had safely reached Guimba, including the small party of Americans who had stayed behind to care for Dr. Jimmy Fisher. Even Edwin Rose, the deaf Englishman who'd been left behind, was now safely lodged in Guimba. Rose had awakened early on the morning of January 31 to find the camp faintly smoldering and littered with scores of bloody Japanese corpses. Finally it dawned on him that the Americans had come to fetch the prisoners, that he'd somehow missed the boat. Rose didn't panic. He shaved and cleaned himself up and then put on his best clothes, confident that liberation day was at hand. He gathered a few of his belongings and then strolled out to the front gate, where he was soon intercepted by a band of Filipino guerrillas who happened to be passing along the main road. "I knew somebody would come!" Rose said cheerfully.

A few days later, a group of Sixth Army soldiers and a Signal Corps photographer would return to Cabanatuan with Herbert Ott to dig up vital camp documents. This expedition, too, was a success. They were able to unearth death logs, cemetery layouts, and medical records. Buried beneath the shack that used to be the library, they found a cache of camp literature, including prison diaries, sketchbooks, and the poems of Lieutenant Henry Lee. Lee's frayed and yellowed notebook was given to Colonel Horton White who, in turn, sent it back to Lee's parents in Pasadena. Lee's poems would be published in November of 1945 in *The Saturday Evening Post*.

During the first week of February, the prisoners gathered strength at the evacuation hospital and were treated to such extravagancies as haircuts and fingernail trims. They underwent various medical tests—one prisoner was told that his stool specimen was "so contaminated it climbed out of the lab and got away." They were seen by a steady procession of Army debriefers, Army photographers, and Army dignitaries. General MacArthur even paid a brief visit. He milled among the prisoners, sobbing at one point to his old friend Colonel Duckworth, "I'm sorry

410

it took so long." Ralph Hibbs, who was sitting one cot away, remembered MacArthur "quietly struggling with his emotions, reflecting in disbelief on the miserable image of his old corps." Aghast, MacArthur listened as the men recounted some of the horrors they'd experienced. "I wondered whether the general's visit was a guilt trip," Dr. Hibbs wrote, "but his grief could not have been more genuine." Stirred by the raid's success, MacArthur awarded Colonel Mucci and Captain Prince the Distinguished Service Cross, observing that "nothing in this entire campaign has given me so much personal satisfaction." The other Ranger officers were given the Silver Star, while each enlisted man received the Bronze Star.

The news media were equally ecstatic about the raid. Reporters from the Associated Press, UPI, the *New York Times,* and *The Times* of London rushed to file stories by wireless. The parade of newsmen through the camp was so overwhelming that, as the official Ranger report narrative noted, "If it lasted one more day, more buttons would have to be sewed on and larger hat sizes secured. The men were walking on air." For the American public, the story carried immense symbolic importance; here was a story of redemption, the first definitive reversal of fortune in the otherwise desperately bleak chain of events that had begun with the fall of Bataan. The famous war photographer Carl Mydans, who was on hand at Guimba, would publish a lengthy photographic essay in *Life*. "It is now American history," Mydans would write of the raid, "and every child of coming generations will know of the 6th Rangers, for a prouder story has not been written." Yet after the initial flurry of press attention, the raid was quickly eclipsed by other developments in the war—Iwo Jima, Okinawa,

Hiroshima—and the story of the rescue would largely fade from public consciousness.

The prisoners were taken to a steel-planked runway near Lingayen Gulf and loaded aboard an olive-drab C-47 transport plane. It seemed to take the old plane forever to get airborne. "The C-47 creaked and groaned as it struggled down the runway," Tommie Thomas recalled. "I wondered if three years as a POW were in vain."

Finally, the plane lifted off, and soon they were banking over the smoking ruins of Manila, where a desperate, door-to-door battle was then raging. As the plane turned southeast in the direction of Leyte, the prisoners craned their necks for their last look at the green volcanoes of Bataan, the long peninsula cutting like a dull, nicked knife into the rippled blue of the bay.

———————

Westward we came across the smiling waves,
West to the outpost of our country's might
"Romantic land of brilliant tropic light"
Our land of broken memories and graves

Eastward we go and home, so few
Wrapped in their beds of clay our comrades sleep
The memories of this land are branded deep
And lost is the youth we knew.

One of Lt. Lee's poems recovered from Cabanatuan

At dawn on the morning of March 8, the *Anderson* bored through a cold, thick scrim of fog. The boat had stopped tacking and was making good time, cruising at flank speed straight up the coast of California. At least the captain said it was the coast of California—the men couldn't see a thing through the mist. They had spotted land the day before, and were told it was Mexico. Their spirits couldn't have been higher as they clutched the railings with their life preservers cinched tight. "The inner doom," said Dr. Hibbs, "was fading." They scrutinized the folds and recesses of the fog, each man hoping to be the first to spot America.

Then, in a flash of gleaming metal, a vent opened in the mist, and they could see the Golden Gate Bridge, only a few hundred yards ahead. The *Anderson* was aiming straight for it. The Marin headlands were clothed in a soft nubby green, the first suggestion of spring. The fog was fast peeling away as though to herald their arrival. When they approached the bridge, they looked up and realized that it was filled with people, thousands and thousands of tiny human specks, waving handkerchiefs, screaming from the rails. When the boat passed beneath the span, all sorts of odd trinkets began to rain down upon the deck—flowers, money, tickets to movies and musical shows, bras and lingerie. A banner on the rail said: GOD BLESS YOU, EX-POWS.

"I tell you," Robert Body said, "there wasn't a dry eye on that ship."

The *Anderson* nosed into San Francisco Bay at exactly twelve minutes past ten o'clock, and suddenly the city was engulfed in what the newspapers would call a "tornado of sound." The men could hear air-raid sirens keening, church bells, a din of foghorns and factory whistles. The bay was filled with vessels of every size and description. Navy dirigibles floated over the water. Fireboats spouted contrails of froth hundreds of feet into the air.

Squadrons of fighter planes swooped down from the sky, tipping their wings in unison. Then an official water taxi came out to meet them. The seventy-five-foot greeting on the side of the boat said WELCOME HOME in letters that stood six feet high. A large group of WACs, wearing yellow scarves, yellow gloves, and high heels, climbed aboard the *Anderson* and milled among the prisoners, distributing kisses and messages.

With seagulls wheeling in the sky above them, tugboats pulled the *Anderson* to Pier 15 at the Embarcadero. The docks were crowded with thousands of people cheering wildly. Schools and factories had been called off for the day. For the ex-prisoners' benefit, a brass band was playing "Don't Fence Me In." Then a telephone call from Roosevelt was broadcast live over the loudspeakers. The President greeted the POWs effusively and apologized for not being there in person, but he noted that every prisoner would be receiving a hand-signed letter from the White House.

When the prisoners stepped off the ramp, they kissed the ground and were promptly attacked by well-wishers. A gorgeous Navy WAVE walked up to Ralph Hibbs and embraced him. She pressed a folded note into his hand, on which she'd written her telephone number and address. She said, "Give me a call if you don't have friends." As the prisoners circulated among the throng, they looked dull-eyed and dazed—the reception was almost overwhelming. Newspapermen tried to interview them about their ordeal but they were frustratingly inarticulate. "It seems as if it were years ago," one prisoner told a newspaper reporter. "It all seems like a bad dream—like something not quite real."

The men were loaded onto buses, which then crept in a long procession up the crowd-lined streets of San Francisco toward the Presidio, where they would have a long, luxurious stay at Letterman Hospital. While they threaded through the hilly city, they opened their notes from the President. "You have fought valiantly in foreign lands and have suffered greatly," Roosevelt's letter said. "May God grant each of you happiness and an early return to health."

—·—·—

ABIE ABRAHAM did not come home aboard the SS *General Anderson*. Instead, he stayed behind on Luzon and reunited with his wife and three young daughters, who had been imprisoned in a civilian internment camp. After the liberation of Manila, Abraham was given an assignment that would significantly delay his return to the United States: the Graves Registration Administration wanted him to head up the effort to locate and identify the bodies of all Americans who had died along the Bataan Death March and in O'Donnell and Cabanatuan prison camps. The bodies were to be disinterred and reburied with full honors in the military cemetery in Manila. It was a monumental enterprise that took more than two years to complete. Abraham retired from the Army in 1955 to become a bartender and a foreman on a highway construction crew. He lives in Renfrew, Pennsylvania.

RALPH EMERSON HIBBS returned home to Iowa. Pilar Campo, his Filipino girlfriend, whom he had hoped to bring with him, was murdered by Japanese troops during the Rape of Manila. Dr. Hibbs moved to Oregon, where he ran a clinic and taught on the medical school faculty of the University of Oregon and wrote numerous articles in medical journals on beriberi and other prison maladies. He retired from the practice of medicine in 1984 and lived in Medford, Oregon, with his wife, Ginny, until the fall of 2000. Hibbs died in October of that year.

TOMMIE THOMAS came home to Michigan and built the exact house he had so fastidiously dreamed about all those years in prison camp. He served as a Grand Rapids police officer and ran a heating and air conditioning company before deciding to enter the seminary to become a minister in the Methodist Church. Thomas retired from the ministry in 1983, and now lives in Tucson with his wife, Dorothy, whom he met at the 1945 San Francisco homecoming.

After an intensive regimen of vitamin supplements, BERT BANK'S eyesight was partially restored. Bank returned home to Tuscaloosa, Alabama, and served for twelve years in the Alabama state legislature. Bank ran an enormously successful radio station that owned the rights to broadcast all the Alabama Crimson Tide football games during the coaching era of his close friend Bear Bryant. He lives with his wife, Emma, in Tuscaloosa.

When HENRY MUCCI returned home to Bridgeport, Connecticut, he was a national hero. Some 50,000 people came out for a hometown parade in his honor. He ran an unsuccessful bid to be a U.S. congressman from Connecticut. He later became the Far Eastern representative for a Canadian oil company, living for many years in Bangkok, and denying all rumors that he was an operative for the CIA. Mucci died in 1997 from complications resulting from a fractured hip sustained while swimming in rough surf near his home in Melbourne, Florida. He was eighty-six.

Shortly after the raid, ROBERT PRINCE joined a group of Rangers on a "bond-drive tour" of America that began in Washington, D.C., where they met with the ailing President Roosevelt in the White House. Prince left the Army in 1946 and went into the fruit-distribution business, selling vast quantities of apples from Washington State's famous Wenatchee orchards. He was inducted into the Ranger Hall of Fame at Fort Benning, Georgia, in 1999. He lives with his wife, Barbara, in Kirkland, Washington.

CLAIRE PHILLIPS was liberated on February 10, 1945, from an internment camp on the outskirts of Manila. The Japanese Kempei Tai had issued her a death sentence but for some reason declined to carry it out. Phillips returned to Portland, Oregon, and became the subject of a Hollywood movie entitled *I Was an American Spy*. The U.S. Senate awarded her the Medal of Freedom in 1951. She died unexpectedly in 1960 at the age of fifty-two.

CHAPLAIN ROBERT TAYLOR survived the long voyage to Japan aboard the *Brazil Maru*. He was sent to a prison camp in Mukden, Manchuria, where he was liberated by Russian soldiers in September 1945. When he returned to the United States, Taylor learned that his wife, believing him to be dead, had married another man. Taylor would later remarry, and would eventually rise to the rank of major general, becoming the highest-ranking chaplain in the U.S. Armed Forces. He died in 1997.

SOOCHOW, the marine regimental mascot that lorded over Cabanatuan, had been transferred to another Philippine POW camp from which he was safely liberated in early February of 1945. The dog returned to the United States and made sergeant before passing away in 1948. He is buried on the grounds of the marine recruit station in San Diego.

Through arrangements made by the family of the late Dr. Jimmy Fisher, DRS. CARLOS AND JULITA LAYUG came to Boston for a year of advanced medical training at Harvard Medical School and then returned to Cabanatuan City to continue their practice. Guerrilla leader EDUARDO JOSON became the governor of Nueva Ecija Province after the war. JUAN PAJOTA was appointed the province's military governor and then moved to America. He died of a heart attack in 1976 just days before he was to receive U.S. citizenship.

In war crimes trials held in Japan, Cabanatuan commandant SHIGEJI MORI and Camp O'Donnell commandant YOSHIO TSUNEYOSHI were sentenced to "life at hard labor." Dubbed the "Beast of Bataan" by the American media, General MASAHARU HOMMA was convicted of command responsibility for the Bataan Death March, although the prosecution was unable to prove that he was even aware of the atrocities, let alone ordered them. Homma's wife personally appealed to MacArthur to spare his life, but the American general, then commander of the American occupation of Japan, declined to intervene. The Poet General was executed by a firing squad in Los Baños, Philippines, on April 3, 1946.

The man widely believed to be most directly responsible for the worst atrocities of the Death March, Colonel MASANOBU TSUJI, escaped all war crimes prosecution and went into hiding in Burma, Thailand, and China, faking his own death and then disguising himself as a Buddhist monk. In the 1950s he reemerged in Tokyo, writing unrepentant accounts of the war and becoming a prominent member of the National Diet. Tsuji mysteriously disappeared in 1961 while traveling in Vietnam.

Today the site of CABANATUAN CAMP is a modest park covered in tropical fruit trees. A memorial wall of white marble lists the names of 2,656 Americans who perished there.

Acknowledgments

This book is, to an unusual degree, a work of thorough-going collaboration between me and the men who populate its pages. I've based the narrative on my interviews with actual participants, on prisoner memoirs and oral history transcripts, on primary documents found in the National Archives and other repositories of Army records, and on personal observation of the landscapes that form the settings for the story. All passages of reconstructed dialogue grow directly from my interviews or from other reliable documentation. Although for reasons of style and pacing I have chosen not to use conventional footnotes, I owe a large debt of gratitude to myriad individuals and sources scattered from Washington to Manila to Tokyo.

First and foremost, I must give enormous thanks to the major characters from Cabanatuan who appear in my book: Abie Abraham in Renfrew, Pennsylvania; Bert Bank in Tuscaloosa, Alabama; Edward "Tommie" Thomas in Tuscson, Arizona; Dr. Ralph Hibbs in Medford, Oregon; Robert Body in Jensen Beach, Florida; Ralph Rodriguez in

Albuquerque, New Mexico; Dr. Herbert Ott in Norwalk, California; John Cook in San Bruno, California; and John McCarty in Dripping Springs, Texas. Without the forbearance and cooperation of these veterans of Bataan, this book would not have been possible. They gave freely of their time even though talking with me often necessitated opening old wounds. I met them in their homes or at reunions and conventions scattered about the country. I spent hours and sometimes days interviewing these men in person or by telephone, and over time we became friends. More than once I wept with them as they trained searchlights, at my prompting, on particularly unpleasant recesses of the past.

I relied on their correspondence, their war diaries and personal scrapbooks, their published memoirs or unpublished manuscripts. They revealed their lives with graciousness and hospitality, introducing me to their wives and children, their hometowns, their favorite cafes and restaurants. In describing these men and their ordeal, I also made direct use of the following autobiographical works: *As I Remember: The Death March of Bataan,* by Ed "Tommie" Thomas; *Tell MacArthur to Wait,* by Ralph Emerson Hibbs, M.D.; *Back from the Living Dead,* by Bertram Bank; *Ghost of Bataan Speaks* and *Oh God Where Are You?,* by Abie Abraham; and *Cabanatuan: Japanese Death Camp,* by Vince Taylor and John McCarty. Meshing my tape-recorded interviews with passages found in these vivid works enabled me to render these men's experiences with immediacy and verisimilitude.

It was often said after the war that all the men of Bataan could well expect to go to heaven because they'd already served their time in hell. These men suffered enough for a hundred lifetimes, and no one in this country should be allowed to forget it. The veterans of Bataan did not merely serve their country in war; they lived through three years of gratuitous and often surreal mistreatment which, as they've come to the end of their lives, they still cannot fully believe or understand. They're old men now, but sometimes they still wake up in the night, sweaty and scared, tormented by visions. For their honesty, their courage, their poise under the merciless burden of memory, and their sense of humor in the face of unspeakable travail, I cannot thank these men enough. Spending time with them was, for me, a tremendous honor.

I was extremely fortunate to have met former prisoners who were willing to talk. The men of Bataan are famous for their iron reticence. They're stoics. Seldom in our history has such a large group of men endured so much and complained so little. Many of them never told their stories when they returned home, not even to their own families. For many of the POWs, it has taken fifty years to sift their experience and begin to make sense of it. Some felt as though they were branded by a certain shame when they returned to American shores—shame for having surrendered in the first place (even though they were ordered to do so), shame for having survived when so many of their friends didn't, shame for having to be walking exhibits of American defeat, like so many wraiths crashing the national party. The months following V-J Day were a time to celebrate the war's end, not to examine the dark asterisks of victory. They resumed their lives, burying the past to the extent possible, suffering quietly. All the syndromes and illnesses that have come to be associated with Vietnam veterans were suffered twenty-five years earlier by the American captives of the Japanese—high rates of suicide and alcoholism, constant nightmares, a litany of mental problems, and all the hallmarks of post-traumatic stress syndrome (although the condition was not then dignified with a name). While their patriotism is beyond question, many of the Bataan veterans have been unable to shake their belief that their country abandoned and forgot them, that Washington for all intents and purposes turned its back. To this day, Bataan veterans continue to feel a sense of bitterness. They're still proud to recite their company slogan—"No mama, no papa, no Uncle Sam . . . and nobody gives a damn." The orphan spirit behind the chant remains understandable, at least from their perspective, yet the sentiment was not entirely true, as was suggested by the great emotional upwelling that accompanied the Ranger raid on Cabanatuan and the heroes' welcome the prisoners received in San Francisco: Americans very much gave a damn. They still do.

There are many other veterans of Bataan and Corregidor whom I had the pleasure to meet during the course of my research and whose insights I relied on both directly and indirectly. Among them: Winston Shillito, James Hildebrand, Oscar Leonard, Andy Miller, Leon Beck, Al McGrew, Robert Lapham, James Bogart, Humphrey O'Leary, and Malcolm Amos. Other Bataan and Corregidor veterans who were helpful to me include Richard Daly, Rev. John Morrett, F. Langwith Berry, Dr. Alex Kelly, Sam Grashio, and Lou Chandler. The following family members of Bataan and Corregidor veterans also assisted me enormously: Ginny Hibbs, Lorna Murray, Barry Beutell, Peter Wainwright, Nicoll Galbraith, Fred Baldassarre, Bob

Taylor, Charles and Jan Wyatt, Sara Leonard, Lanae Hagen, and Dennis Raines, Jr.

I was fortunate to meet with many surviving members of the 6th Ranger Battalion. Robert Prince especially went out of his way to provide helpful details and documents. I thank him for sharing with me his unpublished memoirs and for hosting a meeting with several other Rangers from the Seattle area. Other Rangers I spoke with include Dalton Garrett, Lester Malone, Eugene Kocsis, Leland Provencher, Roy Peters, Vance Shears, Robert Anderson, Mel Schmidt, William Proudfit, Francis Schilli, Thomas Grace, Joseph Youngblood, Homer Britzius, Alvie Robbins, Joe Malatesta, and Howard Baker. My thanks also to the family of Manton Stewart, the family of James Herrick, and the family of Carlton Dietzel. I'm most grateful to Vivian Hixon, the niece of the late Dr. James Fisher, who shared with me copious files of family correspondence and other insightful documents. Also I thank Ken Nicholson of the Dorothy Canfield Fisher Symposium in Arlington, Vermont, for providing valuable materials related to Dr. Fisher.

Among the surviving members of the Alamo Scouts, I wish to extend my thanks to Robert Sumner, Gilbert Cox, Galen Kittleson, Zeke McConnell, Terry Santos, W. F. Barnes, and the families of Tom Rounsaville and Bill Nellist. Thanks also to the late Lewis Hockstrasser, whose manuscript "They Were First: The True Story of the Alamo Scouts" proved revealing.

I particularly wish to thank Forrest Johnson, author of *Hour of Redemption.* Johnson gave of his time and energy and generously shared a number of his contacts with me. Johnson, whose scholarly interest in this story spans nearly three decades, suggested a number of avenues of research which proved fruitful. Colonel John Olson, a Bataan veteran and scholar, offered his valuable perspectives on the POW experience in the Philippines and graciously hosted me at Fort Sam Houston in San Antonio. Another writer, Gavan Daws, author of the acclaimed *Prisoners of the Japanese,* was quite helpful during a research stopover in Honolulu, sharing with me his prodigious insights into this intricate subject. Richard Gordon, author of *Horyo: Memoirs of an American POW,* helped me enormously, both as a conscientiously accurate commentator on Bataan veterans' issues and as a traveling companion during a research trip to the Philippines. Andy Miller, historian of the American Defenders of Bataan and Corregidor, read my manuscript with scrupulous care. I also wish to thank the late John Hersey, a good friend and college mentor who launched his formidable literary career in 1942 with the little-known book *Men on Bataan.*

Cabanatuan survivor John Cook went far beyond the call of duty to assist me with my research by providing key contacts, forwarding me documents, and keeping me apprised of events on the calendar of the American Defenders of Bataan and Corregidor. At great expense, Cook organized an extremely emotional reunion of all living Rangers and Cabanatuan POWs.

I thank Carl and Shelley Mydans, Peter Cook at WGBH in Boston, and Robin Wiener, who helped me keep the home fires burning. Thanks also to Mark Crosby for his photographic expertise, to the radio engineering talents of Jack Loeffler for making my tapes audible, to Dave Byrne at CD Café, and to the crew at *Outside* magazine for their editorial judgment and support, especially Hal Espen, Jay

Stowe, Elizabeth Hightower, Eric Hagerman, Dave Cox, and Kevin Fedarko. Edder Bennett, John Bessone, Andy Court, Walker and Dottie Wilkerson, and Scott Stevens helped this project in multiple ways. Special thanks to Kendra Harpster, my lifeline at Doubleday.

I'm indebted to a number of veterans organizations, archives, museums, and oral history projects which aided me immeasurably. I especially benefited from insights provided by the Battling Bastards of Bataan and by the American Defenders of Bataan and Corregidor, two national organizations that represent World War II veterans from the Philippines. The Oral History Program at the University of North Texas, in Denton, was of great assistance to my project. I wish to thank Helen MacDonald at the Admiral Nimitz Museum in Fredericksburg, Texas, Jim Zoebl at the MacArthur Library in Norfolk, Virginia, and Jerry Rep at the Air Force Museum in Dayton, Ohio. My special appreciation goes to Will Mahoney at the National Archives in College Park, Maryland. Also of vital importance to me were the Army archives at Carlisle Barracks in Carlisle, Pennsylvania, and the National Prisoner of War Museum in Andersonville, Georgia. Sarah Brown, Tim Neville, Sue Terry, John MacKessy, Mike Kessler, and Walker Wilkerson provided important research assistance into a variety of topics related to the book. I owe much gratitude to Rick Padilla at the Bataan Memorial Museum in Santa Fe, whose collection of rare and out-of-print books on the Philippines proved an enormous boon to my project.

Many people helped me during my trip to the Philippines. I am especially grateful to Jim Rush and his wife, Sunny, for taking me under their wings in Manila and providing wise research advice. Thanks also to James Litton,

Bob Reynolds, and the Philippine Tourist Board in Chicago. Journalist Jose Manuel Tesoro read my manuscript with a sharp eye. Luis Taruc, the former guerrilla leader of the Hukbalahap, generously gave of his time. I thank Fred Baldassarre for his many insights into life on Luzon, and Bataan veteran Humphrey O'Leary for giving a lengthy interview at his Manila home and for providing cold San Miguel beers too numerous to count. Finally, I must thank Ellen Weiss, the executive producer of NPR's *All Things Considered,* who armed me with a tape recorder and flew me to Manila to undertake a radio documentary project.

I spent three months living in Tokyo learning what I could about the Japanese perspective of this story. Many people there made my stay enjoyable and constructive. First I must thank Ruri Kawashima and the good people at the Japan Society in New York who offered me a generous research fellowship to study Japanese culture. In Tokyo, I am indebted to Kazuko Kozumi-Legendre at the Foreign Press Center, who was my lifeline for arranging travel and interviews. I thank Calvin Sims of the *New York Times,* Robert Ratcliffe, Alex Wilds, and Donald Richie for helping me negotiate the labyrinths of Japanese society. I am grateful to Bataan veteran and POW Shiro Asada for his insights and his gracious hospitality during my stay in Hiroshima. Professor Ikuhiko Hata was most helpful in elucidating Japanese concepts of surrender and the status of POWs. Mikio Kato of the International House of Japan and Sadaaki Numata of the Ministry of Foreign Affairs especially aided my research. During my stay in Japan I met with journalists, war veterans, politicians, and historians. I thank the following individuals for insightful interviews: Yuji Suzuki, Tadae Takubo, Moriya Wada, Minoru Hataguchi, Akihiro Takahashi, Tsunehiko Miyake, Keiko Ogura, Koji Oda, Norifumi Tateishi, Katsuichi Honda, Noriko Takasawa, Tsuguo Morita, Takashi Itoh, and Murakami Hyoe. Finally, I am deeply grateful to Masahiko Homma, the son of the late General Masaharu Homma. An Imperial Army veteran and a POW who served five years in squalid Russian work camps, Homma met with me for three days at his lovely home on Sado Island, his father's birthplace.

Although in writing this book I consulted hundreds of books and reference volumes, I wish to cite a few sources that were most worthwhile to my research. **The Bataan surrender and Death March:** Louis Morton's *The Fall of the Pacific,* the definitive official account of the siege of Bataan, proved indispensable. Other works that were of enormous benefit include *Bataan: The March of Death,* by Stanley L. Falk; *Death March,* by Donald Knox; *O'Donnell: Andersonville of the Pacific,* by John Olson; *American Caesar,* by William Manchester; and Stanley Karnow's *In Our Image.* **General Masaharu Homma and the Japanese perspective:** I especially relied on two books which vividly explored the remarkable personality and character of General Homma—Arthur Swinson's *Four Samurai* and Lawrence Taylor's *A Trial of Generals.* Noteworthy for their general insights were *The Chrysanthemum and the Sword,* by Ruth Benedict; *The Rising Sun,* by John Toland; and *War Without Mercy,* by John Dower. **Cabanatuan camp:** The two most richly detailed works on the life of the camp are *Barbed-Wire Surgeon,* by Alfred A. Weinstein, M.D., and *Of Rice and Men,* a fascinating and often amusing compendium of camp history and lore edited by Calvin E. Chunn. I made considerable use of *Nothing But Praise,* a collection of prison poetry by Henry Lee, and *Days of Anguish, Days of Hope,* a biography of Chaplain Robert Preston Taylor by Billy Keith. My account of Claire Phillips and her involvement with the Cabanatuan underground was primarily adapted from her autobiography, *Manila Espionage,* by Claire Phillips and Myron B. Goldsmith, and from the article "I Was an American Spy," by Claire Phillips and Frederick C. Painton, which appeared in *The American Mercury* in 1945. A relative of Claire Phillips, Deborah Hagemann, provided copious notes as well. **The *Oryoko Maru*:** My depiction of the ill-fated transport ship was based on numerous interviews and oral histories. Two published works were especially helpful: *Some Survived,* by Manny Lawton, and *Give Us This Day,* by Sidney Stewart. **The raid on Cabanatuan:** My account of the raid is based on my interviews with raid participants as well as hundreds of pages of Army records and "after-action" reports. I also relied on numerous journalistic accounts dating from 1945, including stories that appeared in *Life, Time, The New York Times,* and *The Times* of London. Of special use were two articles written by Colonel Henry Mucci that appeared in *The Saturday Evening Post* and *Infantry Journal.* My reliance on Forrest Johnson's exhaustively researched *Hour of Redemption* (1978) was considerable. I am especially indebted to his research in several passages that concern raid participants who died before I undertook my book project—notably Bill Nellist, Juan Pajota, James Herrick, and Rufo Vaquilar. I would urge anyone who seeks to become a student of the Cabanatuan raid to consult Johnson's account. Other written sources that proved helpful to me include *Silent Warriors of World War II,* by Lance Q.

Zedric; *Spec Ops: Case Studies in Special Operations Warfare,* by William H. McRaven; *From Down Under to Nippon,* by General Walter Krueger; *Lapham's Raiders,* by Robert Lapham and Bernard Norling; *Rangers in World War II,* by Robert W. Black; and *Raider or Elite Infantry?,* by David W. Hogan.

Finally, to my agent Sloan Harris, who judiciously nursed this project from its first day as a half-baked e-mail message, to the estimable Bill Thomas at Doubleday, who believed in this book with a zeal that at times exceeded my own, and to my wife, Anne, who brought this story to faithful fruition with her keen ear and hawk's eye, and who, as far as I'm concerned, now justifiably wears a golden nimbus over her head—*eternal thanks.*

DOUBLE STANDARDS
The Rudolf Hess Cover-up

Lynn Picknett, Clive Prince and Stephen Prior

'A cracking read with every intricate twist and turn expertly researched' *Time Out*

For over sixty years there has been an unprecedented cover-up by both the British Establishment and successive generations of historians about the flight of Hitler's Deputy, Rudolf Hess, to Scotland in May 1941. It has been long dismissed as the misguided attempt of a madman to make contact with a non-existent British peace party.

Based on entirely new material from eyewitnesses, hitherto inaccessible archives and intellignece sources, *Double Standards* reveals that:

- Despite official denials, Hess flew to Britain with Hitler's full knowledge.

- There was a substantial British peace party in 1941, which included most of the aristocracy – and the Royal Family.

- There is substantial evidence that the prisoner who died in Spandau prison was not the real Rudolf Hess.

- The fate of the real Hess was inextricably linked to the mysterious death of the King's brother, the Duke of Kent.

- Winston Churchill guilefully used Hess to influence Hitler and change Britain's fortunes in the war.

Hess's peace mission was a pivotal event in the Second World War, and raises some intriguing questions about the history of the twentieth century. *Double Standards'* mission is to answer them.

Time Warner Paperbacks
0 7515 3220 7

IBM AND THE HOLOCAUST

How America's Most Powerful Corporation
Helped Nazi Germany Count the Jews

Edwin Black

IBM and the Holocaust is the stunninng story of IBM's
strategic alliance with Nazi Germany.

As the Third Reich embarked upon its plan of conquest
and genocide, it faced a cross-tabulation and organizational
challenge so monumental, it called for a computer. Only after
Jews were identified – a massive and complex task that Hitler
wanted done immediately – could they be targeted for efficient
asset confiscation, ghettoization, deportation, enslaved labour,
and, ultimately, annihilation.

Of course, in the 1930s no computer existed. But IBM's
Hollerith punch-card technology did. Only with IBM's
technological assistance was Hitler able to achieve the staggering
numbers of the Holocaust. Edwin Black has now uncovered one
of the last great mysteries of Germany's war against the Jews –
how did Hitler get the names?

'You thought, perhaps, that there was nothing fresh left to write
about the Holocaust. Think, sadly, again . . . [Black] shows, in
compelling detail, that IBM, 'the solutions company', was also the
company of the final solution . . . a distinctive contribution to
the history of the time' *Observer*

'Explosive . . . backed by exhaustive research, Black's case
is simple and stunning' *Newsweek*

'Edwin Black has given Holocaust history an extraordinary new
dimension . . . monumental' Abraham Peck, Director of
Research, American Jewish Historical Society

Time Warner Paperbacks
0 7515 3199 5

HITLER'S BANKER

John Weitz

Hjalmar Horace Greeley Schacht was a genius, an eccentric and an enigma. Single-handedly halting Germany's runaway inflation and freeing her from the crippling reparation debts imposed by the Treaty of Versailles, he gained worldwide fame as the economic guru of Nazi Germany. Yet while he financed Hitler's military regime, he held most Nazi's in contempt and frequently clashed with its hierarchy – and Hitler himself – over anti-Jewish laws and war spending. Before the war was over, he had been imprisoned in Dachau; later, he was one of only three defendants to be acquitted at the Nuremberg trials.

John Weitz's riveting biography brings this complex figure, a skilled manipulator of money, men and governments, to life against the chilling, brutal but often grimly fascinating history of twentieth century Germany.

'Weitz is perhaps at his best in the details of the floundering Deutschmark . . . and in the well-placed reminders of the way in which the Americans, British and French were prepared to overlook the increasing thuggery of Nazi Germany so long as their own interests were safe' *Daily Telegraph*

'A good, vivid read . . . Weitz's judgements are often shrewd' *Literary Review*

Time Warner Paperbacks
0 7515 2666 5

THE TWO KOREAS
A Contemporary History

Don Oberdorfer

Winner of the 1998 Asia-Pacific Book Prize.

While the Cold War is over in the rest of the world, a potentially deadly confrontation continues on the bitterly divided peninsula of Korea. The struggle between the South, economically and democratically fractious, and the closed, communist, militarily powerful North, has repeatedly claimed the headlines of the world, and in 1994 precipitated a nuclear showdown that brought the North perilously close to war with the United States.

Written with the drama and immediately born of extensive experience as a journalist in the area and unparalleled access to leadership circles, Don Oberdorfer's book is a gripping narrative history of the travails and triumphs in the two Koreas over the past quarter-century, and a probing examination of historic events in one of the most dangerous and volatile places on earth.

'This truly important work will, without question, become the standard against which other books on modern Korea will be judged' Donald P. Gregg, former US Ambassador to South Korea

'A valuable contribution to the history of our century, and a fascinating read' *Sunday Tribune*

'The author has produced the best account in English of how the two Koreas have come to be' *Sunday Tribune*

Time Warner Paperbacks
0 7515 2668 1

Other bestselling Time Warner Paperback titles available by mail:

☐ IBM and the Holocaust	Edwin Black	£9.99
☐ The Two Koreas	Don Oberdorfer	£9.99
☐ Hitler's Banker	John Weitz	£8.99
☐ Double Standards	Lynn Picknett, Clive Prince,	
	Stephen Prior	£9.99

The prices shown above are correct at time of going to press. However, the publishers reserve the right to increase prices on covers from those previously advertised, without further notice.

timewarner
paperbacks

TIME WARNER PAPERBACKS
PO Box 121, Kettering, Northants NN14 4ZQ
Tel: 01832 737525, Fax: 01832 733076
Email: aspenhouse@FSBDial.co.uk

POST AND PACKING:
Payments can be made as follows: cheque, postal order (payable to Warner Books) or by credit cards. Do not send cash or currency.

All UK Orders	**FREE OF CHARGE**
EC & Overseas	25% of order value

Name (BLOCK LETTERS) . . . .

Address . . . .

. . . .

Post/zip code: . . . .

☐ Please keep me in touch with future Warner publications

☐ I enclose my remittance £ . . . .

☐ I wish to pay by Visa/Access/Mastercard/Eurocard

Card Expiry Date | | | | |